THE
MILLION
DOLLAR
PRIVATE
PRACTICE

THE MILLION DOLLAR PRIVATE PRACTICE

*Using Your Expertise to Build a
Business That Makes a Difference*

DAVID STEELE

WILEY

John Wiley & Sons, Inc.

Cover Design: Andy Liefer
Cover Art: © Peter Zelei/iStockphoto, © DianaWalters/iStockphoto, © Illustrart/iStockphoto

This book is printed on acid-free paper. ∞

Published by John Wiley & Sons, Inc., Hoboken, New Jersey.
Published simultaneously in Canada.

This publication is designed to provide accurate and authoritative information in regard to the subject matter covered. It is sold with the understanding that the Publisher is not engaged in rendering professional services. If legal, accounting, medical, psychological or any other expert assistance is required, the services of a competent professional person should be sought.

Designations used by companies to distinguish their products are often claimed as trademarks. In all instances where John Wiley & Sons, Inc. is aware of a claim, the product names appear in initial capital or all capital letters. Readers, however, should contact the appropriate companies for more complete information regarding trademarks and registration.

For general information on our other products and services, please contact our Customer Care Department within the United States at (800) 762-2974, outside the United States at (317) 572-3993, or via fax at (317) 572-4002.

Wiley publishes in a variety of print and electronic formats and by print-on-demand. Some material included with standard print versions of this book may not be included in e-books or in print-on-demand. If this book refers to media such as a CD or DVD that is not included in the version you purchased, you may download this material at http://booksupport.wiley.com. For more information about Wiley products, visit www.wiley.com.

Library of Congress Cataloging-in-Publication Data:

Steele, David (David A.), 1957-
   The million dollar private practice: using your expertise to build a business that makes a difference / David Steele.
     p.   cm.
   ISBN 978-0-470-63578-0 (pbk.); ISBN 978-1-118-25907-8 (ebk);
   ISBN 978-1-118-23458-7 (ebk); ISBN 978-1-118-22081-8 (ebk);
   ISBN 978-1-118-08998-9 (obk)
     1. Professions—Marketing. 2. Specialists. 3. Expertise. 4. Consulting firms.
 I. Title.
   HD8038.A1S73   2012
   001—dc23   2012008096

Printed in the United States of America

10 9 8 7 6 5 4 3 2

Contents

CONTENTS

Preface

Private practice professionals typically conduct personal, intimate services that address the biggest, most important human needs, goals, and challenges. In any other industry, the ability to solve such problems would attract venture capital investment far and wide, making wealthy the providers of such critical expertise.

So why are so many practitioners struggling to get clients, make a living, and command fees commensurate with their gifts and contributions?

Simple: They are motivated by ideals, not profits. They shy away from calling attention to themselves, preferring to be of service to their clients. They resist marketing and are uncomfortable asking for money. They unknowingly undervalue their services, and therefore, their services are undervalued.

The social problems of divorce, unemployment, domestic violence, juvenile delinquency, stress, disease, depression, and anxiety are getting worse, not better. Private practice professionals devote their lives to addressing these problems, and it doesn't serve them or society to devalue their contributions.

Just as inventive, entrepreneurial engineers and scientists create wealth by solving problems and advancing technology, private practice professionals can be just as inventive and entrepreneurial. You can build a successful and lucrative business that addresses the most significant problems, needs, and goals within your area of expertise.

Doing good—helping others—and doing well—making a comfortable living—are not mutually exclusive. You may need a little help getting there, but if you choose to do so, in your quest to genuinely make a significant difference in the world, you can absolutely build a Million Dollar Practice.

CHAPTER ONE

Is a Million Dollar Practice Right for You?

As a pioneer and leader in my industry, I am often approached by practitioners for advice on building their business. And I'm glad to help. I'm passionate about making the world a better place and we can't do so as helping professionals if we can't get clients.

Many of the private practice professionals who approach me are struggling and hungry. They want to make the quantum leap to a six- or seven-figure practice, which is great and absolutely possible. However, many are just starting their practice and have stars in their eyes. They want to hit the big time—like Deepak Chopra and Anthony Robbins—though they are unaware of how to get there or what awaits them if they decide to venture down that path.

The Litmus Test

When I conduct my practice-building programs, I start by addressing the need to "embrace your inner entrepreneur." As a way of helping participants understand this concept and tap into the proper mind-set, I designed a litmus test question. It's a question that strikes at the heart of your current willingness to pursue — and your compatibility with — the model of the Million Dollar Practice.

The yes-or-no question of which I speak was not designed to discourage or dismiss you from the pool of potential Million Dollar Practitioners, nor was it designed to give you the impression that you may not be able to cut it. My intention was quite the opposite. The litmus test question was specifically designed to inspire you and help you address any internal elements that may be preventing you from reaching your goals.

So here's the question:

If you were offered a job, making a comfortable living, doing exactly what you wanted to do, with whom you wanted to do it, would you take it?

Now I have put this question to my clients many times. And while the results can't be considered a scientific sampling, since I've never officially measured them, they are nevertheless quite revealing. I'd estimate that 80% of the respondents say "Yes," they would take the job. They would take it with relief: "Oh my gosh, I wouldn't have to worry about how to pay my bills anymore, I wouldn't have to market or stress about building my own business anymore."

So why are these answers so revealing?

First, they corroborate what many people already know deep down but what is often hidden or suppressed:

People who enter a helping profession have a genuine desire to help, but also have a significant level of resistance to being in business for themselves.

Still, please know that if after pondering the litmus test question you feel that you would really rather have a job, it doesn't mean that you are incapable of one day building a Million Dollar Practice. It just means that you currently have some internal resistance to identify and overcome.

Where you are is not where you will always be. And it doesn't matter where you've been, what matters is where you're going and how you'll get there.

THE HERO'S JOURNEY

Building a successful practice is a hero's journey. And what makes it a hero's journey is that it's not easy. But while many people believe the difficult obstacles come from external factors—they don't know how to market, they don't know how to choose a niche, they don't know how to build a Web site—the truth is that most things that prevent it from being easy are inside us. That's right. That's the secret: The biggest obstacles to building a Million Dollar Practice come from within. External factors are merely details, and they are relatively easy to resolve.

The world offers countless possibilities for what your Web site can look like, infinite ways to start a business, a broad range of strategies and tactics that you can employ to thrive in life—so much so that for all practical purposes it doesn't really matter. There is no one right answer. Strategies and tactics for building a successful business are relatively simple to identify and put into place, as will be demonstrated in this book.

Internal obstacles, on the other hand, can be debilitating. It takes courage and will to embrace both the destination and the journey to get there and to confront and slay the dragons that crop up along the way. Practitioners identify with this because they constantly see it in their clients. They get in their own way. The most serious things holding them back are inside them, not outside of them. And it's the same with each of us as builder of a Million Dollar Practice.

When you are just starting out and you don't know what you don't know (which will be addressed in more detail later in this book), you can't possibly recognize or comprehend all of your options. And if you're anything like I was when I was starting out, it can be hard to even imagine that little old you can build a successful practice, reach a lot of people, and make a lot of money, because you simply don't know how.

In addition to introducing you to a lot of the "how," this book gives you much more, because knowing the "how" doesn't make building a Million Dollar Practice happen by itself. You still have to adopt the right mind-set. And you have to be willing to step up and take the necessary action, because, as we've pointed out, it's the internal obstacles—fear of failure, fear of success, and other issues—that get in the way of your goals. My job in this book, in part, is to act as your cheerleader, to provide you with the practical tools and strategies, but also to provide you with hope and inspiration to help you overcome that internal resistance. I want to see you realize your professional potential and get where you want to go.

Processing the litmus test question can bring a wide range of thoughts and emotions to the forefront. And again, if you are leaning toward an answer of "Yes, I would take the job," it doesn't mean that you should give up on your dream of creating a Million Dollar Practice, or any other goal. It just means that you must identify what might get in your way and do something about it. The litmus test question helps you start identifying what factors might get in your way, such as procrastination, distraction, falling back into your comfort zone, or your fundamental belief in yourself. To quote Henry Ford: "Whether you think you can, or you think you can't, you're right." And so begins your hero's journey.

LEAP OF FAITH

There is a scene in *Indiana Jones and the Last Crusade* where Indiana Jones, in pursuit of the Holy Grail to save his father, comes to a huge chasm. It is so far across that there is no way he can jump it, no way he can use his whip to swing across. Matching a clue on the cavern wall—a lion's head—and a passage from his father's Grail Diary— "Only in the leap from the lion's head will he prove his worth"—he realizes what's needed to reach his goal: "It's a leap of faith." Agonizing over what he knows he must do, and with no guarantee of success, Indy steps off the ledge . . . and to his great surprise and relief, he touches solid ground. There is a bridge, a pathway across the chasm, that he couldn't see before he was willing to take that leap of faith. But once he took that step, he could see it, and he made his way across.

This scene is one of the best metaphors I have ever seen for the hero's journey. It completely embodies the necessity to have faith, take a risk, and be willing to go all in. All of us can build Million

4

Dollar Practices; we just have to be willing to embrace our hero's journey. We have to believe.

The world of sports is another way of looking at your journey. Whether it's chess, ice skating, swimming, soccer, or any other sport, you will find talented people for whom it comes naturally and easy, but who don't go the distance at it. Maybe they don't have the self-discipline or the family support, or maybe they don't have the economic ability to sustain their participation because they have to focus more on survival. There are many reasons why somebody might be highly talented at something and still not excel at it, follow through with it, or reach the elite level.

And there is another category of people who are highly talented at a particular sport, do follow through with it, and shine. It comes easily for them. They are just blessed. We all know people like that.

Then there are the rest of us . . . those who have a passion for the sport, and can only wish we had half the talent of other people. But we don't. We may have a long, more-challenging road ahead of us, but we can absolutely excel at that sport. We can get the gold medal; we can win the championship. It's just going to be a longer, harder road than for the people to whom it comes easily. This, too, makes our dedication to our profession a hero's journey.

THE INNER GAME AND THE OUTER GAME

You have probably heard the concepts of an "inner game" and an "outer game," but probably haven't considered that they might apply to you. You have the talents and temperament that you were born with, and then you have the accomplishments that result from what you choose to take on. We can all choose to make a difference in the world and build a highly successful practice doing so. But we must master our inner game and be willing to embrace and play the outer game. We can absolutely do it. And for most of us it's going to be a hero's journey. For most of us it's not going to be that fast rise to the top. But it doesn't have to be hard.

One of the most effective ways to make the journey easier is to adopt the proper mind-set and habits early on. To help you start with a strong foundation on your road to the top, I have crafted what I call the Seven Habits of Million Dollar Practitioners.

Seven Habits of Million Dollar Practitioners

A small percentage of practitioners reach their financial goals with a full-time private practice. Most, however, struggle to make it by keeping their day jobs, accepting part-time employment, working pro bono or for discounted fees—you don't have to be one of them. You can achieve your goals by doing what other Million Dollar Practitioners do.

In my experience mentoring practitioners to build their practices, I have found that Million Dollar Practitioners share all of the following characteristics:

1. Passionate

Million Dollar Practitioners love their work. They are living out their life purpose and are so excited by it that they would do it for free and have no thought or intention of retirement. They truly could not imagine doing anything else, and consider themselves lucky to have the best job in the world. Their passion is easily expressed and very attractive to their potential clients.

2. Positive

Million Dollar Practitioners have "can-do" attitudes. They believe in themselves and trust that they will find a way around obstacles in order to survive and thrive. Thus, they are able to effectively empower their clients to be positive as well. Million Dollar Practitioners assume abundance instead of scarcity. While they may experience fear and doubt, they never view them as reasons for "No."

3. Entrepreneurial

Million Dollar Practitioners have entrepreneurial attitudes, consider their practice a business, and take the trouble to learn and apply the business skills needed to be successful. While most private practice professionals understandably wish to focus on serving their clients and resist the business and marketing aspects of their practice, Million Dollar Practitioners enjoy the challenge of pioneering successful businesses that are expressions of their gifts, mission, and purpose.

4. Playing Large

Million Dollar Practitioners are always expanding by growing themselves and their practice. They desire to play as large as they can and take every opportunity to do so. They get impatient with the status quo and are always in motion seeking to maximize their time, energy, opportunities, and resources.

5. Creative

Million Dollar Practitioners pioneer their work with their clients and their practice. They like to build upon what they've learned and are excited to develop their own approaches to their work that express their gifts, talents, and perspectives. Most enjoy the thought of writing a book or developing a program that would make a unique and powerful contribution to the world.

6. Service-Oriented

Million Dollar Practitioners truly wish to make a difference in the world and are grateful for the opportunity to be of service to their clients. While they may have their financial goals, they wish to practice "right-livelihood." It's more important for them to fulfill their mission and purpose than it is to be financially successful, and as a result— perhaps paradoxically—they help more people and ultimately become wildly successful themselves.

7. Walking the Talk

Million Dollar Practitioners believe in the value of their work and are enthusiastic clients as well. They put time and effort into developing themselves and building the life that they really want, while they are making a living helping others do so. They have walked in their clients' shoes and continue to do so. Here's a related principle: *Investing in yourself will help your prospective clients see the value of investing in you.*

As a private practice professional, you should be able to take a look at any of the Seven Habits of Million Dollar Practitioners and say, "Okay, I can do that if I want to: I can be positive, I can be passionate, I can be entrepreneurial, I can play large, I can be creative, I can be service-oriented, I can walk the talk."

THE LONE RANGER

You can adopt the Seven Habits of Million Dollar Practitioners, no question about it. You probably need help overcoming some of your internal obstacles to do so. Just as you want to help your clients identify *their* obstacles, it's important to recognize that you have *your own*, and you need to deal with them, just as you want your clients to deal with theirs. And what is the most effective way to deal with them? By getting support for them, by not doing it alone.

One of my biggest pains and frustrations is seeing private practice professionals who want people to hire them yet don't get the support that they need. These lone rangers are struggling and flailing around because they don't have the clarity and resources that comes with having a support system, which is absolutely one of the biggest differentiators between being successful and not being successful. Are you getting help and support? No one is successful alone. People who try to do it all by themselves are building castles confined to their own minds. They are creating elaborate internal images that they think are wonderful and that everybody is going to love. But it's a fantasy if these images are not shared with others. Lone rangers lack the reality check that comes with doing something with and for real people, because they are living in their own minds, doing it by themselves, which is often a way of hiding.

There are many ways that we hide. Some people maintain a virtual practice. "I'm going to work from home and deal with people over the telephone and Internet so I won't even have to leave my house or directly interact with anybody." That is very attractive for some people, and certainly many services can be delivered effectively over the telephone. But if there is one thing I have learned in all my years of private practice, it's that you can't hide if you want to be successful. This lesson actually started much earlier, when I was 13 years old, and experienced the most terrifying moment of my life — ever.

PUBLIC SPEAKING

In preparation for your bar mitzvah, you are expected to study for about a year leading up to the actual event. And one of the biggest things you study is called the Haftorah — the portion of the Torah that you will recite for your bar mitzvah. In Jewish temples, they don't just recite it, they sing it. So not only did I have to engage in one of society's most feared activities, public speaking, I had to sing!

There I was, a 13-year-old boy, on a stage, behind a podium, with a microphone, in front of a couple hundred of my closest family, friends, and community members — singing! No joke: By the time I finished my performance, I was so soaked with sweat that I literally had to go home and change before the reception, which is immortalized in our family photos. If you look at a picture of me at my bar mitzvah, you will see me in a suit and tie with a blue shirt. And if you look at pictures of me at the reception, you will see me in a suit and tie with a white shirt.

Now after having gone through that experience you may think that I would never, ever want to subject myself to speaking in public again. But in junior college, in order to complete my requirements, I had to take certain electives, and public speaking ended up being one of them. Predictably, my first couple of talks were horrendous. But that class helped me become a heck of a lot more comfortable speaking in front of a group, even though, for many years as I toiled as a marriage and family therapist in private practice, public speaking wasn't something I had to do.

I went into a profession where all my work was one-to-one. I sat in a private office, with four walls and a door, a couch, a chair, and a desk, and me and one other person, or me and a couple, or, at most, me and a small family. Every once in a while I gave a talk to a group as part of my marketing, but it wasn't something that I sought out, and it certainly wasn't something I perceived myself as doing very well.

Eventually I made the transition to relationship coaching because I was burning out as a marriage therapist. In my new career path, I decided that I wanted to reach singles and figured the way to do so was to start hosting singles events and giving presentations and seminars—public speaking. As frightening a prospect as that was, I knew I didn't want to go back to my life of burnout, so my only option was to move forward. And going forward meant speaking in front of groups. Even though I was uncomfortable doing so, I did it anyway, and it worked out very well. My singles events were successful and I became more and more comfortable with public speaking.

Then, when I started Relationship Coaching Institute (RCI), just about everything I did was speaking to groups. Again, I didn't want to, but I did it anyway. For a long time my goal was to stay in the background. My introverted preference was to be the "man behind the curtain," supporting and empowering everybody else. I didn't view myself as anything special and certainly not as a front man. I'm not especially good-looking, charismatic, or brilliant. I'm just a regular guy and would rather be the supporter than the star. As a result of this mind-set, my business didn't go anywhere—that is, until I was willing to step out front and reveal all. Without getting too much into the psychology of it, there are many ways that we hide and there are many reasons why we hide, but there is one thing that is clear: You cannot hide if you are going to build a Million Dollar Practice. I didn't want to be the front person, but it was unavoidable. For RCI to succeed, I had to be a leader, I had to be out in front. Public speaking was something that I had to embrace to accomplish my goals. It was not something that came comfortably at first. It was not something I wanted to do. But the payoff was that, after working with a speaking coach/mentor (thanks, Burt!), it became something enjoyable, something I looked forward to, and something I became good at doing.

Many people are not comfortable speaking in public. They have tremendous resistance to it. Yet, part of building a Million Dollar Practice, especially as it relates to the one-to-many model that we will explore later in this book, is the ability to speak in front of groups. People who shy away from public speaking and say, "Well, I'm not comfortable," and use that as a reason for "No" are going to stay small. The ones who work through that fear and overcome their internal obstacles to public speaking—as one of many, many examples of what might get in the way—are the ones who are going to make it.

Remember: When I started out, I was scared just like everybody else. But I worked through that fear so as to not let it stand in the way of my goals. In time, I got better at it and was able to reach more people. And when it became apparent that speaking was going to help me get where I wanted to go, I even hired a speaking mentor, one of the top guys in the industry who advises lots of top speakers. He wasn't cheap but he was worth the investment. I worked with him for a year and I'm glad I did because I learned a lot. And the more I got up and spoke in front of people the better and more comfortable I became. Now, speaking in front of groups is something I look forward to and can do without anxiety.

My wife and I travel thousands of miles to speak at professional conferences, and when I'm getting ready to take the stage she always asks me, "Are you nervous?" And my response is always the same and she can't believe it: "No."

She can't believe it because she would be nervous. But when you do something enough, you become comfortable with it, you become good at it, and you even come to enjoy it, like exercise. Embrace the things that are uncomfortable or hard, don't focus on "I can't because . . ." or

"I don't want to." Focus on "How can I?" How can I get that speaking gig? How can I do a good job in that speaking gig? How can I penetrate this niche? How can I build a Million Dollar Practice? Those are the questions to ask. When you ask those questions, you'll find many ways. There are always resources. There are always solutions. There are always strategies. The beautiful thing is that there are usually *many* ways to go, not just one. It's like the marketing triad: speaking, writing, and networking. You don't like to write? You're not good at writing? You don't have to write. There are other ways to market. You really don't want to speak? Okay, there are other ways to market.

We should embrace and say "Yes" to opportunities that come our way. If somebody asks you to speak, say "Yes!" Don't say "No, I don't speak in public," "No, I'm not good at that," or "No, I'm not comfortable."

One day I was approached by a top-notch pay-per-click-advertising guy who wanted me to help market his services to my network. I appreciated his work and thought a lot of people could benefit from it, and I was quite open to the idea. So I said, "Okay, well, why don't you put together a tele-seminar introducing my network to pay-per-click advertising. Explain it to them, give them some tips, and then let them know what your services and programs are." And he wouldn't do it. He wanted the business, but when I told him how to get the business, he said, "No, I'm not comfortable doing that." As a result, he lost the opportunity to reach 20,000 people in a single 1-hour telephone call from the comfort of his home or office.

Again, the people who have the hardest time succeeding aren't the ones who don't know what to do, they are the ones who aren't willing to do it. They (understandably) hold back when they have internal resistance, which causes them to procrastinate, avoid, or delay, which in turn causes them to miss out on opportunities. The ones who are successful are the ones who ask, "How can I overcome this?" or "How can I accomplish this?" and who get the support they need to do it.

FEAR OF SUCCESS AND FEAR OF FAILURE

Most of us understand fear of failure. We recognize that we all have a lower limit, a pain threshold, beyond which things become so uncomfortable that we feel the need to act to protect ourselves to survive. The fear of success, however, is not something that a lot of people really understand, but it's something that we all have. One of the most helpful ways of understanding fear of success is to frame it as an *upper limit*. An upper limit works similarly to the lower limit, except instead of being about survival, it's about happiness and success. Believe it or not, even though we might want it, when we get up there it feels scary. And so what do we do? We do things to bring us back down to a more comfortable level. We sabotage ourselves. Again, everybody has a comfort zone comprised of a lower limit and an upper limit. Our job is to not let those limits dictate our choices. It's unnecessary to live our lives based upon our survival instincts. We don't need to live our lives avoiding too much pain and happiness because when we get near them we become scared. But it's a lifelong journey to raise our upper limits to be able to handle increasing levels of success and fulfillment, because, for most of us, whether it's that relationship, that job, that business opportunity, or something else, when we get far enough outside of our comfort zone it brings up all our *stuff*. Childhood insecurities, family situations, experiences we've had in our past, lack of faith and belief in ourselves, how much or little we feel safe in the world, the amount that we trust ourselves or other people—there are many reasons why we self-sabotage. It all falls under the umbrella of *stuff*. For now, it's enough to be clear that we all have it, that it is triggered when we are outside of our comfort zone, and that therefore it's our biggest obstacle to building a Million Dollar Practice.

And since our *stuff* comes out in fear of failure and fear of success, and since building a successful private practice is an entrepreneurial enterprise and for a lot of practitioners being an entrepreneur does not come naturally, it's something that needs to be learned and chosen and consciously embraced. We don't just walk by the entrepreneurial pool and say, "Wow, that looks inviting, I think I'll jump right in!" No, we look at that pool and say, "Ooh, that water looks cold, I don't know if I'm ready to get in there yet. Maybe I'll put my toe in the water . . . well, maybe not my toe, I'd have to take off my shoe . . . how about my finger?"

In answering the litmus test question, whatever *stuff* comes up for you is just an indication of what you have to deal with. It doesn't mean that you are not able to become an entrepreneur or build a Million Dollar Practice, it just means that you are going to have a hero's journey. Well, congratulations, most of us do!

If it were easy, everybody would have built a Million Dollar Practice by now, and it wouldn't be worthwhile. Anything valuable, special, or exceptional is done through hard work, by taking risks, and with consistent stretching.

So now that we have laid out some principle habits of Million Dollar Practitioners and given you a flavor of the right mind-set, let's delve a little deeper into a key point of view that will guide you along your hero's journey to a Million Dollar Practice.

Technician or Entrepreneur

Three fundamental categories set the stage for how you operate in business: the technician, the manager, and the entrepreneur. Michael Gerber does a fantastic job of laying these out in his book, *The E-Myth Revisited*. For the purposes of determining how your current mind-set might be better aligned with that of a Million Dollar Practitioner—and as a prelude to Chapter 2, as it relates to your mission and message—we're going to examine the technician and the entrepreneur.

Most private practice professionals are technicians. That is, they have been trained in a particular area of expertise, much like somebody trained to fix your refrigerator or your car. They have skills and experience, training and knowledge. But there is a difference between the person who fixes your car or home appliances, and the person who owns a car or appliance repair shop and lives in a mansion on a hill:

The technician just wants to do his work and get paid for it.

The entrepreneur has a dream or vision to create a successful business.

The Entrepreneurial Mind-Set

Building a successful six- and seven-figure private practice is a journey fraught with obstacles. The litmus test question—in addition to helping you identify and uncover inner resistance—gauges your current level of resolve to navigate them. It sheds light on the entrepreneurial mind-set necessary to build a Million Dollar Practice.

Will you embrace your inner entrepreneur or submit to your inner resistance? The litmus test question helps you answer this question.

Again, if you answered affirmatively to the litmus test question, don't be discouraged. It doesn't mean that you can't build a Million Dollar Practice. It just means that what you really want, right now, deep down, is just to be given a job. You currently have inner resistance to the freedom, opportunities, and obstacles that come with being a self-employed entrepreneurial practitioner. If you answered "Yes" to the litmus test question, it means that the things most celebrated by entrepreneurs about being self-employed are things that scare you . . . at this moment. And that's okay.

Most practitioners, myself included, have a measure of fear and resistance at some level. But we also have the ability to identify, address, and overcome that fear and resistance. The litmus test question is one way to begin the transformation from anxiety to prosperity. Because if somebody were to offer you a job doing what you wanted to do with whom you wanted to do it, and you would accept it, that's a strong indication that—right now—you have some resistance to overcome to become ready for a Million Dollar Practice.

Setting business goals that are incongruent with an existing inner resistance to becoming an entrepreneur will lead you along a bumpy road to nowhere. Granted, if you are seeking self-employment you will likely have a bumpy road ahead of you anyway; most practitioners do. But understanding what's coming—to the extent that you can—and having the mind-set necessary to endure it helps you stay on course to where you want to go.

Reaching your destination takes strength of character, clearly defined goals, and an entrepreneurial mind-set. There is enormous pressure to turn around and seek safe passage when the storms rage and the seas swell in front of you. As practitioners, we recognize this. We understand that our clients have obstacles to achieving the results that we want to help them get. We recognize them because we have them, too—in life and in business. Resisting self-employment and the risk and freedom that comes with private practice is among them.

That's why many private practice professionals "sell out" to insurance companies and spend time, energy, and resources doing work they don't love and being underpaid for it.

Of course, if that's the only way you can serve your population, then you have to make some sacrifices. If you want to serve the homeless, you have to accept that the homeless can't pay you. You're going to have to spend your time and effort getting grants and government contracts. But to me, it's a trap, one that can permanently derail your efforts to build a Million Dollar Practice, one that has a significant social impact. When the focus of your organization is about survival, about getting paid, it takes time, energy, and resources away from serving your population, being creative, building your organization, and making a wider difference in the world.

But there is a workaround:

Build a wildly successful organization and then *contract with the government.*

To some, this may sound paradoxical, but it's like getting a loan at the bank; the bank wants to lend you money only if you don't need the loan. In the same vein, the government is most eager to give grants and contracts to people or organizations that don't need the grants or contracts. Everybody likes success.

CASE STUDY: THE SCREAMFREE INSTITUTE

Hal Runkel is cofounder and the public face of The ScreamFree Institute, an organization that promotes the idea that keeping your cool is the way to a happier home life and a successful marriage. Hal and his partners are worth emulating. The ScreamFree Institute is indeed a Million Dollar Practice. It also happens to be a not-for-profit organization.

The ScreamFree Institute helps tens of thousands of people all over the world have better marriages and families, including the men and women of the U.S. Armed Forces. The government is happy to give Hal and his organization money to work with military families because ScreamFree—in addition to being a brilliant brand—is a tremendously successful business model, albeit a not-for-profit one.

It's catchy. It's "teach-out-of-the box." It's effective. Lenders and keepers of the purse happen to like it when you offer measurable results and a discrete solution. By discrete I mean it has a beginning and an end. It's not a black hole for time and money.

Make no mistake, the success of the ScreamFree Institute is no accident. Hal Runkel is a licensed marriage and family therapist, and he is also a savvy businessman. Hal and his partners have surrounded themselves with a team of intelligent and experienced people. They know what they are good at and empower each other to excel in ways that best support their mission. While they have certainly made their share of mistakes like everyone else, everything they have done—including adopting a not-for-profit business model—has been the result of careful consideration. If Hal and his team had started out pursuing government contracts, they likely would have hit hard times when the contracts expired or the funding ran dry. Instead, they built an organization and became visible and successful *first*. Jumping to the next level of reaching tens of thousands of military families was a natural progression. It wasn't based on survival, it was based on mission. And it's a perfect illustration of an important principle to bear in mind as you pursue a Million Dollar Practice.

THE LONG WAY IS THE SHORT WAY AND THE SHORT WAY IS THE LONG WAY

One of my mentors adapted a passage from the Talmud[1] that has become one of my favorite sayings and principles:

In life, sometimes the long way is the short way and the short way is the long way.

---

[1]Solomon, Norman (2009). *The Talmud: A selection.* Penguin Classics. Gemara: [53b] "I was on my way when I saw a boy sitting at the crossroads. I asked, Which is the way into town? He said, This way is short but long, and that one is long but short. I followed the short but long [route], but when I arrived at the town I found that it was surrounded by gardens and orchards, and I had to retrace my steps. I said, My son, didn't you tell me that was the short [route]? He said to me, But didn't I tell you it was long! I kissed his head and said to him, Happy are you, Israel, for you are all astute, from the greatest to the smallest!"

Hal Runkel displayed knowledge of this principle in building the ScreamFree Institute, and it can be applied in all sorts of situations. I often remind my kids about it in relation to their homework. Invariably, when my kids take shortcuts and rush through their homework to get it done as soon as possible so they can play video games, it needs to be redone. It's sloppy and incorrect. I try to instill in my kids that if they would just take their time and do a good job on their homework from the outset, they would be done with it and able to play much faster.

It's funny; at parent-teacher conferences, the teachers tell me, "I only give 10–15 minutes of homework a night." And then I see my kids spending *hours*. Why are they spending hours when it's only designed to take 10–15 minutes? Well, partly because they have a tremendous amount of internal resistance to doing their homework. And who can blame them? However, if they would just choose to embrace the task with a positive attitude and say, "Okay, I completely commit to this and will do the best job I possibly can on this assignment," they would be done a heck of a lot faster.

It's the same with building a private practice. Seeking government grants and taking on managed care clients is often chosen over marketing to get private pay clients. It's the short way. But it's also the long way. Unless the managed care approach is in keeping with your original goals and interests, you are likely not going to be happy with where you end up, which, in effect, will be way off course from where you originally intended. Besides, the money wouldn't necessarily always be there anyway, so it's best to take the time to create a strong foundation.

Similarly, that's why I referenced the "stars-in-the-eyes" practitioners at the opening of this chapter. If you want to leapfrog straight to seven figures without paying your dues and laying your foundation, you are in for a rude awakening. If, on the other hand, you methodically build your business on sustainable, scalable principles, like Hal Runkel and his partners did with the ScreamFree Institute, then you can command all the contracts and get all the business that you want. In building a sustainable, successful Million Dollar Practice, the long way is the short way, and the short way is the long way.

IT's AN EVOLUTION

Before you are ready to claim the mantle of the Million Dollar Practice and the lucrative contracts that come with it, there is an evolution that must take place. It takes time to create a Million Dollar Practice. There's a progression. And it should come as no shock to you that undergoing such a progression is not easy. It's not impossible . . . but it's not easy. That's why having a positive mind-set is so critical. And as we mentioned earlier, shaping that mind-set starts with recognizing and overcoming your internal fears and resistance. To assist you to do so, I'm going to rely on one of my colleagues to help demystify some of what lies ahead in your practice-building journey.

If you are going to pursue a Million Dollar Practice, the most critical piece of advice I can share with you is that you must understand and embrace the stages of practice building. You must recognize and accept not only where you are, but also where you want to go and what it takes to get there.

My friend, renowned conscious business expert and entrepreneur, Brian Whetten, PhD, of SellingByGiving.net, has created a comprehensive description of the progression for building a successful practice he calls *The Seven Stages of Practice Building*. With his permission, and because I have used it to such great effect with my clients, I would like to share the nuts and bolts of it with you now.

THE SEVEN STAGES OF PRACTICE BUILDING[2]

Stage 1: Student

Your private practice career starts as a student pursuing your degree or certificate in your area of focus—psychology, finance, spirituality, etc.—and you are developing the requisite knowledge to prepare you for your quest to make a difference in the world. The developmental goal of the student is to "develop trust in the value of what you've

---

[2]Adapted from *The Seven Stages of Practice Building* with permission from Brian Whetten, PhD, MA, www.sellingbygiving.net © 2010. All rights reserved.

learned." This stage is marked by a comfort level some find tough to get beyond. Practitioners often revert back to this stage when they encounter obstacles or get in a jam: "I need to go back to school." "I need more training."

Stage 2: Intern

You are an intern when you graduate from your degree or certification program and are focused on gaining experience. Here the developmental goal is to "develop trust in your ability to provide exceptional value." The intern level is reached when you have successfully delivered exceptional value to at least five repeat clients. Getting paid for your efforts is not necessary at this level. What's important is that you receive positive feedback affirming your ability to deliver effective services to your clients.

Stage 3: Apprentice

Here is where you start getting paid. You know you are an apprentice when you are finally earning some or most of your income through your chosen profession, consistently. This level can be achieved simultaneously with stage two. The developmental goal of the apprentice is to "develop trust in your ability to get paid for your services."

Stage 4: Practitioner

This is the first stage of full-time private practice. If you haven't done so already (as many practitioners jump the gun in this regard), your efforts are designed to build your practice to the point where you can quit your day job. Some may think that leaving your day job early (before your practice pays your bills) to work full time in private practice gives you a tactical advantage in building it. But that's not necessarily the case. Leaving your day job too soon often creates undue stress and prompts you to act hastily and erratically, which in turn detracts from your ability to deliver quality services. Remember the survival mode we mentioned earlier? The goal of stage four is to "develop trust in your ability to support your basic financial needs with your practice's income."

Stage 5: Master Practitioner

In this stage, you have a successful practice and are refining your business to coincide with your vision, mission, and message. The developmental goal of the master practitioner is to "develop trust in your ability to enroll clients at will." You are confident in your ability to get clients, you only work with your desired clients, and you might even have a waiting list. This is the six-figure practice level.

Stage 6: Teacher

If you are in the Teacher phase of practice building, your focus is to "develop trust in your ability to effectively enroll groups of people and to function as an entrepreneur." Here we are getting to the crux of a Million Dollar Practice; the idea of a technician vs. an entrepreneur, a one-to-one model vs. a one-to-many model (to be covered in Chapter 2). This is where the rubber meets the road and where the entrepreneurial mind-set really kicks in. This is where the transition takes place for building a Million Dollar Practice.

Stage 7: Leader

At this stage of the game, your goal is to "develop trust in the systems you've built for effectively enrolling participants as well as building your organization to the place that you are no longer needed for day-to-day operations." But remember: This is not the endgame. You don't ever stop building your practice. You must continue to grow and expand your ability to serve your chosen niche. There is no limit to the degrees of leadership and how far you can expand your mission.

Again, the progression laid out in Brian Whetten's *The Seven Stages of Practice Building* is designed to put things in perspective so you can see where you are, where you want to go, and the steps and time investment needed to get there. So where are you now? While the primary audience for this book is Stage 4 Practitioners and above, those in the earlier stages can benefit from knowing what's ahead in order to "begin with the end in mind."

What is a Million Dollar Practice?

Many private practice professionals see a "six-figure practice"—or Master Practitioner as viewed through the lens of *The Seven Stages of Practice Building*—as the pinnacle of their professional and financial success. And there is nothing wrong with that. In fact, this was my goal years ago as a marriage and family therapist in private practice. Since then, however, I've learned that you can go beyond the six-figure level. You can indeed build a Million Dollar Practice. But what does that mean, exactly?

A Million Dollar Practice is not a numerical measure of success. It's a scalable business model. Sure, some practices reach the literal, seven-figure, quantifiable dollar value, but we are talking about much more than dollars. In addition to the inevitable financial compensation that comes along with it, we are talking about leveraging your expertise to not only build a successful business, but to make a significant difference in the lives of others.

Comparing the Six Figure Practice and the Million Dollar Practice

SIX FIGURE PRACTICE	MILLION DOLLAR PRACTICE
The Six Figure Practice typically exchanges time for dollars (one-to-one)	The Million Dollar Practice has multiple revenue streams (one-to-many)
The Six Figure Practice typically provides a standard service commonly found elsewhere	The Million Dollar Practice provides unique and creative services unavailable anywhere else
The Six Figure Practice typically emphasizes quality services and benefits	The Million Dollar Practice emphasizes life-changing results
The Six Figure Practice is typically composed of one practitioner and a few staff	The Million Dollar Practice is a collaboration of motivated partners providing complementary talents and contributions
The Six Figure Practice seeks to make a comfortable living	The Million Dollar Practice seeks to make a social impact

What is a Million Dollar Practice?

The Six Figure Practice Typically Exchanges Time for Dollars (One-to-One) If you are practicing at the six-figure level, there is a good chance that you are still operating under the one-to-one model. This is the mind-set and method of the technician. When your primary means of service is conducting one-to-one sessions, exchanging your time for dollars, you limit not only your income potential but also the number of people you are able to reach.

The Million Dollar Practice Has Multiple Revenue Streams (One-to-Many) By opening up your practice with products and programs, you instantly make yourself available to a much wider slice of your niche. This creates multiple revenue streams that can help others, generates income while you sleep, and leverages your time to help more people.

The Six Figure Practice Typically Provides a Standard Service Commonly Found Elsewhere Practitioners at the six-figure level are no doubt providing a valuable service. But they tend to offer a level of service that people can readily get elsewhere. This poses problems on several levels, not the least of which is that it forces the practitioner to compete on price. On one hand, why would you pay more for the exact same service when you could get it down the street for less? On the other hand, if you want ScreamFree Parenting, you can only go to Hal Runkel's organization.

The Million Dollar Practice Provides Unique and Creative Services Unavailable Anywhere Else When you make the switch to the Million Dollar Practice model, you begin to look for ways to customize your products and services. This adds more value to your constituents, who are not necessarily averse to paying higher fees for added benefits and a custom program unavailable anywhere else.

The Six Figure Practice Typically Emphasizes Quality Services and Benefits There is no quicker way to lump yourself in with every other provider that does what you do than to tout your quality service and benefits. That's what everybody does. And while it's important to do it, doing that alone won't lead to a Million Dollar Practice.

The Million Dollar Practice Emphasizes Life-Changing Results If you truly want to set yourself and your business apart from the rest, you would be wise to highlight the transformation that you deliver for your clients (and you do!). Again, excellent customer service is no longer enough; it's expected, a given. Today, in addition to clearly communicating the benefits and results of your services, you must deliver on your promise to change people's lives.

The Six Figure Practice Is Typically Composed of One Practitioner and a Few Staff If there's one mistake that I see over and over and over again with my practice-building clients, it's that they try to do everything themselves. Whether it is to hide, to maintain control, or to save money, many practitioners keep too tight a grip on administrative and other tasks that would be better suited for others.

The Million Dollar Practice Is a Collaboration of Motivated Partners Providing Complementary Talents and Contributions If you want to jump to the level of the Million Dollar Practice, you're going to need help. You can't do it alone. Taking advantage of skilled and knowledgeable employees, contractors, and partners is the way to grow your business efficiently, reach more people, and allow everyone to stay focused on their areas of expertise to benefit all involved.

The Six Figure Practice Seeks to Make a Comfortable Living If you are just looking to get by and live a fairly easygoing life—which is perfectly fine—then you will likely find yourself hanging around the periphery of the six-figure level. This mind-set is shared by many helping professionals who never really look beyond their desire to be a technician in their chosen field.

The Million Dollar Practice Seeks to Make a Social Impact Private practice professionals who are in touch with their inner entrepreneur are more prone to wanting to make a broader difference in the world. While it may be one component of a larger mission, they are not satisfied to see their contributions stop within the walls of their office.

Those pursuing the Million Dollar Practice seek to have a much larger and more significant social impact.

IS A MILLION DOLLAR PRACTICE POSSIBLE?

Now that you see what a Million Dollar Practice involves, does it seem like it's worth pursuing? In your eyes, does a Million Dollar Practice seem possible?

We've already touched upon one example of someone who has built a Million Dollar Practice, Hal Runkel with the ScreamFree Institute, but there are other examples that may be more familiar to you. And they all share something in common with Hal and, more important, with you.

Deepak Chopra. Anthony Robbins. Jack Canfield. You name it. These are just ordinary people who have leveraged their expertise to build a Million Dollar Practice. These helping professionals have brought passion to their work. They have created their own approaches to helping people that make a difference. And they have built successful businesses around them.

While many practitioners might not believe such professional and monetary success is even possible for them, we know that it is. We know it because we have seen people do it. And we have much to learn from them. They serve as inspiration. They provide a roadmap. Their methods and techniques can be applied and built upon with your own special talents and areas of expertise to make a larger difference in the world and to touch the lives of many—that is, to build a Million Dollar Practice.

Again, this is not to suggest that building a Million Dollar Practice will be easy. While most private practice professionals dream of earning six and seven figures, it takes a specific combination of passion, understanding, risk-taking, entrepreneurial spirit, and overcoming obstacles and resistance to pull it off.

Let's examine some cases in more detail.

Case Study: Deepak Chopra

No practitioner has better leveraged his expertise to build a successful business and make a difference than Deepak Chopra. And you won't find a better example of a Million Dollar Practice than the Chopra Center for Wellbeing. While its reach now stretches around the globe, it wasn't always that way.

Founded by Deepak Chopra and David Simon, the Chopra Center began with two physicians who stood for something bigger than themselves, the concept of combining Eastern spirituality and Western medicine to bring a unique and holistic health approach to the world. Deepak Chopra and David Simon started with merely an idea and the passion to see it through. And they turned that into an empire that impacts millions. How did they do it? Well, along with leveraging the principles laid out in this book, they did it with the help of a great team of people, one of whom, Max Simon, is not only a friend of mine but a valued mentor.

Max Simon currently serves as Chief Enlightenment Officer of GetSelfCentered.com. And while he is a brilliant guy in his own right, he is also the son of Chopra Center cofounder David Simon. Fresh out of business school, Max was tapped as the Chopra Center's new Director of Consumer Products—a tall order for a 21-year-old. Max accepted the challenge and turned a fledgling products division into a multimillion dollar market. He revamped 49 products and tripled online sales. Max knows a little something about business.

During a recent conversation, Max gave me an inside look at the Chopra Center's transformation. He provided insight into how two ordinary guys, physicians intent on helping others through mind-body medicine, banded together and managed to leverage their interests and expertise to not only build a business around it, but also evolve their practice into a global phenomenon.

Through his experience with the Chopra Center, and through the principles and philosophies he teaches in his own business, Max is clear on what an entrepreneur needs to do to go from a one-to-one model (seeing people individually) to a one-to-many model (serving groups), one of the principal tenets of building a Million Dollar Practice.

First, let it be known—and Max will be the first to tell you—that the Chopra Center for Wellbeing is a bit of an anomaly. Not because they did something that you can't do, but because they were actually willing to do it. They stood for something that nobody else dared stand for at the time.

Back in the 1980s, mind-body medicine, meditation, yoga—even vegetarianism—were not commonly accepted. Deepak Chopra and David Simon championed a methodology and philosophy that was completely new to the Western world—a rarity in this day and age. As Max maintains, "There are very few things these days that are completely new to the world."

Most of what's new to the world these days is more good marketing than it is new concepts.

Deepak Chopra and David Simon were trained in Western medicine. They were also exposed to mind-body medicine. They trained in meditation and yoga. They explored and experienced a particular form of enlightened living and raising consciousness. And they were profoundly moved by it.

As physicians, Deepak Chopra and David Simon started to look deeper into the scientific and medical opportunities and implications of their philosophy. They believed that mind and body were connected and that much of the way Western medicine was being delivered to the world was incomplete. They felt that spirituality and mind-body medicine needed to be integrated into our modern health-care system.

While they certainly had a lot of the right ingredients fall into place over time, Deepak Chopra and David Simon's success came from seeing an opportunity to do something they genuinely believed was going to help people. And because they were innovators, they weren't immediately seen as popular or even credible. They were seen as eccentric, even crazy. It wasn't until Deepak Chopra went on *The Oprah Winfrey Show* that they gained some real traction. It started with Deepak Chopra's books. His books led him to Oprah. And Oprah led him to the world. Once he received that overnight recognition, everything just took off. Deepak Chopra's books became bestsellers, and Deepak Chopra and David Simon opened the Chopra Center for Wellbeing.

Neither Deepak Chopra nor David Simon ever planned to create a worldwide movement. They just took a stand for what they believed.

And while it's clear that a bit of good fortune came into play, as it does with every international sensation, it's also clear that Deepak Chopra and David Simon weren't just doctors waiting in their offices for people to come so they could heal them. They both took a firm stand, they were both teachers at heart, they both put themselves out there—in books, in classes, and in products—and they built a following in the process.

In addition to being an integral part of the Chopra Center's growth, being the son of one of the cofounders, Max Simon has been given a ringside seat to the personal side of the public face of the Chopra Center. Max has known Deepak Chopra all of his life and has been deeply influenced by him. Max is well aware that Deepak has a lot going for him—his charisma, his brilliant mind, and his ability to wrap language around the way he has come to look at the world chief among them—but Max also knows the man behind the public persona. He knows Deepak Chopra as a person. But just how important is that in growing a Million Dollar Practice?

When I interviewed Max for this book, I wondered what practitioners can learn about building a Million Dollar Practice from Deepak Chopra. I asked him what draws people to Deepak and what makes him so successful:

> *"Where does he come from inside that causes people to be attracted to him? Do you think that it's genuine? Is it manipulative? Is he just a good salesman? Is he truly as spiritual and compassionate as he seems?"*
>
> *"I think Deepak is all of it." Max said. "I think we all are."*

"He's got his flaws as well," Max continued. "He does things wrong. Yes, he's at times manipulative. He's just another person who's doing the best he can. People are often surprised about that. But I've known Deepak pretty much my whole life. Underneath the superstar is just another guy. But he truly is brilliant and charismatic, and he has certainly managed to do a lot of good things in the world. He's screwed up a lot of business deals and done a lot of things wrong. He's just like you and me. He's had lots of successes, and he's had lots of failures, too. And that's okay."

As you can see, while Deepak Chopra has his unique gifts and talents — just like you do — he is also a person who has made mistakes and who has built his practice from the ground up, just like you plan to do. His story is not unlike another Million Dollar Practice builder you may recognize.

Case Study: Anthony Robbins

Anthony "Tony" Robbins is more than a name. He's an institution. The world of personal growth owes a tremendous debt of gratitude to this pioneer.

Tony Robbins grew up in the Los Angeles area, a child of divorce, in a poor household. When he was 13, a stranger left an anonymous gift of food on his family's doorstep so they could properly celebrate Thanksgiving. Tony Robbins was so taken by this act that he vowed he would one day be successful enough to return the favor to others.

Like Deepak Chopra, Tony Robbins has always been a charismatic person. But his success comprises more than that. He, too, believed in what he was doing and put himself out there to champion it. By the time he was 19, he was making $10,000 per month as a salesman for motivational speaker Jim Rohn. But for Tony, it was too much too fast. As he achieved more and more financial success and recognition, he felt isolated and started sabotaging himself. He began missing meetings and overeating. He became an overweight recluse. Tony Robbins essentially hit rock bottom at the ripe old age of 21.

Out for a walk on the beach one day, Tony Robbins made the decision to pick himself up, take control of his life, and make the most of his talents and knowledge. With a foundation in Neuro-Linguistic Programming (NLP), Tony Robbins began hosting personal growth seminars that steadily grew in popularity and got himself back on track inside a year. His signature seminar was called Fear into Power, where he walked barefoot on hot coals and had people do the same. Over time, he revamped and improved his seminars and workshops, many of which were sold out months ahead of time.

One day he met a literary agent who was attending one of his seminars. This meeting eventually led to the book *Unlimited Power*, a huge bestseller that cemented his presence as a self-help guru. You may be familiar with Robbins's next marketing attempt, as he was an early adopter of the infomercial. Through these extended television broadcasts, Robbins sold his products, tapes, books, programs, and seminars and created an enormous following. He became extremely wealthy, amassed an elite client list from professional athletes to heads of state, and had a worldwide impact. He also charged top dollar for his personal time and ongoing daily group presentations. Tony Robbins built a Million Dollar Practice.

While things were certainly not all roses for Robbins, who, as we are all vulnerable, suffered heartache, skepticism — even lawsuits — there is no question that his rags-to-riches story serves as an inspirational example of the possibility of the average person to build a Million Dollar Practice. But it's important to note that — like Deepak Chopra and Hal Runkel — Tony Robbins didn't do it alone. He had mentors and a team of professionals to help him with his mission, some of whom actually now work within my organization to serve our clients and further our mission.

Case Study: David Steele

If you still doubt that building a Million Dollar Practice is possible for the everyday practitioner, allow me to direct you to another, lesser-known, example: yours truly. And believe me, no one was more surprised than I was at an ordinary person's ability to build a Million Dollar Practice.

Starting down the path of becoming a marriage and family therapist, I had no idea I would end up here. I never thought I would hit the big time. In fact, you could say that founding Relationship Coaching Institute was a bit of a fluke.

My mission started when I was a child, being unhappy and confused about my parents' divorce and why they were so unhappy and why my mother was so mean to me and why my father didn't have any interest in being a father. There was a lot of pain in my childhood. I was trying to understand it all. It was liberating to me when I realized, eventually, that it was not about me. It wasn't my fault. There was nothing wrong with me. That one realization, which occurred sometime in my teens, freed me up tremendously. But there was a lot of pain that caused me to enter my profession, a lot of healing that I had to do, a journey that I had to take to become the person I wanted to be, have the life I wanted to have, and get my needs met in ways that they weren't met when I was a kid. So I embarked on a mission that propelled me to get my degree and license as a marriage and family therapist, start my own practice, and share what I learned to help others who were struggling in similar ways.

I started out working with clients in the hopes of helping them resolve their relationship problems and dreamed of maybe one day hitting the six-figure level. Since then, I've met and exceeded that original aim by building a successful relationship coaching business in my local area, founding Relationship Coaching Institute (the first and largest relationship coach training organization), publishing relationship and practice-building books, developing numerous products and programs (*Conscious Dating*, *Private Practice Marketing on a Budget*, *Private Practice Magic*, etc.), and founding MillionDollarPractice.net to help private practice professionals build their ideal practices and fill them with their ideal clients. In short, I've built a Million Dollar Practice . . . but, like the other examples cited, it didn't happen overnight.

MY EPIPHANY

Back in 1997 when I was a marriage and family therapist in full-time private practice, sitting in my four-walled office in Silicon Valley, my days and nights were filled with stress. I was burning out, my bank balance was heading south, and the reason I started my career in the first place, to help change people's lives (I had committed to single-handedly bringing down the divorce rate in this country), had been met with mixed results.

That's when I stumbled upon coaching—and fell in love with it. Suddenly, I realized that an entirely new helping profession had developed completely off my radar. After first taking a weekend workshop, and then completing a comprehensive training in personal coaching—sometimes called life coaching—my perspective completely changed. I started to see new possibilities. As a therapist, I found it an attractive and novel approach to work with functional people who had goals and wanted fulfillment in their lives. So when I first looked at relationships from a coaching perspective, it struck me as more effective to help people succeed in their goals than to attempt to help them fix their problems. It seemed so logical all of a sudden: Singles become couples!

How could I have overlooked this niche—singles in Silicon Valley—for so long in my mission to help people have successful marriages and families? *If we could help singles learn about themselves and relationships, including how to make good relationship choices, their chances for long-term success would be greatly increased.* It was settled: Working with singles was the critical starting point.

Shortly thereafter, I started holding weekly singles events, and word quickly spread throughout the community. The events consistently filled to capacity. Before long, my colleagues caught on to what I was doing and they wanted me to train them.

No, no, no, I thought. *I'm having a lot of fun here. I just want to build a successful relationship coaching practice and work with my clients.*

After all, until then, it had never occurred to me to train anybody in anything. I had never dreamed I would ever come up with something worth teaching. Unfortunately, this mind-set is all too common with helping professionals. As practitioners, we are often in awe of other people who conduct trainings and who have originated things. But not in a million years do we think *we* can originate something. *All the good ideas are taken . . .* or so we think.

The truth is, we are all brilliant. We all have the potential to create our own brand—and our own branded programs—that we can leverage into a Million Dollar Practice, one that is helpful to a great many people.

Thankfully, along with my epiphany that singles become couples, I realized that to build a Million Dollar Practice you must leave your comfort zone. You must say "Yes" to things that you would otherwise shy away from. So, when I was asked to help train my colleagues— even though I was originally against it—I said, "Yes." And years later, here I am.

WHO'S ON YOUR BOOKSHELF?

It's almost impossible to become a helping professional without accumulating shelves and shelves of books, and to admire and be influenced by certain leaders in our profession.

Thinking about all of the experts and industry leaders who have written books that have influenced me over the years, I started going through my bookshelf to identify those who have a Million Dollar Practice. As a result, I quickly identified a host of role models who have successfully reached the public and brought their expertise into the mainstream. And here they are in no particular order:

Rhonda Britten is a coach. She wrote a book called *Fearless Living: Live Without Excuses and Love Without Regret*. And she followed that up with *Fearless Loving: 8 Simple Truths That Will Change the Way You Date, Mate, and Relate*. She also wrote *Change Your Life in 30 Days: A Journey to Finding Your True Self*. Rhonda created the Fearless Living Institute, similar to the ScreamFree Institute, created by Hal Runkel, whose books I also have in my bookshelf. Fearless Living is Rhonda's brand, and she is definitely in the one-to-many space and has been on top TV programs. She has taken her passion, experience, and expertise and spent many years getting people to push past their fears, embrace their passions, and live their best lives. Now she is a franchise. She is an accomplished woman with a Million Dollar Practice.

Harville Hendrix wrote a book called *Getting the Love You Want: A Guide for Couples*. He took his relationship theory and created a whole approach to relationships called Imago Therapy. He created the Imago Institute, which conducts training and certification of professionals as well as workshops and seminars for the public. He has been called "Oprah's favorite therapist." Harville packaged his approach to couple relationships just like I packaged my approach to singles. An intellectual with a ranch in New Mexico (which I visited at his invitation), Harville has the life of a rock star and makes a difference in people's lives on a huge scale.

Marsha Wieder founded Dream University. She is a coach like Rhonda Britten and wants to help people live their best lives by finding and living their dreams. She has been called "America's Dream Coach." That is her brand. She is Jack Canfield's coach. She conducts seminars and workshops and has a one-to-many model in terms of helping the public. She also trains and certifies dream coaches. She is a Million Dollar Practitioner.

John Gray brought relationship information to the mainstream with his book, *Men Are from Mars, Women Are from Venus: A Practical Guide for Improving Communication and Getting What You Want in Your Relationships.* He also wrote many follow-up books and has been widely seen on TV. John offers workshops and seminars for the public and trains and certifies other people to be Mars–Venus coaches. And he has franchises that are Mars–Venus counseling centers. He has leveraged all of this into a Million Dollar Practice.

John Assaraf came from the world of multilevel marketing and real estate sales and investments. Now he is "Mr. Law of Attraction" and "Mr. Spirituality." John was featured in the best selling book *The Secret.* He is a sought-after speaker with one-to-many programs for helping people generate wealth and make their lives better. He, too, has a Million Dollar Practice.

T. Harv Eker, who reaches the masses with his *Millionaire Mind* books, products, and workshops, teaches you how to attract, grow, and manage your money. Similar to Anthony Robbins, he started from nothing, owns his niche, and leveraged his interest and passion into a huge franchise.

Chris and Janet Attwood wrote a book called *The Passion Test.* Their whole approach is "follow your passion." And they train "Passion Test facilitators." They have leveraged their desire to help people identify their passions, get in touch with their passions, and live their passions into a Million Dollar Practice.

Marshall Rosenberg is the guy that I most want to be like. He created an entire approach to relationships and communication called "Nonviolent Communication." His passion is helping people communicate effectively in a way that facilitates connection and harmony and productive relationships. He also does it on the macro level, between countries and governments. Marshall established the Center for Nonviolent Communication and has written many books and created satellite centers all around the country and all over the world.

Sue Johnson is a relationship therapist in Canada. She developed an approach called Emotionally Focused Therapy (EFT) for helping couples. She started the International Centre for Excellence in Emotionally Focused Therapy (ICEEFT) and conducts seminars and workshops for the public and she also trains practitioners in EFT. She has written good, solid, credible books with genuine value. Sue Johnson is the real deal. And as far as I'm concerned, she has a Million Dollar Practice.

John Gottman is a psychological researcher who chose to focus on relationships. Through his research he ended up writing books, conducting workshops, and training other people who conduct workshops. You know you have arrived when you can start an institute and put your own name on it because your name is adequate by itself to be the brand. John created the Gottman Relationship Institute. Through it he has helped lots of people and generated significant income for his contributions to the relationship world. He has a Million Dollar Practice.

Terrence Real got his start working with some of the heavyweights in the area of codependency. He then went out on his own and founded the Relational Life Institute, where he writes popular books, conducts workshops and seminars for the public, and does trainings for professionals. He has been on all the big talk shows. He is a sought-after speaker. He is brilliant, insightful, and able to communicate his approaches clearly and compellingly to the public. He creates paradigms that make sense to people. He also has an edge to him. He is direct, he challenges people, and he is successful. He has gone from the clinical world to the mainstream, a necessary step for developing a Million Dollar Practice.

Gay and Kathlyn Hendricks are two of my favorite people. They have influenced me tremendously. They wrote a seminal book years ago called *Conscious Loving: The Journey to Co-Commitment,* and they have written many books since then. *Conscious Loving* was my landmark exposure to the world of relationships outside of the clinical realm. They showed me where I wanted to go, setting me on the path to be a relationship coach. When you are trained as a therapist, and you are looking at couples and relationships from a clinical point of view, and then you read a book by people who are writing about the emotional and spiritual potential of relationships to bring love and trust and intimacy to higher levels, it is inspiring. Gay and Katie are pioneers in their field. They dug the well. Today they still conduct seminars and workshops as well as professional trainings. And they definitely have a Million Dollar Practice.

All of these professionals, whether a coach, a therapist, or something else, have something in common: they have a mission and a message and genuine expertise, and they managed to leverage it to success-fully reach the public, the mainstream, by leveraging the one-to-many model. They all have a Million Dollar Practice. They may have been ordinary before, just like you and me, but they are not ordinary any-more. Now they can be found on my bookshelf and on the book-shelves of many others who look to them as true experts whom they admire and respect and from whom they want to learn. Perhaps you are attracted to the idea of writing a book that has the same impact, but don't think it is possible. But everybody started someplace. You just have to make the most of who you are and who you want to reach.

OPPORTUNITY LOST: LEADING EXPERTS UNSUCCESSFUL IN BUSINESS

There are two authors I have on my bookshelf whom I highly respect, whose books and work have made a huge difference for me. But in business they are examples of what not to do. In fact their stories are almost tragic examples of lost opportunities and unnecessary struggle.

The first example is considered to be the leading pioneer in his spe-cialty and works for a prominent university. He is a professor. He does research. He has lots of students and interns and fellows hanging on his every word. But he has not been able to leverage his expertise and his accomplishment and his acclaim into money or a business. He does not have an organization and he doesn't even have a Web site. Despite my prodding and attempts to support him, he has convinced himself that he doesn't have the time or resources to set it up.

This person is a leader and pioneer in his field. He is well liked, respected, and intelligent. But he is holding himself back. He writes books, but he doesn't leverage them. He teaches classes, but he doesn't train anybody. He's a sought-after speaker for professional conferences, who pays his own way to share what he knows with his colleagues. He works with clients, but he doesn't show anybody how to do what he does. He has a tremendous potential legacy that will be greatly diminished because, while his work will live on in his books, he could have a much bigger impact. Additionally, he could be much, much more financially successful than he is.

If goodwill in terms of how many people think you are great and contribution in terms of how many people you have helped could be turned into money, this gentleman would be among the wealthiest. But goodwill, respect, and professional accomplishment do not automatically translate into business and income. Yes, the more people you help, the more money you make, as we will discuss later in this book, but you have to leverage it. He is just not leveraging it. And it's such a tragedy, not just for him, but for all of the people he could be reaching but is not.

The other example is someone whose career I have been following for decades, ever since I got into this field. He is great. He has written books that I liked and appreciated. I even wanted to feature him as a speaker at my Conscious Relationship Tele-Summit (a virtual conference by telephone and Internet). I tracked him down. I got him on the phone and told him how much I admired him, what I was up to, and asked him to conduct a presentation over the telephone at his convenience. What he told me blew me away. He said: "I'm old. I'm tired. I still have a full caseload of clients. I don't have the energy to do anything else." He couldn't even muster up the passion or the energy to get on the phone and do a presentation from the comfort of his home or office.

Here is a guy, like Terrence Real, who tells it like it is and is not afraid to shake people's trees, and he writes books that challenge the status quo and complacency. He should be at the time of his life where he is reaping the rewards for his expertise, his books, and his contributions. If he had built an organization, if he had leveraged who he is and what he does and what he teaches, and packaged it and managed it and created a Million Dollar Practice around it, he would have plenty of time, plenty of money, and plenty of energy. But that's not what happened. And I feel so bad for him. Here is one of my heroes, a guy whose work and books have influenced me from almost the beginning. And now he is sad, old, broken down, and still working full time.

So in looking for inspiration, and for what to avoid, you need to look no further than a collection of expert authors from your profession, and what they have done, or not done, to leverage their passion, mission, and message. And the examples I have cited in this chapter can all be found in my bookshelf. What's in yours?

Likely you will identify, as I did, a series of books from professionals who have leveraged their expertise into Million Dollar Practices of one kind or another. You may also find examples of the two tragic cases who held themselves back by working in their businesses instead of on their businesses, by being technicians rather than entrepreneurs, by coming up with all the reasons why they can't rather than trying to figure out a way that they can. They have been absorbed in all of the "gotta-do" tasks. They have made time for clients, but they have never made time for anything else. And the world will be less because of it.

So is the Million Dollar Practice Right for You?

Now that you have seen what I and others have been able to do, you should have a better idea of your own possibilities. You can create your own program. You can write your own book. You can create something significant that makes a difference in the world in a way that other people can't, because they are not you.

As a private practice professional, you have priceless expertise that can solve significant human problems, enhance quality of life, and make the world a better place for all of us. Your audience needs you and is waiting for you to show up. And you deserve the professional and financial success that results when you do.

Paving a new path, taking a stand that is not mainstream, being a pioneer—we all have the potential to do so in our particular specialty. You have your own unique mission and message, and pioneering your own approach to helping your clients is the best way to grow a Million Dollar Practice—not by being the same as the other guys, but by doing something uniquely yours.

So is the Million Dollar Practice Right for You?

All private practice professionals have the potential to make a unique and significant contribution to their niche, as well as to our profession and the rest of the world. We all have a gift, a passion, an area of expertise and a reason why we pursued it—often motivated by our own pain. We gain experience with our clients, who stimulate us to be creative. They challenge us to figure out how to effectively help them. In doing so, we often develop our own spin on things. We create our own interventions or systems of helping them—regardless of our training. Often we amaze ourselves. We come up with something and think, *"Wow, that was good. That was brilliant! Did that come from me?"* And it's all in response to helping our clients.

All private practice professionals do this, and we know we do it. But we don't always understand what to do with it. We don't understand the potential. We don't understand what it means. What it means is that we need to embrace our inner entrepreneur. We need to capture our ideas and expertise, leverage them, turn them into systems, products, and programs to broaden our reach, help more people, and make a larger difference in the world.

Can you do that? Are you willing to do that? Then the Million Dollar Practice just might be for you.

Million Dollar Questions for Chapter 1

1. Are you a technician or an entrepreneur?

2. What forms of internal resistance do you have toward building a Million Dollar Practice? How will you overcome your internal resistance?

3. Which of the Seven Habits of Million Dollar Practitioners are weak areas for you? How can you strengthen them?

4. Where are you in the Seven Stages of Practice Building, and what is needed to get to the next stage?

5. Looking in your bookshelf, who are your top role models and what about their accomplishments and businesses would you like to learn from and emulate?

CHAPTER TWO

Your Mission and Message

Picture this: A private practice professional, a marriage and family therapist who is passionate about helping his clients have successful marriages and families, sitting in his office in San Jose, California, near the intersection of Saratoga Avenue and Highway 280—literally the center of Silicon Valley—struggling to make ends meet, working long hours with couples in trouble and managed care referrals. All around him is a display of wealth the likes of which most people have never seen.

That was me in 1996 during the height of the dot-com era, prior to becoming a coach. Most of my clients lived and worked in the area, which, in Silicon Valley, meant they were doing something in the high-tech industry. Most of them were making three to four times what I was making—with far less education and training. Even the average entry-level factory, on-the-line, high-tech quality-assurance person—with, maybe, a 1-year certificate in electronics—was making twice what I was making at the time. This I pondered as another Ferrari drove by outside my office window.

Believe me, I thought about it often: *How much more could I be making simply by getting a job at one of the local companies surrounding me?* But if it were about the money, I would have picked up and left the marriage and family profession a long time ago.

Money is like oxygen — necessary for life but not the purpose of life.

For me, as well as for most helping professionals, it's not about the money. It's about something more. We pursue our profession for a reason. We go through all those internships (3,000 hours' worth in my case) and sometimes work odd jobs (I drove a taxicab for a couple of years) for a reason. We seek to make a bigger difference in the world.

YOUR PURPOSE

No behavior is random. There is a reason for doing it, a purpose. A purpose can be many things, like creating a world of love and empowerment, living a life of compassion, serving God, or providing for your family. Whatever it is, your purpose is yours and yours alone.

Your purpose must be clarified and understood in order to serve as your life's compass. This need for clarity extends to your business when your purpose is tied to building a Million Dollar Practice. So not only is it helpful to have a purpose statement for our business, but it also helps to have a purpose statement for our life that resonates with who we are. Here's mine: *The purpose of my life is to create a world of love and empowerment by loving and empowering myself and others*. That's my reason for getting up in the morning, for everything I do in my life and business, including writing this book. Your purpose guides you toward your goal, which is where vision comes into play.

YOUR VISION

Your vision is the internal image of where you believe your purpose will lead you. It's what you want your life to look like. By extension, if you are an entrepreneur, it's what you want your business to look like. You must know what you are aiming for in order to hit it. The trial-and-error method of throwing stuff against the wall to see what sticks may have worked for some people, but it's not a solid strategy for building a Million Dollar Practice. Generally, a successful practitioner will have an internal image, a vision, of what it is she wants to create. And often that vision isn't clear and needs to be uncovered.

42

If you take part in my practice-building program, one of the first things I will have you do is clarify, in detail, your vision for your ideal practice. Your vision is what it is you want to create. It's what is inside you that you want to manifest in the real world. It's your big picture. And it's incredibly important in helping you get where you want to go. The clearer you are about it, the more successful you are going to be.

To get in touch with your vision, you only have to look within yourself. It's already inside you before you start, and it generally reveals itself on its own, like it's always been there. It just needs to be given room to rise to the surface. Vision is seldom made up on the spot as if you were shopping for paint at Home Depot: *Let's see . . . I'll choose this color and this color and this color for my house. That should work.* No, your vision usually comes from an image that appears from within: *Ooh, I want my house to look like this!*

YOUR MISSION

If your vision is what you want your business to look like, and your purpose is why you are doing it, your mission, then, is how you are called to carry it out. Your mission is exactly what you want to accomplish. This can change over time. I was originally called to carry out my purpose as a marriage and family therapist, then as a relationship coach, then as founder of Relationship Coaching Institute. Because I'm a guy, I tend to think of mission as being like a military mission. When a platoon of soldiers goes out on a mission, it is sent to accomplish a concrete, tangible result. It has specific routes, instructions, and orders, which help it accomplish its task. That's your mission: It's how you are specifically called to realize your vision and carry out your purpose.

And just as you should have a purpose statement for your practice, you should have a mission statement, too. Here's a simple and effective format: "I help [who] to [achieve what]." My mission statement for my practice is "I help singles and couples to have successful, fulfilling relationships." It's simple, to the point, and drives everything I have done for the past 30 years.

Million Dollar Practitioners know who they want to help and why and how they want to help them. There is power to clarity. And in the coaching profession we know this, so we start working with our clients around their vision of what they want to create. If someone says, "I want my relationship to be better, or I want my business to grow, or I want to lose weight," the first thing a coach does is make the goal measureable and clear: "What does that look like for you and by when do you want to achieve it?" There is magic in specificity, because it gives you clarity of vision. And with clarity of vision comes clarity of choices, ideas, and resources to accomplish that vision.

YOUR MESSAGE

Your message is the conversation you want to have with the world about your purpose and your vision. It's how you accomplish your mission. It's how you connect with people. So while some may cringe at the thought, your message is the core of your marketing—essential to building a Million Dollar Practice—because *marketing is simply communicating what you do.*

We have deep-seated experiences or factors that have shaped our mission and that drove us to become helping professionals, and we naturally have something to say about it. We have a personal story and a message to deliver from that story. We have something we want to express, something that excites us and that is deeply meaningful to us. It's a conversation, not only for the sake of connecting with others, but for the sake of making a difference in the world.

Your message is in your books and your articles. It's on your Web site. It's in the seminars you conduct. It's in the conversations you want to have with people, to help them, to affect them, to connect with them. And you will find that these conversations come easily and are deeply fulfilling to you. They are driven by a genuine source that comes from within.

YOUR PASSION

If you hang out with me and you're in the mood for some light banter, you're going to be disappointed. I'm a terrible small-talker. I don't chat. I like deep, meaningful conversations. And if they are about relationships, they can keep me going for a long time. Those conversations are interesting and fulfilling to me.

When I meet people for the first time, if the conversation goes where I'm interested in going, within a short time we will be talking about their love life, or their being single and that journey, or their relationship history and what it is they want in their life and relationships. That's just who I am. That's where my mind wants to go.

Now, don't get me wrong, there are lots of other things I like to talk about. I have many other interests and things that excite me, like sailboats and the military—get me going with an old World War II Navy vet and his experiences in the war and you can't get me to stop asking questions. But there are conversations that are simply enjoyable ways to pass the time, and then there are conversations that are deeply meaningful and that help us make a difference in the world. The conversations that I have with singles about relationship requirements—and other topics—are deeply meaningful to me and make a difference to them. They are fueled by passion.

To recap, as related to building a Million Dollar Practice:

- Your purpose is why you are pursuing it.
- Your vision is what you want it to look like.
- Your mission is how you specifically are called to realize it.
- Your message is what you have to say to the world about it.
- Your passion is your source of energy to see it through.

The clearer you are on these terms and concepts, the stronger the foundation of your business from which you can create systems, products, and programs that promote change and make a significant difference in the world.

MISSION IN PRACTICE

Let's look at a massage therapist: A massage therapist gets paid to massage people's bodies. And maybe she is happy with that and that's all she wants to do. Perhaps one day she will burn out and decide she wants to do something different and move on. Referring

YOUR MISSION AND MESSAGE

to our definition from Chapter 1, she's a technician. She massages people's bodies and gets paid for it. Her focus is as simple as, "I want to help people feel good by massaging their bodies." This is not a bad mission. There is nothing wrong with it. It's just that its limited scope does not currently correspond with the model of the Million Dollar Practice.

It's the same with a chiropractor. A chiropractor has studied and become a doctor of chiropractic. He is a true believer. He is passionate about wellness and the role of the spine and alignment in the body and helping people in that way. Still, if all he is doing is practicing chiropractic, if that's as far as he sees, if his reach and desire never extend beyond the walls of his clinic, he, too, is a technician. Again, while this is a perfectly noble endeavor, it is not, at this time, in alignment with a Million Dollar Practice.

Working with one person at a time, exchanging time for dollars, limits your reach. It prevents you from leveraging your time and your talents. Now, I have seen people employ some tricks. Instead of having individual exam rooms, I have seen some chiropractors have a number of their chiropractic tables out in a big open room, side by side. The patients come in, they get on the tables — *crack-crack-crack* — and 5 minutes later they're up and gone. The chiropractor goes to the next table — *crack-crack-crack* — and 5 minutes later they're up and gone. You can serve a lot of people that way. But it still requires putting your hands on people, so it is still a one-to-one model. If you stop working because of illness or vacation, your income stops. Not only does this limit your earning potential, but having a limited mission and message precludes you from making a larger difference in the word, the kind that comes from building a Million Dollar Practice.

However, while it's not across the board, most helping professionals tend to want more — and they are surely capable of it. Many helping professionals (especially private practitioners) are also evangelists and entrepreneurs and don't even know it. We have a mission and a message far beyond just helping the clients who come to us. We long to make a bigger difference in the world. We long to help more people than we could possibly help in our offices on an hourly basis.

We want to save the world in our own way. We are in touch with the unique contributions we can make in the world. This is the foundation of a Million Dollar Practice.

RESONANCE

But know this: Just because you have a clearly defined mission and message, it doesn't mean that they will be universally accepted.

Some people will resonate with your message. They will be attracted to it. They will gladly hear and benefit from it.

Some people will resonate with your mission. They want the results that you are passionate about helping them achieve.

Others, well . . . they won't see things the way you see them, and believe it or not, they won't want what you want for them at all. They will walk a different path. That's the way it's meant to be.

My mission for singles is to help them find and have a successful, fulfilling relationship. While most singles want this, many don't. They would rather be single, don't resonate with my mission, and are not a fit for my services. When I conduct Conscious Dating seminars for singles, I have a message for them that is in keeping with my mission to help them:

You gotta know your requirements!

It's imperative to align relationship choices with those requirements, because if one requirement isn't met, the relationship is doomed. But first, "You gotta know your requirements!" In fact, you already have them. You know you have them. And they are nonnegotiable deal-breakers. Want proof? Think back to your last relationship breakup. That's proof right there.

One day I was giving a seminar to singles and I was sharing my message about requirements when a guy raised his hand and said, "I don't believe we need requirements. All relationships would work if we just practiced unconditional love."

Here's someone with whom my message of requirements obviously did not resonate.

And his message of unconditional love did not resonate with me — or, as it turned out, with most of the people in the room.

From my perspective — while it's a great ideal — unconditional love is impractical. You are not going to put up with just anything because of the higher ideal of unconditional love. This is the real world. Rather than trying to reach some unsustainable ideal, I prefer to be pragmatic and say, "Well, we've got to deal with how we *really* operate, not how we *should* operate. Maybe we *should* practice unconditional love, but that's not *really* how it goes. Life doesn't work that way."

So your mission will resonate with people who want the results that you help people achieve in your work, and it won't resonate with those who don't want those outcomes. Your message will resonate with people who need it and are attracted to it. And your message will not resonate with people who don't need it and aren't attracted to it. That's all right. You can make a tremendous difference with the people who need *your* mission and message. When you are clearly different and you bring something different to your work, you attract people who resonate with who you are and with what you have to offer. As helping professionals, it's why we do what we do.

YOU ARE UNIQUE. EMBRACE IT. USE IT.

The great fear of would-be Million Dollar Practitioners is "I'm not going to make enough money doing what I'm passionate about. There are not enough people who are going to resonate with me and who want what I uniquely have to offer." As a result, they try to follow formulas. They try to be like everybody else. They try to compete for what they envision to be finite slices of an existing pie. Yet the true path to success is not to follow the crowd and conform to an existing business model, but instead to create business where there was none before and to fill a need that people didn't even know they had. Instead of competing with your colleagues for clients, you will attract and create your own following and clientele.

When I started a singles organization in Silicon Valley (we will get into this in more detail later when we cover niche communities), I targeted personal-growth-oriented singles who wanted to learn something about relationships, have a good time, be among like-minded people, and be part of a community that supported each other rather than in a "meat-market" environment. At the time, people didn't really know that they wanted or needed those things. But when they discovered it, they flocked to it. They were grateful for it. I had people coming up to me all the time, saying, "Thank you so much for doing this." While this principle certainly relates to finding your niche, doing market research, and other ideas (which we will also explore in future chapters), it also has to do with allowing yourself to accept who you are and to bring your unique gifts to your work. If you try to be like everybody else, or if you're afraid to follow through on your true mission and share your unique message, then a Million Dollar Practice is going to be an uphill battle for you. To successfully overcome the obstacles and reap the benefits of a Million Dollar Practice you must allow yourself to be unique and authentically share your gifts with the world.

If you have a purpose for being on this Earth that's strong enough, and you're clear enough about what it is, you don't really have a choice about what you do and whether or not to pursue it. The only questions are "How do you go about making it sustainable?" and "How large do you want to play?"

As much fun as I had driving a taxicab while I was earning my master's degree, I wouldn't want to do that for a living. Not because I find it an unworthy profession, but because it's not part of my mission. It's the same with the restaurant business. I worked in restaurants when I was younger and even managed a fast food franchise when I was 20. I left that profession, not because it's not a noble calling—it is—but because it didn't give me juice. My passion is in helping singles and couples. Following my passion allows me to approach my work from a genuine place of service. There is nothing else I want to do. Even when I was frustrated and having trouble making a living at it, there was still nothing else I would rather have been doing.

Having a clear mission and message is what separates the men from the boys, the women from the girls, the wheat from the chaff—pick your metaphor. I have survived three economic recessions as a private practice professional. I stuck it out and thrived while many of my colleagues experienced fear and left their private practices, and even their professions, to take other jobs. Well, I guess they had a choice. Not me. I am firmly rooted in my mission and message. I have no choice.

PASSION AND SERVICE

As mentioned earlier, your mission and message are fueled by your passion. And the stronger your passion, the stronger your desire to be of service. It comes from within. It's who you are, and you can't deny who you are. But it's something that you need to determine and pursue on your own, and that's not easy. When you genuinely come from a place of service—meaning it's from your purpose, you have a clear mission, you have a message to share, and you have passion—then (a) you really have no choice but to pursue it because there is nothing else you could do or want to do, and (b) because you have no choice, you gut it out. You do it even though you are afraid or frustrated.

In my case, even though I was burning out with a full caseload of couples in trouble, there was nothing else I wanted to do. Sure, I had fantasies about getting a job in Silicon Valley and making a lot more money and having an easier life. But I couldn't do it. My mission and message wouldn't allow it.

When you are coming from a place of service, you are following your calling. It's who you are. You are passionate and have a strong sense of mission and purpose and message. You become creative and make it work out of necessity because you know you want to do it and there is nothing else that will do.

COMING FROM EGO

Practitioners motivated by ego are dangerous. They want status. They want to be called "Doctor." They want to make a lot of money. They want to have an impact on people not out of service to them but as a way of acting out their own agendas.

All politicians claim to be advocates for the people, to be public servants. And some of them really are called to serve. But some are not. They are interested in power, money, recognition, and status. For them, it's ego driven. And it's easy to spot. It's the same with helping professionals. The ones who are ego driven and totally blind to it scare me the most. They are unconsciously oblivious to what they are doing. Their goal is to influence everybody else and to get them to believe what they believe, to get them to fall in line with their vision of the world. It's coming from ego, no matter how well intentioned. "I'm doing this for your own good." My attitude is a bit more humble: "Who am I to want everybody else to conform with my vision of the world?"

When motivated by ego, we try to implement our own agenda instead of being of service. We unconsciously act out a script instead of supporting others to be who they are. We come from a place of wanting status, money, accomplishment, and control. We want to enforce our agenda and have our clients conform with how we think they should be.

Let's take the institution of marriage. Marriage is one of my highest values and goals. It's been a significant part of my pain and my desire. It's a large part of my work. But I don't assume that everybody wants to get married. I don't assume that everybody who *is* married should *stay* married. People have a right to their own journeys, their own paths and decisions. Sure, I'd rather see people get married, stay married, and live happily ever after. But that's idealistic. That's not the real world. However, for people who do want to be married, I want to help them. I want to help them find their soul mate, make a good partner choice, and live happily ever after. I love marriage!

Now, I could combine my purpose, mission, message, and passion, and I could really beat people over the head with it. "Everybody should be married. Marriage is the state of being that we should strive for. If you're *not* married you should find a partner and get married. If you *are* married you should work to make your marriage the greatest marriage it could possibly be. If you're *not* married, then you're deficient." But that's not coming from a place of service.

LENSES AND FILTERS

The biggest challenge of being of service is to be aware of your lenses and filters. Many helping professionals are not aware they even have their own filters. And the stronger your passion, the stronger your filters. Until you become aware of your own lenses and filters, take responsibility for them, and stop assuming that everyone else should look through them, too, then you can't genuinely be of service. If you are going to be of service to people, you must respect who they are with compassion and empathy. You must see the world through their lenses and filters. And you must help them achieve what they want to achieve, not what you want them to achieve.

When you are truly coming from service and you authentically want to make a difference by helping your clients find *their* way—it's not for you, it's for them—then you know you are on the right path and will naturally become attractive to potential clients. To get there, we as helping professionals must go through the necessary developmental step to become aware of our own filters. It's tempting to impose our view of the world on others and think that they should look at the world that way, too.

Here's an example: As a couples therapist I've had many couples contact me and say, "Yeah, we were seeing a therapist who said that our relationship is unhealthy and that we'd be better off divorced." This happened much more often than it should have. It was not an anomaly. If there were only one unethical practitioner saying that I wouldn't have been getting all those cases.

It's scary to me that there are so many well-intentioned couples' therapists who are imposing "professional opinions" such as "Your relationship is unhealthy and you'd be better off divorced." Garbage! That's not coming from service. That's doing damage. If your intention is to help a person or a couple resolve their pain and deal with a relationship that is dysfunctional or not working for them, you can't argue with that. But if you are looking through your filter of healthy versus unhealthy—stay together if it's healthy, get divorced if it's not—you are coming from ego. That's a very black-and-white view of the world. There are many well-intentioned but ego-driven helping professionals out there. Unfortunately, you can't trust them. They do get business and make a living doing what they do. But they are not candidates for a Million Dollar Practice, because they can't really get the trust factor working for them. They can't get enough referrals and develop the social proof (testimonials and endorsements) of many people willing to stand up and say, "Hey, this person's great. You should work with him." And, similar to corrupt politicians and greedy televangelists, their self-serving approach to their profession isn't sustainable and will eventually trip them up.

Trust Is Key to Success

When you are authentically coming from service, people trust you. They feel safe with you. They will refer to you. And they will gladly pay your full fee. If you are coming from ego, people tend not to trust you. Often, they can't even put their finger on why. They may be attracted to your mission and your message. They may be receptive to your promises and your products and your business. But they are uncomfortable. If they do hire you or buy from you, they often feel uneasy, as if they didn't receive the full benefit, and these are the ones who request refunds.

If you want people to gladly pay you money, feel good about you, and get the full benefit of the transformation that you are able to help them create, then you must establish trust. Think about it: How long would an ice cream shop stay in business if it sold bad ice cream? Regardless of how great the pictures looked in the window or how low the prices were, it would still have to deliver a good product. If an ice cream shop made a promise of providing excellent ice cream and charged half the price of the stand down the street—even if it had a huge advertising budget—and then broke people's trust by selling bad ice cream, people would not come back. And then they would tell all their friends, "Hey, don't believe it, that ice cream sucks . . . don't go there." In today's world, with the power of the Internet to instantly spread word-of-mouth information far and wide (for better or worse), that place would be out of business in a day.

Yet there's a different way:

When you establish trust by fulfilling your mission and spreading your message to meet people's needs, you are a hero to them, and they are inclined to tell their friends about you.

When people are looking for a support resource and don't know where to go, it's scary and confusing for them because they don't know whom to trust, so they contact a lot of people and research them online. That's where social proof comes in. *What are other people saying about them?* Here are two sides of the same coin:

Referrals: People trust you because somebody whom they trust has referred them to you.
Social proof: Other people say great things about you.

If you are to build a Million Dollar Practice, people must know you, like you, trust you, hire you, and pay you out of pocket to help them. Most practitioners mean well and don't believe they are coming from ego. If you're not sure, simply look at your results. If you are unconsciously acting out your agenda, people aren't going to trust you, they aren't going to refer to you, and they aren't going to want to work with you. You might somehow find a way to get clients, but they are certainly not going to talk you up in a good way. That's why I don't worry too much when the charlatans go into business and hang their shingles and market themselves as the next guru. They tend to wash out pretty fast, because people lose trust in them. They may be able to take advantage of a few people, but as practitioners, they don't go very far. People intuitively do not trust professionals who come from ego and don't have a handle on their own lenses and filters. They are not comfortable with them, even if they don't know why.

Is this uncomfortable for you to read and think about? I hope so. This is the shadow or dark side of being a helping professional and we all must look in the mirror and be honest about our lenses and filters, and about our motivations — service or ego.

There are people who are truly inspirational people, truly people of service. I'm thinking of Billy Graham. What a guy! Over the years he has amassed a huge following, including many sitting presidents. He has deserved every award, all the attention, and all the accolades, and he has remained humble through it all. Unfortunately, for every one Billy Graham, you can probably find 20–50 "professionals" who are indicted for fraud and other serious offenses. People who come from ego tend to trip themselves up. Though some people might be impressed by them, and might even buy what they're selling, people tend to catch on eventually and sever the relationship. It tends not to be a long-term relationship or even a productive relationship.

A PRODUCTIVE, LONG-TERM RELATIONSHIP

When there's something wrong with my car, like most people, I take it to a mechanic. But when it's time to change my oil, like most people, I have historically found it much more convenient to go to a quick-change outfit. It's inexpensive, and I'm out of there and on with the rest of my day in a short time. My perception had always been that my car mechanic would charge a lot more to change the oil, and, for some reason, I had this feeling that changing the oil would somehow be beneath him. *He's a car mechanic. He maintains and fixes complicated cars. A 5-year-old can change the oil. I don't want to bother him for that.*

One day, as I always did, I went to a quick-change outfit—which shall remain nameless—and got the oil changed. A short time afterward I noticed that the "check engine" light was on. And I didn't make the connection that it was a result of the oil change. So I took it into my mechanic, Jack, whom I trust implicitly. I've been going to him for 20 years. He takes good care of me and I take good care of him. "Hey, Jack, the 'check engine' light's on."

"Can you leave it?"

"Yeah, I can leave it."

Twenty-four hours later, after all the inconvenience of having to go home and be without a car, Jack called me up: "Okay, it's fixed. Come get it."

When I got to his shop, Jack reported that there was a disconnected hose to the air filter. So I slapped my forehead and said, "Oh, that's all it was? Well, thanks, Jack. How much do I owe you?"

"No charge. Took me 10 minutes to figure out."

All right! That's the Jack I know and love—no charge—what a guy! Only a mechanic with whom you have a long-term relationship and with whom you have established trust would do that kind of thing.

Fast-forward 6 months later. It happens again.

"Hey, Jack, the 'check engine' light's on."

"Can you leave it?"

"Yeah, I can leave it."

Twenty-four hours later, Jack called me up: "It's ready, come get it."

When I got to his shop, Jack told me what the problem was. "There was a hose disconnected."

"Hose disconnected? How'd that happen?"

"You know the same thing happened the last time you were here. Remember that?"

"Oh . . . yeah."

"It was that same hose."

Now, it was Jack who remembered this. I had no recollection of the previous incident. I don't have an elephant memory, or, apparently, even a memory as good as my car mechanic. I'm a busy guy. I do a lot in my day. This was just an errand.

So Jack asked me a question: "Where do you go to get your oil changed?" He knew I didn't take it to him.

"Well, I go to XXXX. It's cheap. It's convenient. I drive in, get my coffee, and by the time I'm finished with my coffee, the oil's changed and I'm on my way. Yeah, they try to sell me stuff I don't want or need. But if it comes to a transmission-fluid change or differential or any of that kind of stuff I go to you for that."

"Well, I'm not sure if you're aware of this, but in order to look at your air filter, they have to disconnect a bunch of hoses. And they are not reconnecting them all when they put it back together. And this happened twice in a row."

"Oh . . . ."

"David, I want you to bring your car here and let me change your oil. Those guys over there don't know what they're doing. They are underpaid and undertrained. I know your car. I'd be happy to change your oil. Just drive by, and if I have a free lift, I'll do it without waiting."

"Wow, what a great offer. Thanks, Jack!"

From that moment on, I would just drive by and say, "Hey, Jack, got time to change the oil?"

"Sure!"

A Productive, Long-Term Relationship

He would drop what he was doing, or have one of his guys drive the car right in, and 15 minutes later the car was ready.

And I look at what he's charging me for it, and he's only charging me $29 to change the oil. I was paying $45 at the other place—and I thought I was getting a good deal! Jack charges me less than the other place, and Jack knows my car. He's able to check things like the belts and the brakes and the tires—just to make sure things are up to snuff—for $29!

Jack provides this service to me not because I'm special, but because he comes from a place of service. He does that for all of his customers. Certainly Jack wants business and likes money, but that's not his sole motivation. He truly wants to do a good job for his customers and to be their mechanic and take good care of their cars. He cares about his work. He hates it when the folks at the quick change outfits screw things up. And I appreciate that about him. I trust him.

So guess what? Even though I knew I was going to get sticker shock, when my daughter's car needed a major overhaul, who do you think I went to for the service?

When I brought it in, Jack helped us decide whether the car was good to keep or whether it was time to get rid of it, what could be put off until later and what needed to be done right away. Jack's value doesn't come in the form of discounts. I pay his going rate like any other customer. His value comes in the form of exceptional service and in working with a guy I trust, a guy who cares about his work and does a very good job. He's honest and he goes the extra mile for his customers. It's a true relationship.

Those of us in private practice need to be authentic and trustworthy and have expertise and help people. But there is a little bargain going on here. The bargain is this:

When you are truly being of service and doing a good job, you make a good living.

Of course, you can sabotage yourself by giving away your services or not charging enough. But if you are going to succeed in business as a helping professional, you need to be trustworthy, you need to have expertise, and you need to come from a place of service. This means being of service in ways that truly work for your client rather than from your ego and what you think they should want (this concept, which I call the Platinum Rule of Marketing, is addressed in more detail in the next chapter).

Jack is not just a car mechanic. He doesn't just care about my car and what needs to be fixed. He cares about me. He cares about the whole experience. He cares where I have my oil changed. He doesn't need the $29; changing the oil is just part of taking care of my cars. It gives him a regular opportunity to check them over, and it gives me a regular opportunity to be at his shop.

It's just like cleaning your teeth at the dentist. You don't need dental work every time you go to get your teeth cleaned. The dentist will check things over and let you know whether something needs to be handled now, whether it can wait until later, and whether there's something you need to watch out for. I have my teeth cleaned every 4 months. My dentist takes good care of me. I put myself in his hands. I trust him. And what's more, he and his staff trust me as their patient.

I've known my dentist, Dr. Smith, even longer than I've known Jack, my mechanic. In fact, I've been going to him since 1979 — more than 30 years! This is the longest relationship I've ever had. His wife is the receptionist/office manager. Every time I have an appointment, she calls to confirm, which is what dentist's offices do. But it used to drive me crazy because when she called she would leave a message that said, "Hi, this is Diane from Dr. Smith's office. I just wanted to remind you of your appointment. Please give me a call back to confirm."

Finally, one day I said, "Diane, why do I need to call back to confirm? I know the appointment. Have I ever missed one? Calling back is a hassle. It's on my calendar. I'll be there."

She said, "Okay, David. You don't have to call back."

Now, when she calls me to remind me of my appointment, she says, "Hi, David. This is Diane from Dr. Smith's office, just reminding you of your appointment, no need to call back."

That's one of many reasons I love my dentist and his staff. And that's the value of having a real relationship with people. They trust me — and I appreciate that trust. I'm a real person to them. They know my story. They know my wife. They know my exes. They know my kids. They know the books I've written. And I know their story. I know Dr. Smith's son, who has now joined the practice. In fact, at first I gave him a hard time because he is a lot younger and a fairly new practitioner. And I've come to trust him just the same. So we're onto the next generation now.

It's this kind of productive, mutually beneficial relationship that we all need to strive for over the long term. It's based upon purpose, mission, message, passion, and service. And it's the foundation of a Million Dollar Practice. You want to have an ongoing, productive relationship with the people whom you serve. If you're (still!) reading this book, I'm confident that you don't just want to take their money, get the quick fix or transformation, and then say good-bye. In the helping profession we don't believe that a quick fix is possible or even a good idea. We want to have long-term, productive, mutually beneficial relationships with our clients. And to do that, we can take a cue from the other experts out there—the car mechanics and the dentists—the ones who truly are coming from a place of service, grounded in their mission and message, who go the extra mile and take good care of us. We need to do that, too.

THE RAZOR'S EDGE

Again, we will get into this a little deeper in subsequent chapters, but I must caution you, that there is more to building a Million Dollar Practice than passionately following your bliss and screaming it from the rooftops. There is a lot more to it than coming from a place of service. It's not that easy. You must charge what you're worth. You have to be creative and devise a service delivery system. You must create a one-to-many model of service. And all of this must appeal to your desired customers or clients. There's a razor's edge between doing what you want to do and doing what people want and need and will buy. Even if you are genuinely coming from a place of service, pursuing your mission, and sharing your message, you must factor in what your clients and customers want and package your services in ways that resonate with them. If it's all about "*me, me, me*" and "*what*

I love and want," because *"hey, I'm passionate and just following my bliss,"* then you will be your one and only best and loyal customer—not exactly the one-to-many model of the Million Dollar Practice.

There's a balance between bringing your unique gifts to your work and not being so absorbed in following your bliss that you are oblivious to those whom you want to help. You must base your efforts on sound business principles, and you must truly serve the needs of your clients.

When Max Simon, as brilliant as he is, left the Chopra Center and struck out on his own, literally, he failed. So, how did this rising star, who helped the Chopra Center achieve such great success, originally fail so miserably when he tried to follow his bliss?

"I went too far to the side of 'I'm going to do what I love,'" said Max. "And I didn't have a good business model in place. We're always taught to 'just do what we love and the money will follow,' and it's bull****. What you have to do is 'find out what it is you love, and then create a solid business strategy to support it.'"

When Max first formed his own company at GetSelfCentered.com, his philosophy was to teach young people how to meditate, because he loves meditation—a noble mission. But Max ignored some fundamental business principles that revolve around three simple questions:

1. What's the business model (for generating income)?
2. Are the people you're going after interested in buying what you are selling?
3. How do you create something that's scalable?

When he started out, Max didn't have any of those answers. Instead, he just said, "Well, I want to teach young people to meditate, so that's what I'm going to do." He spent a lot of money and a lot of time, and he lost a lot of money and wasted a lot of time, doing things that put him on a path to failure—even though people were saying, "This is really cool!" He lost $80,000 and became disenfranchised with his purpose. He went from being excited and passionate to a place of desperation. And that's when he started to realize it was time to get some help. Over time, by investing in coaches, trainings, and programs, Max was able to reconnect with his purpose, redefine his mission and message, revamp his business, and turn things around. In fact, Max exceeded the million dollar mark in his second year of business, and during his latest promotion he generated more than $186,000 in 7 days and reached more than 1.5 million people. Not bad.

The point I'm making is that you cannot simply arm yourself with a mission and a message and expect to be wildly successful. You must also have a sound foundation, market your business effectively, and employ a service delivery system (all of which I will show you in the chapters to come) to build a Million Dollar Practice.

You Don't Know What You Don't Know

One day I was having lunch with a friend and a local entrepreneur when I was given my single best piece of business advice—ever.

As we sat around the table we explored ways to take Relationship Coaching Institute from a position of stagnation to sustainability. I knew RCI was tremendously important and that it had tremendous potential, yet it was struggling. It was struggling for a couple of reasons: Partially, it was struggling because I'm not a great salesman. I don't like to sell people things that they don't want or that they are not convinced are good for them. Another reason RCI was struggling was that members of my target audience have limited funds. Other coach-training programs command thousands and thousands of dollars, because their target audience is comprised of people coming from the business world (i.e., people who have the money to invest in a new profession). They view those training programs as business opportunities. My audience, however, for the most part, saw RCI programs as continuing education, or just another way of helping people. I knew RCI also offered a business opportunity and a whole new world, but I had a hard time getting it across to my constituents.

That all changed during lunch when this Silicon Valley entrepreneur turned me on to an idea. To this day I have no idea where he came up with it, because within his area of expertise, with the businesses he was familiar with, it was not a common practice. But he took one look at my business model and suggested a membership system. And it completely changed the face of Relationship Coaching Institute.

Before we were a membership organization, I provided training and had a staff of trainers. I wanted to help people build successful practices, and that involved a practice-building program. I wanted people to sign up for it, but in order to sign up for it, they had to pay something—I couldn't do it for free. Of course, I priced it as low as possible, because I wanted them to say "Yes" to it. But it was painful to me that lots of people who needed and could benefit from my practice building program weren't signing up for it because they felt that they couldn't afford it. The membership system eradicated all that. No longer would we have to worry about selling initial training or upselling the next training . . . and the next training, to our market. They would make one decision to join and get it all.

Developing a membership system made marketing and enrollment a lot easier. And my work became a lot more fun. Because rather than trying to continually upsell to my enrollees, I was able to provide them additional value. Now, every time our members have a problem or a question we concentrate our efforts on addressing it. We are fully focused on our mission and our message.

Plus, a membership system is scalable and sustainable. You get members and they keep paying you every month for years and years. Your bottom line grows with every new member you get. And to me, a membership system is a much more fun, fulfilling, and effective way to do business than trying to sell training and practice-building programs. You are able to focus on your mission and your message by giving your members lots of benefits and being accountable to them and keeping them happy.

All of a sudden Relationship Coaching Institute became a much more attractive and compelling value proposition and, in turn, began helping a lot more people: "When you join RCI you get training, certification, practice-building support, and marketing support. We take care of you. We help you build and market your coaching practice."

RCI is now a membership organization and a leader in practice-building and marketing support, and it has different levels of membership. People who joined in the infancy stages are called Charter

Members. They paid to enroll, but don't pay a monthly fee. We also have Lifetime Members, people who joined at a slightly higher price and don't have to pay a monthly fee—for life. Other levels of membership involve an enrollment fee and a monthly fee. The enrollment fee depends upon the level of membership, and that's an investment. We also offer payment plans so members can pay off their enrollment fee in installments to make it easier for them. They are also required to pay a monthly fee for maintaining their membership and benefits, like a health club. The point is that we are able to provide options and benefits for a wide range of budgets.

Here's an example: A common challenge of new members when they first join RCI is that they don't have a Web site. If they do have a Web site they often don't have the money or expertise to create a good one. After years of trying to support our members to find affordable alternatives for putting up Web sites, we launched a project to provide fully functional, prepopulated Web sites for our members, complete with multiple template choices.

As an organization, RCI wants to make a big difference in the world. We want to help you have a successful practice, because that's how you will make a difference in the world. It's all in service of the mission and in spreading the message. We come from a place of service. Our services also include MillionDollarPractice.net, the practice-building program for our members. And the Conscious Relationship World Tour, discussed later in this book, is a series of launch events for Conscious Relationship Communities, a project designed to help our coaches build substantial, highly visible, highly successful practices in their local areas. This is all in service to the RCI mission and message. And it all came about from a lunch in Silicon Valley.

This story serves as a great example—which, in many ways, is the foundation and the purpose of this book—that "You don't know what you don't know." That one piece of advice, that one door that a random Silicon Valley entrepreneur opened for me, really solved a huge problem. And it took a struggling business that was losing money and financed on credit card debt and turned it around quickly.

So even though I didn't know it when I sat down for lunch that day in Silicon Valley, it turns out that providing a membership program is a great model for the Million Dollar Practice. It's a one-to-many model, and it's scalable. You can add members, and you are able to offer your services, products, and programs affordably. And every new person who comes in adds to your bottom line because it's recurring income. There's momentum. Once individuals make the decision to join, they are set. Their credit card is billed each month until they say "Stop." It's an effective model that enables you to focus on your mission and message, to be of service.

So, if you are a private practice professional who is just doing it for the money (e.g., because you would rather do this than dig ditches, because you were given a scholarship, to follow in your father's footsteps, because it just seems like a good thing to do), if you are not mission-driven, don't have a message, and are not coming from a place of service—well, then, you are a technician at heart. And that's okay. There is nothing wrong with being a technician. Most people in the world are technicians. They dig ditches. They fix televisions. They fix cars. They build buildings. They build widgets. They do a job in exchange for money. They might enjoy their job, but they are not on a mission. They "work to live" and are not out to transform anybody or change the world. They don't have an important message for the world that people need and can benefit from. They are not change agents. That's all right. But for those of us who have a mission and a message, who truly want to be of service, and who want to change the world, we have the foundation for building a Million Dollar Practice.

YOUR PASSION SPEECH

Earlier in this chapter we discussed how passion ties into your mission and message and how that relates to service. As you now have a better understanding of the relationship, I will leave you with a practical exercise to put this knowledge into action to best capitalize on your mission and message.

Many entrepreneurs are familiar with the "elevator pitch," which is explaining what you do within 30 seconds (about a paragraph or so) in a concise and compelling way to capture the interest of a prospective customer or investor in the time it takes for an elevator to travel between floors. In the world of coaching, this practice was refined to be a "laser speech," which is a shorter version of only a sentence or two. Many participants in my practice-building programs struggle to craft their laser speeches. When they do create their laser speeches, they end up memorizing them and delivering them in a manner more like reciting their home address than expressing a world-changing mission and message.

I recommend you craft a laser speech for your practice, then forget it and instead simply share your passion about who you help and how you help them in a "passion speech."

Remember the simple mission statement template from earlier in this chapter? "I help [who] to [achieve what]." This can be expanded a bit into your passion speech:

Part I: Ask an engaging question (e.g., "Do you know people who . . . ?").

Part II: Describe who you are passionate about helping (include descriptive adjectives).

Part III: Explain how you help them (what you help them to achieve).

When the opportunity arises, simply think about the people you dedicate your life to serving, get in touch with your passion for your mission and your message, and extemporaneously speak from your heart. Here's an example:

Do you know how singles over 50 really want to find true love but often think it's too late or not possible? I help discouraged, mature singles who really want to live the life they love with the love of their life to find their soul mate and live happily ever after.

Can you spot my mission, message, and target audience in the preceding statement? Your passion speech doesn't need to be smooth, it just needs to come from your heart and express your passion for your mission and message. Your energy and emotion will resonate with people more than your words will. When people experience your passion, they will be attracted to you, inclined to trust you as authentic, and — if it's a fit — will eventually want to work with you and/or refer to you. Communicating your mission and message with passion can be your best marketing and enrollment tool, as long as you do it with sincerity and with a genuine desire to help.

Most helping professionals do come from a place of service and choose their specialty for very important personal reasons. What are yours?

What is your mission? What is your message? Figure that out, and you have taken the first step to building a Million Dollar Practice.

Million Dollar Questions for Chapter 2

1. What is your purpose? Why did you choose to dedicate your life to your profession?

2. What is your ultimate vision for the Million Dollar Practice you want to create?

3. What is your mission? What transformation are you called to help people accomplish?

4. What is your message? If you could only share one pearl of wisdom or inspiration with the people you want to help, what would it be?

5. What is unique about you as a practitioner in your specialty and niche? What makes you the perfect helping professional for your target audience?

6. What is your passion speech? Carefully script one, but use it as a guide—don't memorize it.

CHAPTER THREE

Owning Your Niche

The Platinum Rule of Marketing in Action

When it comes to marketing and building a practice, it's difficult to be a generalist. People looking for solutions want to work with individuals or organizations with skills and experience related to their specific needs, problems, and challenges. They want a specialist.

In the old days, you might have had the village blacksmith who did just about everything with tools. Today, you have people working in factories who put one little widget on another little widget all day long. There was a time when a cleaning solution was a cleaning solution was a cleaning solution. It was multipurpose. Today, when we go to the store, we look for a specific product with a specific purpose. If you have a mark on your wall you're not going to settle for rug-cleaning solution to get it off. You're going to look for something that cleans walls. That's just how our society is and works. We are highly specialized. We have a huge division of labor and innovative products to address any given scenario, and we've been trained and accultur-ated over time to accept it. To be a generalist and put yourself out there as a professional who "works with everybody" just plain doesn't work. We need to specialize and we need to communicate that specialty to those who can benefit from it.

And the same principle of clarity from the last chapter applies here: The more clearly you define yourself as a practitioner, and the more specific you are about your niche, the more quickly and efficiently you will attract people who can benefit from working with you. People who "get" that you "get" them are easy to spot. It's as obvious as Santa Claus waving on a street corner in July; it's going to stand out—big time—you can't miss it.

When you are in your brilliance, when you define yourself as a practitioner by aligning who you are (the "what"—your specialty), the niche you've chosen to serve (the "who"—your target audience), and the method by which you've chosen to serve them (the "how"—your program), the people in your niche will notice. Remember Max Simon from Chapters 1 and 2? He is a great example of this. He is unapologetic about wanting to work with spiritually oriented entrepreneurs. And he has been wildly successful because of it. He loves his niche, and they love him. Max serves them well. It's similar to his dad and Deepak Chopra. They were unapologetic about being spiritually oriented mind-body physicians at a time when nobody else was. Max likes to use the refrain, "Find your tribe, find your tribe, find your tribe." That's his way of talking about niche. So, how do you become wildly successful and build a Million Dollar Practice? Find your niche, find your niche, find your niche.

Lacking a well-defined niche usually means that you are providing a service to anybody you can find who wants it and that you are getting paid by the hour. While you may be able to get by doing this, it's not going to help you build the necessary foundation for a Million Dollar Practice. To build a highly successful practice you need a niche. What's more, to "own" your niche, you need to apply the Platinum Rule of Marketing.

While I don't claim to have the last word on the niche subject, this chapter covers what a niche is, how to choose one, and how it can become your key to professional success and financial freedom. We cover 11 specific strategies for choosing a niche. We also cover how to own your niche, which is one of my favorite subjects, since I've done it several times, and putting into action what I call the Platinum Rule of Marketing. But first, let's start with a fundamental definition.

WHAT IS A NICHE?

Despite being an important part of a successful practice, to the folks in my practice-building programs, whether or not to have a niche continues to be one of the biggest bones of contention, creates the most resistance, generates the most questions, and poses the biggest challenges. Worse, most practitioners don't even know what a niche is!

When I'm conducting my practice-building programs and I ask participants to define their niches, they say things like "single women, ages 35–50, who've been through a divorce and are looking for their life partner." While these are certainly *characteristics* of the people in their niche—and their ideal client—in and of themselves they do not constitute a niche. To qualify as a niche, it's got to be narrowed down further. And it can be as simple as just adding a geographical area. "*Seattle* single women, ages 35–50, who've been through a divorce and are looking for their life partner." That's a niche—you know where to find them.

Quite simply:

A niche is an identifiable group of people.

It has to be identifiable because, as we mentioned in the last chapter regarding your message, *marketing is communicating what you do.* And to effectively share your message you must direct your marketing to a particular audience. You can't just communicate about yourself and what you do to everybody in the whole wide world and expect your message to resonate, because most of the people in the whole wide world are not interested. They are not a fit for you, nor are you a fit for them. Your message will be wasted on them—and, more important, you will lose an opportunity to resonate with your true market. Whether you are paying in some way to reach them through advertising or some other avenue, or you are taking a "no-cost" approach that still taps into your time and effort reserves, you likely will be just spinning your wheels and reaching no one. The idea of niche marketing, of having a very clear and defined market, allows you to design your message and your channels to resonate with those whom you want to reach. Again, a niche is an identifiable group of people; the key word is "identifiable." So, if you know how and where to find them, you have found yourself a decent niche. However, if you have no idea where they are or how to reach them, then you don't have a workable niche yet.

People often confuse specialty and niche. "I'm a relationship coach for single women." That's a specialty, not a niche. Specialty is what you deliver. Niche is to whom you deliver it. Specialty is service. Niche is people.

Here is how I break it down: You have your profession, your specialty within that profession, and your niche that you serve within your specialty. Then you have your services that you provide to your niche and then you have your brand. Let's look at each one in more detail.

Profession

First, we have a profession. Your profession answers the question, "Who am I?"

For me, I'm a licensed marriage and family therapist who has transitioned to relationship coaching. So I'm a relationship coach.

Think of it this way: When you're doing your tax return and you get to the box that says "Occupation," what do you enter? Even though I do a lot of different things, I put "relationship coach." That's my primary profession. Again, your profession is the answer to the question of "Who am I?"

Specialty

Next, we have specialty. This answers the question, "What do I do?"

A profession is huge. It's broad. It covers a tremendous variety of people and problems and solutions and theories and techniques and strategies. Specialty focuses on a particular service within an area of expertise.

Most of us don't do everything possible in our profession. We specialize. For example, as a marriage and family therapist, I chose to specialize in couples. I have colleagues who specialize in children, divorce, domestic violence, anxiety disorders, and the like. Your specialty is what you do within your profession. It's the narrower area on which you focus.

Niche

Then comes your niche. This answers the question, "Who do I help?"

As a brand-new relationship coach, I asked myself the questions, "Who needs it? Who wants it? What can I do with this new profession of mine?"

Looking at my work with fresh eyes, I had an epiphany—the biggest epiphany I've ever had in my life, though you might laugh because it's so simple. The epiphany was this: *Singles become couples.*

This got me thinking: *If I want to make a huge impact in relationships, the place to start is with singles, because a single person doesn't have a relationship and wants one.*

Coaches help people get from where they are to where they want to be. I knew nothing about working with singles, so I was able to approach that with fresh eyes as well. Starting with a blank slate, I developed a whole specialty around helping singles, which I call Conscious Dating®: classes, workshops, seminars, products, a coaching program, training and licensing for professionals, an online community for singles, a Web-based "virtual coaching program," an app for mobile devices, and more. I even wrote a book for singles: *Conscious Dating: Finding the Love of Your Life and the Life That You Love,* and I obtained a registered trademark.

In the old days, your prospective clients expected to find you in the Yellow Pages, and if you weren't listed they questioned your legitimacy. In today's world, your prospective clients expect to be able to easily learn about you by conducting an Internet search. Here is an exercise: Pretend you are a prospective client and enter your name in any Internet search engine. If your name shows up on the first page along with your specialty and niche, congratulations! This means your business is well-defined and visible enough to reach your target audience. If not, you have some work to do.

Services

And then come your services. Ask yourself this question about your niche. How do I help them?

Okay, I have this niche of people, singles in Silicon Valley; how do I help them? What am I going to do with them?

For most practitioners, this seems like a very easy question. "I'm going to do counseling," "I'm going to do therapy," "I'm going to help them do their taxes." You're going to do what you're trained to do.

However, since a niche is a specific group of people, they have specific needs. Wouldn't it be nice to know what those needs are and tailor your services for them? Then you are guaranteed success, because you designed your services specifically for the individuals who want and need them. You differentiate yourself from others. This is how to own your niche, and we talk more about that later in this chapter.

Brand

Your brand is what you call your services, products, and pro-grams and how you communicate them. It's whatever is tangi-ble about your business. It's what it might look like as a logo, a graphic on your Web site, or a brochure. It's what people see. It's your image. I chose to brand my relationship coaching for singles as "Conscious Dating." Now, I could have branded it as "David Steele's Relationship Coaching for Singles," but who the heck is David Steele? A brand answers the questions, "What do I call my business and its services, products, and programs?" and "What is the tangible image?"

If you are single in Silicon Valley, are you going to respond more to an invitation to come to a gathering called "David Steele's Coaching for Singles," or "Conscious Dating for Silicon Valley Singles?" Your brand has a lot to do with how you resonate with the people you want to reach and the image you want them to have of you. You want it to resonate strongly and be attractive to them. I want to reach singles who are attracted to the idea of "Conscious Dating," and I don't have much to offer those who prefer "How to Find a Husband," "How to Date Beautiful Women," or other approaches.

In the local section of my newspaper, the *San Jose Mercury News*, there was a one-third-page spread that caught my attention. Along with the article was a picture of a woman who looked like a very nice, but fairly ordinary, person. And I'm looking at this picture thinking, *Why is there a whole article about her?* Well, it turns out that her name is Shannon Silva, and she is a coach, and her story provided the best example of the power of branding and rebranding that I have seen in a long time.

Shannon Silva is a Dale Carnegie–trained speaker, a certified self-discovery coach, and a business skills trainer. She started a meetup group in my local area called "Overcoming Stress in San Jose." She focused on helping working women manage the stress of juggling careers and families and relationships. While this was a noble approach, it wasn't exactly cutting-edge. All life coaches, on some level, want to help their clients achieve balance, and Shannon Silva was one of them. Her basic approach was: "These women are stressed. We need to address their stress and we need to help them enjoy their lives by managing their stress." And she was doing *okay*, as it's not hard to find women with a problem who want to get together and support each other. But that all changed when she made a fundamental shift in her branding.

According to the article, Shannon delivered a talk one day titled "Unstoppable Women" that resulted in a complete change in the group's energy. With that, "Overcoming Stress in San Jose" became "Unstoppable Women of Silicon Valley." What a difference! Shannon's subtle yet massive change completely revamped her business and garnered the attention of the *San Jose Mercury News* and a slew of new clients. So, not only is this a great example of branding as it relates to niche, but it is also a prime example of the Platinum Rule of Marketing, which is discussed in more detail later in this chapter.

So, on the road to owning your niche, you must not only understand what a niche is, but the context in which it exists.

Recap:

A profession answers, "Who am I?"—Example: relationship coach

A specialty answers, "What do I do?"—Example: coaching singles

A niche answers, "Who do I help?"—Example: personal growth–oriented singles in Silicon Valley

A service answers, "How do I help them?"—Example: workshops, classes, coaching, and the like

A brand answers, "What do I call my business or service?"—Example: Conscious Dating, or Unstoppable Women of Silicon Valley

A Million Dollar Practice Is a Business Fueled by a Niche

As a private practice professional, your niche is your key to professional success and financial freedom. It's your key to a Million Dollar Practice. The problem comes when you neglect to see your practice as a business.

A practice is simple. It's where you see clients. A *business*, however, is much more than that. It has multiple streams of income and a service delivery system. To reach the level of a Million Dollar Practice, it's not enough to have a full practice. You must know that you deserve to be well-paid for delivering tangible results and want to sustain that payment over time. Think of it this way:

If you retired or couldn't see clients anymore, would your income stop? If so, then you don't have a business, you have a job.

A business is not dependent upon exchanging time for dollars. That's how you know when you've built a business—when you can go on vacation and still generate income, and generate income while you sleep. One of the building blocks for doing so, for creating the Million Dollar Practice, is to find your niche.

Still feeling internal resistance to a choosing a niche? To motivate you and give you a friendly nudge, here are my seven benefits for choosing a niche.

SEVEN BENEFITS OF CHOOSING A NICHE

Benefit #1: You Get to Push the Boulder Downhill

Let's address the biggest benefit right up front: It's a lot easier to achieve success in private practice and build a business around it when you choose a niche. That's right, it's simply the path of least resistance, or, as I like to say, when you choose a niche, you get to push the boulder downhill.

Generalists—the people who don't want to choose a niche—try to do everything for everybody. They don't want to rule anybody out, they don't want to narrow themselves, and they don't want to define themselves. As a result, they push the boulder uphill, which adds to the already difficult challenge of building a business. This approach is not impossible; a lot of people do it, but it's really hard. Choosing a niche makes it far easier and leads to far greater success. So, benefit #1: You get to push the boulder downhill—nice and easy.

Benefit #2: You Get to Follow Your Passion

This is the fun part. Bringing more fun into your business means bringing more positive energy along with it. But that only comes when you choose a niche that is in alignment with your passion. And make no mistake: You *do* have a choice. So you might as well choose a niche that you want to serve, that you're *excited* to serve, that makes you leap out of bed every day. "Oh, boy, I get to follow my passion!"

Basing your business on what you think you need to do to survive, or what you think will generate the most income, is absolutely the most *ineffective* way to choose a niche. The key is to choose a niche that you have the most passion for: "I'm so excited about this I'd do it for free!"

Of course, we don't want you to do it for free. In fact, I will come to your house and prevent you from doing it for free. The point is that you *would* if you had to because you love it so much. Really, if you find a niche you would love to serve, you will find that you will be unable to do anything else. It's just so exciting—and so mandatory. That is when you know you've chosen the right niche. So, benefit #2: You get to follow your passion, which is also a lot of fun.

Benefit #3: You Get to Be Creative

When I transitioned my practice to relationship coaching, the field was wide open and I looked at everything with fresh eyes. I tapped into ideas and strategies for working with singles and created the Conscious Dating program and a whole training curriculum involving five stages of relationship coaching.

I got creative like I had never been in my life. That creativity helped me build my business and become wildly successful—much more successful than I would have been if I had stayed in private practice, in my office, seeing clients as a therapist or even as a coach.

Like following your passion, expressing your creativity is fun. And it's fulfilling when you get to express the potential that is inside you. So, benefit #3: You get to be creative, which leads to success.

Benefit #4: You Get to Be of Service

If you choose a niche, you truly get to be of service to a particular group of people in much more effective ways than you could if you did not choose a niche. You get to make a difference in the world in your unique way.

If I were still a therapist in private practice, seeing just about anybody that walked through the door, I would be making an immediate difference in my clients' lives, but my contributions wouldn't extend much beyond that.

As David Steele, relationship coach for singles, author of *Conscious Dating*, creator of the Conscious Dating Program for Singles, who gives Conscious Dating seminars all over the country—and on and on and on—I make a *huge* contribution to singles. I'm able to be of service to them outside of my office, nationally, internationally, now and forever. You can do the same with your niche. So, benefit #4: You get to be of service—and change people's lives on a much larger scale.

Benefit #5: You Get to Create a Legacy

Conscious Dating is a registered trademark. It's my intellectual property. It's a program, a book, an app, and a workbook. It's a tool and a set of strategies. It's an entire ecosystem of trainings, products, and programs—and it's going to continue and endure far beyond me. I train other people to implement the system, and my kids will inherit the trademark. As a result, I've created a legacy.

If you are seeing clients in your office, exchanging your time for dollars, you might argue that you, too, are creating a legacy, because your work with your clients will endure. But for me, I have always had the goal of reaching "the public." Yeah, I care about my clients and I get a lot of fulfillment out of working with them, supporting them, helping them, and making a difference for them. But it's never been enough. I have always wanted to spread my wings and stretch my capabilities to reach people who wouldn't ordinarily see a therapist. That has always been my goal, and it will live on in my name. By choosing and serving a larger niche, you can, too. So, benefit #5: You get to create a legacy, which abides.

Benefit #6: You Get to Be Unique

With or without a niche, you are unique. But choosing a niche allows you to express that uniqueness and leverage it into creating a successful business.

You are the pioneer of your work and of your practice. You have a specific personality, a specific bevy of experiences, and a specific skill-set. Sure, you have the same training that a lot of other people have. Yes, you share a job title with a lot of other people in the world. But you are unique. Only you do it the way you do it. That's why there's plenty of business to go around. Because there are many, many people with whom you can work but whom other professionals aren't going to be as effective in helping.

So, the more unique your marketing—you choose a niche, you express your creativity, you deliver your message your way—the better you will attract people who resonate with you and your message and your uniqueness. You will own that niche, with no competition, because there's nobody else like you.

Embracing your uniqueness is a source of self-esteem. It's a source of individuation and fulfillment, because you already feel unique and different. You know you are not like everybody else, and there is an alignment when you are able to have that be respected and appreciated by others.

No, not everybody will appreciate you. But the ones with whom you resonate will. They will be attracted to your work and benefit from what you have to offer them. They are your people and they recognize that you will take good care of them. They appreciate you and know that you have gifts for them. And it will be extremely fulfilling for you to give your gifts to them. That's why I'm giving you the information in this book. It's fun for me. It's fulfilling to me. I couldn't imagine not doing it. I don't want to hold anything back or leave anything out. I want to give it all to you, and more. And that's how you will feel when you serve the niche that is right for you. So, benefit #6: You get to be unique — and be fulfilled in helping others.

Benefit #7: You Get to Make More Money

Pursuing a niche is much more profitable. It lends itself to sustainable, multiple income streams and passive income, so you end up making more money from your practice while making a larger difference over the long term.

I went from being a therapist in private practice, in my office, seeing clients, exchanging my time for dollars, getting paid by the session to help people with their marriages and families and children, to having programs for singles, conducting seminars for singles, hosting gatherings for singles, training and certifying other people to do it, licensing them to do it, writing a book, selling books, and having workbooks, professional manuals, e-books, mobile apps, and many more products.

When you choose a niche and focus your energy and creativity on that niche, you are able to reach and help more people. And the more people you help, the more money you make. So, benefit #7: You get to make more money, which you deserve.

And that's my best effort to motivate you to choose a niche, to get beyond whatever resistance you might be feeling to doing so, as a way to propel you toward building your Million Dollar Practice.

A NICHE IS A BUSINESS . . . AND YOU CAN HAVE MORE THAN ONE

Many practitioners pursuing a Million Dollar Practice are tripped up before they even begin the journey. They are under the impression that they must figure out the one "right" way to do things before setting foot on the path to success. But this is not the case. This rings true especially when it comes to choosing a niche.

Like a practice, a niche is a business. And as an entrepreneur and a private practice professional, you are allowed as many businesses as you want, and as many niches as you can handle. You don't have to have just one.

One of my niches is relationship coaching for singles and the Conscious Dating Program. But you know what? That is not all I do. I do a variety of things with my day (such as writing this book!). I have several niches. And you can, too.

In my practice-building programs, I encourage participants to apply what they're learning to one niche at a time. For instance, if you take my Million Dollar Practice Mentoring program, you will hear me encourage you to go through the entire program, apply it to one niche, and then spend 3 to 6 months focusing on that one niche. Then, once you have launched that niche and gotten it off the ground, and you have time and energy, you can go on to start your next niche. Because once you have launched and set up your niche correctly by putting your systems in place, your business can almost continue on automatic pilot, which frees you up to then start your next business or niche.

So, remember:

- A niche is a specific line of business.
- You can have more than one niche.

Keeping these two items in mind will help tremendously in your pursuit of a Million Dollar Practice. But the question remains: How do you choose a niche?

11 STRATEGIES FOR CHOOSING A NICHE

Anyone who has ever been told, "You should choose a niche," at one time or another, wondered, *How? How can I narrow it down? How can I possibly choose? How do I proceed when I have no idea where to start?* These are all common questions, and I have devised 11 strategies to answer them—at least one of which is guaranteed to work for you.

As you read through the different strategies, remember: You might end up having a cornucopia of possible niches. That's fine, because this is your profession. You likely will be doing this for years and years and years, so there is plenty of time to get around to everything you want to do. Me? I have no intention of retiring. This is too much fun!

Strategy #1: The Mirror Strategy

If birds of a feather flock together, and if you can probably benefit the most from working with somebody who speaks your language—who comes from a similar place, who has similar values and background and goals and whatever else it might be—then the best mentor for you is likely somebody like you. So, when you look in the mirror, what do you see?

Now, there is no question that it might also be effective to have a mentor who is different from you. But the mirror strategy is about choosing a niche of people like you. They are your people. If you think about it, you might find that you have clients you have worked with or friends you have made who were attracted to you or to whom you were attracted because you were so much alike. That group of people could be your niche.

When I was transitioning to coaching in Silicon Valley and putting together a Friday night social for singles, it wasn't a guess as to what singles wanted, nor was it a long-standing desire of what I wanted to give them. I conducted a pilot project first. I did market research on what the singles of Silicon Valley wanted and needed.

I learned that Silicon Valley singles needed a place to go at the end of their workweek on Friday night. They needed a place that was safe and fun, and where they could meet other singles. They wanted a place where they could learn a bit about life and relationships, and where they could express their desires to have great lives and relationships. They wanted something that would support them to go in that direction, but they didn't want something heavy. They didn't want a Friday night seminar or workshop; what they wanted was a Friday night social.

So what did I do? I launched a weekly Friday night social for singles.

Being Silicon Valley, the social attracted a lot of engineers, which worked for me because I'm a bit of a geek, a technical guy. I love machines and electronics and gadgets, and I ended up getting a lot of like-minded men as clients. It was the mirror strategy in action. There was something about them and me that was strongly mirrored. They saw in me a good mentor, because I was like them, yet I knew things that they wanted to know, and I had accomplished things that they wanted to accomplish.

This approach can work for you, too. It's a compelling way to enroll clients: Seek clients with whom you have a lot in common. That's the mirror strategy.

Strategy #2: The Calling Strategy

What do you feel called to do? Who do you feel called to help?

I know people—these wonderful, wonderful people—who give up their lives and travel to third-world countries and work with their people. They live in squalor. Why? They grew up here. They had all the experiences that you and I likely had. Yet they feel compelled to be someplace else, doing something else, helping someone else. It's a calling. And if you feel this calling, you cannot deny it.

Early in my life, I felt called to be a therapist. Not only that, I felt called to have a *private practice* as a therapist. Everybody I knew, including my family, said, "Oh, no, you'll never make it. There's so much competition. It takes years and years and years just to get a license and set yourself up. You're better off getting into business." But I felt called. I had no choice. Do you?

Strategy #3: The Testimonial Strategy

What do people say about you?

If you get testimonials or ask people for them, what do they say? How do clients respond—at the end of a great session or in an exit interview with somebody with whom you've worked—to questions like, "How did you benefit from working with me? What have you been able to accomplish? What difference did I make for you? What did I do that worked for you?" You can also ask them, "What did I do that did not work for you?" That would be good feedback.

What your clients say about you is gold. Write it down. Ask them for permission to use it. In some professions, soliciting testimonials is frowned upon because of privacy rules. But, where permitted and appropriate, it's always a good idea to collect testimonials, if nothing else for your own positive energy. You can look at them when you need a boost.

What people say about you might help you determine your niche. A lot of people I have met in the relationship coaching field have just naturally fallen into their roles with their friends. Friend after friend had been telling them things like, "You know what? I wouldn't have met my husband if it weren't for you." Hearing this enough times gives you a strong clue to what your niche might be. The ways in which you show up for people and in which they benefit from their contact with you, and what they say about those interactions, can really help you identify your niche.

Strategy #4: The Attraction Strategy

The attraction strategy is simply what you are attracted to or what is attracted to you. It happens. It happens all by itself. You don't have to do anything to initiate it, and you don't have to control it.

Here's an example: I am not, nor have I ever been, an alcoholic. I am not an addict—although I have some experience with it in my family—and I have never been in recovery. And yet, at one time my private practice attracted recovering alcoholics. Why me? I never wanted to work with addictions, and I never sought training in it. It was not one of my specialties. And still they came, couples—and a lot of men, especially—who were in recovery. They wanted to work with me even though I had no expertise in working with them, and it was certainly not something that I chose. But they came to me anyway, perhaps because they wanted to go beyond the 12-Step model, and it just became a part of my practice. It was a niche that found me.

Paying attention to what is attracted to you, or what you are naturally attracted to can give you some strong clues to your niche.

Strategy #5: The Life-Story Strategy

What in your life story could be a possible niche for you? What tragedies have you overcome? What peak experiences have you had? Something in your life story might point to a niche.

As a kid, my dad, who's an artist, used to take me to marinas and paint boats. He liked to talk to the captains, and sometimes they invited us onto their boat and we went for a ride. As a result, I grew up in love with sailboats and sailing and the water. To this day, whenever I see a boat or talk to somebody who owns a boat, I get excited. It's a part of my life story that could help me choose a niche. *I could be a coach for boaters.* It's a niche that is easy to identify and market to. Boaters hang out together. You know where they are. You know where to find them. If you speak their language, you are one of them. You are in. You are one of the club. In fact, I know a member of RCI who lives on a boat with her husband and specializes in coaching boating couples, and she's writing a book for couples who share the boating lifestyle.

Boating is just a small piece of my life story. There are many, many others, any one of which could be a niche.

What is your life story?

Strategy #6: The Serendipity Strategy

The serendipity strategy involves being aware and taking advantage when something just falls into your lap.

Sometimes, if you are not looking for it, you won't even recognize it as a serendipitous opportunity. But if you're paying attention . . .

Here's an example: I used to write a regular column in a local parent magazine. Parenting was a specialty that I had in the past, and leveraging that specialty by writing the column was one way to build my practice. Parenting wasn't what I wanted to specialize in forever— I wanted to specialize with couples and families. But since people who have children are couples and families, it was one way to reach my desired audience.

One day I had a serendipitous event. A social worker from a local hospital read one of my columns and invited me to give a presentation to her new-moms group. Every woman who became a new mom and gave birth at that hospital had contact with this social worker and was invited to this new-moms group—every one.

At the time, I was giving lots of talks, all over, and thinking, *Sure, this is just another one.* So I showed up, gave the presentation, and the new moms loved it. The social worker loved it, too. She gave me great feedback and asked me back to speak again. I came back and gave another presentation, and the new moms enjoyed that one, too, and got a lot out of it. The social worker, again, raved about my performance. Soon I started getting referrals from her.

Now, this could have been just another referral source or just another presentation. But I recognized it as a huge opportunity. When you have a baby, not only does it change your life, but it, perhaps, stresses your marriage because you are in transition. This sometimes presents a need for seeing a therapist.

This social worker became the biggest referral source I've ever had. It seemed as though every stressed-out mom and every couple having trouble who went through that hospital was referred to my office. It was serendipitous. But I recognized it and acted on it.

Sometimes, something falls into your lap—it might have already fallen into your lap—but sometimes you don't recognize it because you are too preoccupied. The next time something falls into your lap, are you going to recognize it and jump on it?

Strategy #7: The Pipeline Strategy

The pipeline strategy is thinking about your niche as a pipeline.

Given a choice of niches, it's advantageous to have a niche that has a long life and a number of stages to it. In my case, singles are a great pipeline strategy because singles become couples . . . and then they get married . . . and then they have children . . . and then their children get married, and their children have children . . . and then they may get divorced and become single again.

So, my epiphany that singles become couples—in itself a great place to help people with their relationships—ended up being a huge pipeline of clients, because they kept coming back, again and again. They had future needs, so they became my clients for a long time. They worked for a while, stopped, came back, worked for another while, stopped, then came back again.

If I had just one thing to offer, that would have been the end of the relationship. Take hypnotherapy for stopping smoking: If that was all I did, if my profession was a hypnotherapist, and my specialty was hypnotherapy for stopping smoking, and my niche was smokers in Silicon Valley who wanted to quit, I wouldn't have much of a foundation. I would conduct one or two sessions, my clients would quit smoking, and they would be gone. That's it. No pipeline. In this case, the more people you help, the smaller your niche becomes. It makes it very hard to have a successful practice, because you continuously need fresh, new prospects (smokers) to sustain your practice. You need larger numbers of clients, because you serve them over the course of a few sessions and then turn them over.

If you have a variety of niches in mind, think about which one has a longer life to it. Which possible niche would serve as a better pipeline into your practice and beyond?

Strategy #8: The Gateway Strategy

Similar to the pipeline strategy is the gateway strategy. The gateway strategy poses several key questions, "What is the most successful gateway into your practice?" "What group of people can you reach most easily?" "What is the easiest service for you to market and generate business?" Simply put, "What is the path of least resistance?" While the answers may not be at the top of the list of what you ultimately want to do, you must survive before you can thrive, and over time you can leverage your growing business into your preferred specialty and niche.

In Silicon Valley, when I transitioned to relationship coaching, I wanted to work with couples, but I found singles to be—by far—the most successful gateway. I simply didn't know how to market to functional couples, because it's hard to convince them to get professional help unless they are motivated by pain and frustration. In fact, that was my niche—and my Yellow Pages ad: "Couples in Crisis." And boy, did I get them. So much so that I eventually burned out.

In my experience, most couples are not motivated to hire someone to help them with their relationship unless they are in serious trouble. Through relationship coaching I'm in the process of changing that. People are starting to see the value of being proactive in their relationships. But working with singles was far easier for me as a gateway strategy to reach new couples—couples who wanted to have a great relationship and whose relationship wasn't yet in trouble.

The gateway strategy: What is the easiest, most successful gateway for clients to enter your practice?

Strategy #9: The Replication Strategy

The replication strategy centers around the questions, "What niche is most easily replicable?" and "What can you do over and over and over again?"

Here is an example of what not to do: Develop a niche around a one-time traumatic event and its syndrome, like individuals with 9/11 posttraumatic stress disorder (PTSD). These therapists focus on the niche of people who have coping issues related to 9/11. Well, 9/11 was a one-time event, and so the niche is not going to have a long life, and it's not replicable—that is, until the next time there is a big terrorist event.

The replication strategy centers around that which is most replicable and staying away from things that are one-shot deals or that may have a short life. The stopping-smoking specialty is an example of something that is not replicable. Yes, you can repeat it with more and more people who want to stop smoking, and you can expand to more and more areas and other stop smoking clinics. But you are going to run out of clients, because you are essentially working yourself out of business. And society is helping you work yourself out of business, as smokers are becoming fewer and fewer every day.

Given the number of niches that you can choose from, which is the most replicable?

Strategy #10: The Unmet-Need Strategy

The unmet-need strategy is choosing a niche with an unmet need that you could penetrate, which, in reality, is the key to success for any business and certainly applies to the Million Dollar Practice. Identify an unmet need and fill it well.

Take a look around as a professional with your specialty. What unmet needs can you find?

As a relationship coach, I wanted to specialize in singles in Silicon Valley. The unmet need I saw through my market research was a safe, fun, educational place for singles to meet. This is what they said they wanted. There was nothing like it. There were bars and singles events that were scary to a lot of the singles with whom I talked. But they didn't want that. They wanted a safe, fun, educational place to meet.

So, guess what? That is exactly what I put in my advertisements: A safe, fun, educational place for singles to meet. That was the unmet need and, therefore, that was what I put together for them. This helped me develop a wildly successful practice in Silicon Valley as a relationship coach in an amazingly short period of time.

What unmet need can you identify and fill?

Strategy 11: The Quick-Start Strategy

The quick-start strategy is very simple. From a practical standpoint, it asks the questions, "What can you launch the fastest?" "What do you have the most contacts for?" "What do you have the most in place for?" "What can you get started doing quickly?"

This is the strategy that I suggest when you transition from a job to private practice.

My quick-start strategy — when I started my private practice — was to focus on parents of children with behavioral problems, because that was what I was doing in my job. I started doing private consulting with schools and agencies, and then I started getting private-pay clients. It was the quickest way for me to get my private practice going.

Granted, this might not be what you have the most passion for, or what you want to do in the long run, but it will get you going the fastest. Again, you have to survive before you can thrive. It is far easier to leverage and expand a successful business than start a new one from scratch. In fact, 90% of small businesses fail. The reason is that they run out of money before they are able to achieve profitability and sustainability. I have seen a lot of practitioners struggle because they have big dreams and believe in the law of attraction. They believe "If you build it, they will come," which I do believe. But if they don't have a way to pay their bills, their dreams can't get off the ground. It takes 2 to 4 years for a typical business to make it into the black, so you need to be prepared to be in a building process for at least that long before it will support you.

I was able to build a successful relationship coaching practice within 3 months. However, I already had a successful practice as a therapist. I had already learned valuable marketing lessons, including what *not* to do. And I had an exciting new niche to penetrate, which, as I also learned, can actually work against you, because if nobody understands it or knows what it is, they may not take it seriously.

It is my great pleasure to help people let go of jobs or situations they don't want and become successful at what they do want to do. I want to help you build a Million Dollar Practice, and one of the crucial elements to that is finding a suitable niche. The quick-start strategy is the shortest route from A to B.

What can get you going the fastest? What can shorten your ramp-up time as much as possible?

Those are my 11 strategies for choosing a niche. If you take these strategies, sit down, and start brainstorming ideas for the mirror strategy, the calling strategy, the testimonial strategy, the attraction strategy, the life-story strategy, the serendipity strategy, the pipeline strategy, the gateway strategy, the replication strategy, the unmet-need strategy, and the quick-start strategy, I guarantee that you will have more ideas than you will know what to do with.

From there, it's a matter of narrowing them down—which is a good problem to have—and choosing the niche that is best for you at this point in time. Don't worry about being locked in forever, as you can change, expand, and add niches at any time. Just choose the niche that is most exciting to you, right now, that you believe has the best odds for success. If you wish, you can select two or three, do market research on each, and make a more informed choice after you have investigated them. Once you have reached that milestone, you can move on to the next phase: Owning Your Niche, which is driven by one of the most important lessons you will ever learn in business.

THE PLATINUM RULE OF MARKETING

Earlier in this chapter we introduced you to Shannon Silva, founder of Unstoppable Women of Silicon Valley. Not only was Shannon's success due in large part to branding and rebranding, but it was a prime example of the number one secret to success, and what I like to call the Platinum Rule of Marketing.

We have all heard the Golden Rule: *"Do unto others as you would have them do unto you."* While this practice civilizes us and helps us get along in society, it doesn't work in marketing and building a service-oriented business. Here's an analogy: If you wanted to give someone a present ("do unto others") and you followed this rule, you would give them something you would like to receive ("as you would have them do unto you"), which only works if they're exactly like you! However well-meaning and unintentional, the message you're sending your target audience is:

I care more about what's important to me than what's important to you.

Ouch! Most helping professionals don't intend to send this message at all!

Here is the good news: There exists a rule that is even better than the Golden Rule. It's something I like to call the Platinum Rule of Marketing. While the Golden Rule states, "Do unto others as you would have them do unto you," the Platinum Rule states, "Do unto others as they want to be done to." To do so requires connecting with others and learning what they really want rather than what you want to provide them. Your sales will be much higher when you provide programs and services that address what your customers want rather than what you think they need. Your message to your target audience is:

I genuinely care about what's important to you.

Shannon Silva applied this perfectly, in correcting the course from her original venture. "Overcoming Stress in San Jose" illustrated the golden rule—that's what she wanted to help people do. It was a problem that *she* identified. But the people whom she wanted to serve likely saw stress as normal and unavoidable: "I have a lot going on. I can't overcome or get rid of stress. What are you talking about?" But as soon as Shannon took the approach of the Platinum Rule of Marketing—speaking to what her target audience wanted, using the language that they used or wanted to use, zeroing in on how they wanted to think about it and what they wanted to achieve, and branding her program as "Unstoppable Women of Silicon Valley"—they not only listened, they flocked.

With the Platinum Rule of Marketing mentality firmly in place, there are a series of specific strategies you can implement to select a niche and own it.

SEVEN STEPS TO OWNING YOUR NICHE—MAKING THE PLATINUM RULE WORK FOR YOU

Step 1: Do Your Market Research

There are two words that differentiate successful practitioners from unsuccessful practitioners, two words that we mentioned earlier in this chapter, two words that will help you own your niche: *market research*. In fact, these words are so important in creating a successful business that I cannot possibly overstate their value. More than any other strategy in this book, in conjunction with the Platinum Rule of Marketing, I consider market research to be *the key* to building a Million Dollar Practice.

As helping professionals, we live and breathe what we do every day. We are inside our head, inside our skin. We have our own thoughts and judgments about what works and what doesn't work and what we like and what we don't like.

If you want to be of service to a niche, a specific group of people, you need to learn a few things first: who they are, what they want, what works for them, and what doesn't work for them. That is market research. It's a concept I stumbled upon by accident, because when I transitioned my practice from therapy to relationship coaching, I learned that my programs were only as good as my market research. So, step one, if you want to own your niche and be successful in it, is to do your market research.

As a brand new relationship coach, I talked to my niche about their experiences of being single and dating in Silicon Valley and what they wanted and what they needed. The answers I received through market research helped me launch my Silicon Valley relationship coaching business, which became successful very, very quickly.

On one hand, over and over and over again, I see practitioners— blinded by their lenses and filters—fall flat. On the other hand, I see practitioners succeed who are really tuned in to the needs of the folks they want to serve and what works for them, and who really want to be of service to a niche of people—to the point where they ask them, listen, and follow through.

Quality market research is done through one-to-one conversations with people who fit your niche, or through a focus group. And let me say bluntly: Surveys are useless! Especially e-mail or online surveys sent to a large group. The information you receive won't help you. Your goal is to learn about your niche from the inside out and get to know them so well that it becomes clear how to market to them and what services to provide. E-mail and online surveys won't do this.

Ideally, you will conduct market research continuously on your existing programs, new programs, ideas for programs, and so on. Just as large corporations use market research to effectively market and serve their customers, this is a key to your success.

Five Steps for Conducting Market Research

Step 1: Research your niche for their demographic information, other professionals/organizations that serve them, other approaches to helping them, Web sites, online social networking groups, books, and workshops. Call or meet with similar and complementary professionals and organizations to learn more about how they help the people in your niche. Do your work and become an expert on available information about your target clients.

Step 2: Put together some ideas for programs, branding, and services. Come up with a variety of program names to find out which they prefer. A great exercise is to brainstorm answers to this question: "If I were to write a book or deliver a workshop for my niche, what would I call it?"

Step 3: Identify three to five people who fit your niche. Ideally, these are people you know. If not, then ask your network for referrals. Contact them for informational interviews.

Step 4: Conduct your informational interviews and ask for feedback about your ideas from Step 2. Ask what they read, where they hang out, what groups and organizations they join, and what publications they read. Ask them about their experiences, needs, goals, and challenges. Ask them about what they have done, where they have gone, and with whom they have worked to get support for the need or goal you will address in your practice. Listen closely to the language they use to describe their needs and goals. Ask for their top three problems and top three goals. Ask them to describe their ideal support services or programs to address their needs or goals.

Step 5: Compile your data and ideas and use them to design the services, branding, and programs for your niche. Follow up with your market research participants and get their feedback on your ideas, plus ask them for referrals. Remember; "people support what they help create," and when you follow up with those who helped you along the way, you will be pleasantly surprised by their excitement and support. In fact, a common and delightful by-product is that some of them might sign up for your program!

While most practitioners understand the importance of market research, they seem to have a hard time implementing it. I have seen many conduct diligent market research (because they know they need to design their services for their niche) and then completely ignore their data. As a result, their marketing flops. It pains me to see such passionate, talented, well-intentioned professionals struggle to make a living because they have such a hard time connecting with the people they want to serve.

Remember: *Do not use surveys!*
Remember: *Do not ignore your market research* and do what sounds good to *you* (seems obvious, but this is all too common).

Diligent market research, along with implementing what you learn from that research, is the first step to making the Platinum Rule of Marketing work for your clients and for you. And it is a crucial element that puts you on the path toward owning your niche.

Step 2: Conduct a Pilot Project

As part of my market research for Silicon Valley singles, I put together a pilot project. It was a succession of four meetings, one a week for 4 weeks, where I invited a group of 12 singles — as many as I could fit in my office. Based upon your market research, put on an introductory event (a seminar, class, workshop, clinic, etc.), give your niche something to experience, then follow up with more market research to get their feedback and refine your approach. This process will help you design your services and programs for your entire business. Design your pilot project and invite folks to join it. It can be low cost, or it can even be free. It's a tremendous service they are doing for you, helping you build your business. And you are going to deliver great value in return. So, conduct a pilot project.

Step 3: Create a Brand Identity

Earlier in the chapter I discussed brand. The idea being that David Steele, Relationship Coach for Singles, has limited value as a brand.

Sure, this might attract some people who want to work with me, but I can reach many more people as Conscious Dating Silicon Valley. Overcoming Stress in San Jose pales in comparison to Unstoppable Women of Silicon Valley. Hal Runkel, Licensed Therapist, doesn't hold a candle to ScreamFree Parenting. Your brand identity is what you are communicating about you, your business, your services, and how you can help your niche. It's the name you call it. The image it has. So, based upon your market research and your pilot project, create a brand identity.

And please, don't hide behind your brand. It drives me crazy when practitioners have Web sites to market their services and I can't find who is behind them. I can't find their names. I can't find their photos. The most effective approach is to do both: Have a strong brand, but also have a strong presence. Have your photo on every page of your Web site. Have a section called "About the Coach" or "About Us."

I'm not saying you want your Web site to be all about you, but you want to make it easy to find out about you. Ultimately, your business and its Web site still need to be about your niche, not about you. David Steele, Relationship Coach, is all about me. Look at me: I have a degree. I have a license. I have a title. I charge money. You want to work with me, don't you?

Not if I approach it like that you don't.

A brand is about the niche: Conscious Dating Silicon Valley. This says, "If you're single, and you'd like to consciously find your soul mate, and you live in Silicon Valley, this is the place for you."

Create a brand identity.

Step 4: Design a Service Delivery System

This is discussed in more detail in Chapter 5, but I will whet your appetite here. A service delivery system boils down to one thing: creating choices that make sense.

If you go to a restaurant, everything the restaurant offers is on the menu—all over the place. There may be some organization to it. You have the beverage category here and the appetizers there, but it's all in front of you. And it's up to you to choose. "Okay, I want this, I want that, I want one of these, I want two of those."

That is *not* what to do in a private practice, because it puts the entire responsibility on the clients to choose what services they want, when they start, where to go next, and where to go after that. You must tailor your services for your clients. You must design a service delivery system: "This is where you start, this is where you go next, this is where you go after that."

My service delivery system started with a weekly Friday night social for singles. The next thing that they could do was take part in a Conscious Dating class that I conducted once a quarter. After they graduated from the class, they were eligible to join one of my coaching teams, a group of people who supported those who had learned the Conscious Dating techniques and strategies by helping them apply these tools in their everyday lives to be successful. Beyond that, we addressed any remaining sticking points with individual coaching. The successful outcome of the Conscious Dating program resulted in a relationship, which meant they would need my Partners in Life program for precommitted couples. And it continued from there. It was a service delivery system for singles.

What service delivery system can you design for your niche that makes sense to them and serves them well?

Remember: It's a *system*; it's not a restaurant menu. Don't get caught up in "Would you like this, this, this, this, or that?"

An example of what not to do is offer a client two sessions a month for $200 a month, three sessions a month for $280 a month, or four sessions a month for $350 a month. That is an example of what not to do because you know what people need to be successful—especially if they are in your niche—because the people in your niche have a lot in common. Your clients should participate in your program at the level needed to get effective results, not choose how many sessions to meet with you per month.

To develop a Million Dollar Practice, you must design a service delivery system for your niche that makes sense to them and that sets them up for success. When they need weekly meetings, then you offer and charge for weekly meetings. Don't offer anything else and don't give them a choice, because forcing them to choose is not a service to them. If you are a client, you may say, "Well, I'll choose the two sessions a month for $200 a month because it's cheaper." But is it more effective? Not necessarily. Design a service delivery system that makes sense and is effective for the folks in your niche.

Step 5: Host a Niche Community

I created a niche community in Silicon Valley and it quickly set up my practice for success. The Friday night socials became a mixed community of singles in Silicon Valley. Here are 11 benefits of how a niche community can benefit your practice:

Benefit #1: External marketing attracts people you don't know who don't yet know you. If you have a niche community, it will attract people within that niche. These folks wouldn't necessarily want to call you for services right away, but they are attracted to the community. We need community. We are attracted to community. Birds of a feather flock together. This is the reason why social media (Facebook, Twitter, etc.) is so popular in today's world.

Benefit #2: Internal marketing helps build your relationship with your prospects so they hire you. When you host a niche community, people will get to know you, like you, and trust you. You will become the go-to person for that community. It gives you automatic credibility and builds your relationships with them. That's how you get clients, by the way: through enrollment and building relationships.

Benefit #3: Stimulate word of mouth. Participants tell their friends more readily about a community resource than a private, for-profit resource. Think about it: Are you going to more readily refer your single friend to David Steele, Relationship Coach, or to Conscious Dating Silicon Valley? By far, people more readily refer to a community resource than to an individual practitioner who charges $150+ an hour.

Benefit #4: Build strategic alliances and invite other professionals to participate in a cross-referral system. Approach your practice from an abundance mind-set. A community has room for everybody, including partners and alliances.

Benefit #5: Increase visibility and become the go-to resource associated with your niche. When it came to singles in Silicon Valley, I was the go-to person. I don't do it anymore, because I moved on to provide relationship-coaching training worldwide. But when I was doing it, I was the go-to person. The media came to me. I was invited to speak. I was the go-to person when it came to conscious dating for singles, people who wanted to find their soul mate and have an alternative to the meat-market singles scene.

Hosting or sponsoring a niche community doesn't have to cost anything and is a viable service that cannot only pay for itself but can generate a profit. Years ago, I started out with an online Yahoo group, and Yahoo groups still exist. But now there are many more resources such as Google Groups, Facebook Groups, Ning, and the like, which is another whole area of discussion.

Benefit #6: Generate low-cost marketing to grow your business. Developing a niche community really is low-cost marketing. You can even charge admission to the community. For my Friday night socials, I charged about the same price as going to a movie. The Friday night socials paid for themselves.

Even if I didn't charge, the marketing was priceless. I got clients from it over and over and over again. It was the most successful marketing I have ever done in my life, and it paid for itself many times over.

Benefit #7: Increased credibility in a niche community reflects upon your ability as a service professional. The qualities of your community—what people say about it and the experiences they have—reflect upon you. The community's success will earn you increased credibility. People will trust you because of their positive experiences in your community.

Benefit #8: Increased effectiveness of your service delivery system is the way to a Million Dollar Practice. More people are exposed to more opportunities to engage you and benefit from your services. When I added a niche community to my service delivery system, I reached many, many more people than I possibly could if the first and only way in the door was for individual sessions with me.

A group is another alternative. It expands the options of how people could come in your door and be motivated to work with you. A class or a workshop: even more. And a niche community: exponentially more. The barrier to entry is very, very low. Anybody can join—anybody who is attracted, who wants to, and who can benefit from it. They don't have to invest a lot of money and time up front. It is a gateway. Remember when we talked about the gateway niche?

Benefit #9: Increased traffic means increased business. Free and low-cost gatherings attract more people and create more prospects. I did not want to work every Friday night, so I brought on partners and associates. After a couple of years, I didn't need to show up on Friday nights at all.

The increased traffic from free and low-cost gatherings and the prospects created from that activity led me to have a wildly successful practice within a very short time. It filled not only my calendar, but it filled the calendars of three associates and a business partner I brought on board. It filled all of our practices. How else can you do this? And to think I discovered this by accident! Building a niche community is a very effective way to a successful practice . . . a wildly successful practice . . . a Million Dollar Practice.

Benefit #10: Attract partners/collaborators to help you focus on your mission. Recruit partners and collaborators, other like-minded professionals, who recognize the value to your niche and who want to participate. Success breeds success. People are attracted to it. One thing I have found is that most people are followers. The ones who are willing to step up, put themselves out there, take a risk, create something new, and be a leader will be handsomely rewarded for their efforts. Followers will just . . . well, follow. They gravitate toward success because they want a piece of it. But they wouldn't step out front in a million years. It's too risky. It's too scary. It's too hard. It's too much responsibility—whatever is going on for them. But the fact that you have done it draws them to you because they think you are great and they want to be part of your success.

Benefit #11: Transform your practice into a business and watch it grow. Have community presence, cultivate multiple revenue streams, and do more than simply work with your clients on an hourly basis, exchanging your time for dollars.

I went from being a therapist seeing clients in my office on an hourly basis to having a relationship coaching business with multiple revenue streams and partners and associates within 3 months.

For much more about how to build your own niche community, I invite you to visit www.milliondollarpractice.net/nichecommunity, where you can download the .mp3 audio recording of "Owning Your Niche by Building a Niche Community," which lays it all out for you.

Step 6: Provide Group Services

Providing group services is your fastest way to a Million Dollar Practice.

From what I have experienced—speaking to groups, offering group services, classes, workshops, tele-classes, conference calls, tele-clinics, coaching groups, coaching teams, support groups, any kind of group you can imagine—going from meeting one client at a time on an hourly basis to serving many at once is one of the most effective ways to serve your niche. It attracts people who are willing not only to pay for your time, but to participate in a resource that can support them.

Step 7: Leverage Your Niche to Build Your Platform

What is a platform, and why is it important?

A platform consists of everybody who knows you. For instance, when you want to publish a book and you shop a book project to publishing houses, the first thing they want to know before they even look at your book is, "What is your platform? Who knows you? What do they say about you? What do you already have in place?"

It's the same for building a Million Dollar Practice. Your goal is to constantly build your platform, to have more and more things in place, to have more and more people know you and more and more people on your mailing list. When you have a niche, you can much more easily leverage that niche to build your platform.

Who is going to sign up for David Steele, Relationship Coach's newsletter? Maybe some people. But who is going to sign up for free membership in the Conscious Dating Online Community? Big difference.

I send out a newsletter to this community. I host tele-seminars and tele-clinics for this community. I have an annual Conscious Dating Success Story of the Year Contest for this community. They download my Conscious Dating app, purchase my Conscious Dating book or e-book, sign up for my Conscious Dating Virtual Coaching Program, and hire my trained Conscious Dating coaches.

There are so many things you can do once you choose a niche. You can leverage that to build your platform. The media will find you. They use the Internet just like you and I do. They search for resources and expertise and ideas online. Own your niche and they will come.

Let's say you have an area of expertise helping Silicon Valley unwed pregnant mothers to start home-based businesses so they can earn a living and spend more time with their children. This is your niche. This is your passion. This is your calling. This is what you are good at. If you publish articles about it and you have a Web site about it and you get referrals for it and you build a niche community around it, people will find you. The media will come to you. This is how you end up on television news and talk show programs. I call this going "an inch wide and a mile deep." You become big by choosing a niche, becoming an expert for that niche, and eventually owning that niche. It's how you develop a Million Dollar Practice.

The alternative to "an inch wide and a mile deep" is an inch deep and a mile wide. This is a generalist. If you are a generalist and your prospective clients are searching for information about your area of expertise, your Web site is going to be way down the list. The ones who specialize in a niche are going to be among the top search results and get that traffic and get those clients. The generalist will never be found. If you want your marketing to be fun and easy and effective, if you want your work to be fun and profitable, if you want to build a Million Dollar Practice, you need to choose a niche. And then, using the Platinum Rule of Marketing, you can own it.

Million Dollar Questions for Chapter 3

1. After brainstorming using the 11 niche identification strategies, what are your top three niche ideas? Which one rises to the top as the one for which you are excited to build your Million Dollar Practice?

2. What are three possible brand names for your niche?

3. Is your market research giving you all the information, feedback, and ideas you need for owning your niche? If not, do more!

4. What kind of niche community would help you attract and serve your niche?

CHAPTER FOUR

How to Create Services, Products, and Programs That Promote Change

Nearly everything we do at Relationship Coaching Institute (RCI) involves creating one-to-many programs. But it wasn't always that way. While there is certainly value in eagerly and ambitiously jumping straight into the pool and beginning with the end in mind, this chapter highlights important principles of client-centric growth and development and a different and more natural approach to building a Million Dollar Practice than you might expect. Instead of initially setting our sights on a preconceived service delivery system and then going back to fill in the pieces based upon a prescribed formula, we're going to ease into the water. Incrementally addressing the real wants and needs of your niche on an ongoing basis in response to your work with your clients allows things to evolve naturally and is (in my opinion) the best way to build a Million Dollar Practice. I call this *the organic approach*.

Here's a snapshot of what the organic approach looks like:

1. Choose your specialty and your niche.
2. Conduct market research to identify its wants and needs.
3. Come up with an idea for a service, product, or program to address those wants and needs.
4. Launch a pilot project to test your offering.
5. Continually add value by identifying and addressing any new and ongoing needs in response to working with your clients.

Even though the organic approach is simple enough in theory, it's not easy because you can't force it. Remember Brian Whetten's *Seven Stages of Practice Building* from Chapter 1? You must know where you are and where you want to go at all times. This takes discipline and patience. The good news is that you absolutely can do it. And you don't need a guru by your side constantly whispering in your ear. All you need to do is remain focused on meeting the needs of your clients. Do that and you will be well on your way to creating services, products, and programs that promote change—the foundation of a Million Dollar Practice (MDP).

MDP PRINCIPLE: SELL PROGRAMS, NOT SESSIONS

So why all the emphasis on creating services, products, and programs anyway? Can't you just do what you do best: advise your clients through their challenges and have them love you for it? No, you can't—not if you want to build a Million Dollar Practice.

People don't want to buy hours from you; they want solutions. Clients don't want to listen to your theories; they want results. Members of your niche are not interested in how well-intentioned you are or how nice your degree looks hanging on the wall; they want assurance. People need confidence that you will successfully help them achieve their biggest, most important goals. And the assistance they are looking for is best delivered in the form of services, products, and programs—tailored just for them.

So how do you do it? How do you satisfy your clients and promote change on a broader scale? Simple: Sell programs that are tangible and structured. Sell products that have concrete benefits and solve specific problems. Sell a package of specialized services and charge what you know they're worth. If a Million Dollar Practice is what you seek, you must:

Sell programs, not sessions.

The development process that will help you create these transformational programs, when coupled with the organic approach outlined previously, boils down to its purest form with two simple questions.

TWO SIMPLE QUESTIONS FOR ORGANIC PROGRAM AND PRODUCT DEVELOPMENT

Simple Question #1: What Works?

As practitioners working with different clients over time in similar situations, we develop the ability to uncover patterns. It comes from our experience and expertise. So any time I set out to address a need, I ask myself, *In this particular situation, because of who I am and how I help my clients, what have I done that has produced the best results? In trying to help members of my niche accomplish their goals, what works?*

Referring back to an example in Chapter 2, tackling relationship problems through lenses and filters of "unconditional love" is not a winning strategy in the real world. It's not that I don't believe in the *premise*—I think it's great—it's that I don't believe it *works*. At the risk of sounding politically incorrect—and as much as people may want it to work—conducting rituals or praying for a healthy relationship simply won't get it done. "Well, I'll just do a magical incantation over these herbs and put them in a little bag and hang it around my neck ... that should do the trick." No, as practitioners we must deal with the real world, real clients, and real solutions.

Designing programs for your niche is not about what is attractive. It's not about what feels good or what makes the most sense to you. It's not about hope and it's not scientific. And you know what? It doesn't have to be. It just has to work. Your ability to effectively serve your clients, and by extension your own success as a private practice professional, is determined not by what you believe *should* get results, but what really *does* get results. Solutions don't have to be grandiose or all-encompassing, they just have to serve your niche.

- What works to get the attention of prospects in your niche?
- What works to entice visitors to your Web site to opt in?
- What works to compel prospects to sign up for your program?
- What works to stimulate referrals?
- What service delivery system works best for your niche?
- What interventions work best for specific situations in your specialty?
- What works for other professionals that you can adapt to your niche?

You get the idea. Capturing and leveraging this knowledge will not only help you design your services, products, and programs, it will help you easily make all decisions related to helping your clients.

Simple Question #2: What's Next?

Whenever I'm faced with a challenge or have just done or created something, I continue to look ahead. I have learned the value of following the *what works* question with one that goes hand in hand to best meet the needs of my clients: *What's next?* The *what's next* question has helped me develop services, products, and programs to help close the loop in serving my clients' needs.

Here's an example: In tough economic times, RCI members often come to me concerned that they'll be prevented from getting new clients. They say, "People won't be able to afford my services." This is an understandable fear, but a myth. A tough economy is when your niche needs you the most. So what to do about this?

Instead of letting negativity define and discourage your behavior, try a more innovative and productive approach, one that is fueled by the *what's next* question to foster a sustained approach to serving your clients: Okay, I'll put together a seminar for them and call it *How to Get Clients in Challenging Times*. But what's next? I will record the seminar and offer the recording as an opt-in on my practice-building Web site *milliondollarpractice.net*. Great, so it's on my Web site as an opt-in offer. What's next? How about when people download the recording, I will have autoresponder messages inviting them to join my practice-building program? Now that the autoresponders are programmed, what's next? Well, practitioners feeling challenged by the economy might also need help learning effective strategies for getting potential clients to say "Yes" to hiring them. So I will take the data from my intense study on the subject over the past 10 years, distill that information into a five-step enrollment strategies and tactics system and put that into a special report. All right, now I've written the special report. Now what am I going to do with it? What's next? It's much too valuable to give away. Should I sell it on my Web site? No, as a product, it would detract from motivating people to sign up for my programs. I know: I'll use it to actually motivate people to join my program. First, I'll make it available to my RCI members. Then, I'll make it available in my preview calls as an enticement for people who are interested in joining RCI. Excellent, now I have that in place. What's next?

MDP Principle: Create Leverage

Years ago I got the idea of doing a workshop for fathers and spent a couple of months putting together a comprehensive program. The manual was about an inch thick. I marketed it to my clients and former clients, my men's community, everybody I knew, and conducted the workshop—*Fatherhood in the 90s*. It was fun, and the men in the workshop really appreciated it.

But after the workshop, I didn't do a thing with it. The manual went on the shelf and the marketing material was filed away. I never followed up on it and I never did it again.

What a waste! As I look back on that episode I kick myself. I could have easily leveraged that workshop by encouraging the graduates to join me in an ongoing group or program. I could have offered advanced classes expanding upon the first workshop. I could have conducted encore presentations as a way to get new clients into my practice. Leveraging the success of that workshop was a huge opportunity to play large, get lots of men into my practice, promote change, and help a great deal of people—and I threw it all away.

At the time, my focus was misdirected. In fact, it was backward. I didn't do the workshop for the participants, I did it for me. I did it simply because I was excited about the idea and it was something I wanted to do . . . that one time. I didn't ask myself the *what's next* question. I just moved on to the next shiny thing that captured my attention. As a result, I missed a chance to create a sustained service, product, or program that not only would have helped me, but would have made a bigger difference in the lives of others.

Always close the loop. Always leverage your efforts and follow up. Always look for ways to create a service, product, or program that better serves your niche. If prospects call you and you have a nice conversation with them, but they decide not to hire you, don't forget about them. If you provide a successful program, look for ways to make it even better and offer it to more people. Ask yourself: *How can I follow up with that? How can I further help this audience? What's next? What's next? What's next?* With everything you do, always ask, *"What's next?"*

Armed with these principles you now have the guiding philosophy on how to build your Million Dollar Practice. But remember: It doesn't happen overnight and it can't be forced. So rather than start with a complete service delivery system from scratch, backfilling it with components to fit your vision, it's better to organically design and develop a cohesive system, piece by piece, in response to the needs of your target audience and through working with your clients.

The remainder of this chapter provides real-life examples, firsthand accounts, of just how you can do this.

CREATING A SERVICE—ONLINE MEMBERSHIP PROGRAM

One day when my wife Darlene and I visited Miami, we decided to sit on a bench and people-watch, one of our favorite things to do. As we sat on the bench, we noticed how most couples walk down the street. They walk without holding hands and seem bored with each other, or they seem to be more friends than married. Every once in a while we would spot a couple holding hands who seemed happy to be together, but it seemed all too rare.

Now, Darlene and I hold hands all the time. We love being together. It feels like something is missing if we are apart, and if we are together we want to be holding hands, touching, or in close proximity. We talked about this as we people-watched and the conversation evolved. We talked about how sad it was when couples have meals together in restaurants and it seems like they never look at each other or even say a word. And then there are other couples who seemingly can't get enough of each other, which led me to think, *We need to create a club. We need to promote couples holding hands and couples being affectionate and couples being closer. We need to create a movement — the anti-boredom movement.*

Immediately when I got to my computer — like I always do when I get an idea like this — I registered a bunch of possible domain names. We thought of using social media resources such as Facebook to host our club, but decided that jumping into a crowded pool would devalue membership. I wanted this club to be initially free, but with a perception of exclusiveness. Shortly thereafter, on Valentine's Day, I got inspired and decided to write a manifesto. I thought: *If you were committed to your relationship, and to your partner, and you were not only committed, meaning you weren't going anywhere, but you were committed to making your relationship the best it could be, what things would you need to do? What promises would you need to keep to make this happen?* And so I wrote them out — *Five Promises to My Beloved*. Then, I looked at all of the different domain names that I had registered. Some of them sounded okay, and some of them sounded like they would be good for a swingers club. Eventually, it came to me: *The people I want to reach want to live happily ever after. They want to be together forever*. So, I called it the *Together Forever Club* and registered togetherforeverclub.com.

Even though I ended up not using any of the domain names I initially registered, they were all part of my creative process. With my newfound domain name, I went to work building my Web site. Today, if you take a look at togetherforeverclub.com, you will see the result — the entire thing was done in a couple of hours on Valentine's Day.

The Web site is basically a squeeze page (no links, just an opt-in box). And I already had squeeze-page templates, so they were not something I had to find. The premise of the club was simple: If you look at these five promises and they resonate, then this is the club for you. And if you want to be a part of this club, all you have to do is opt in with your name and e-mail address. It's free, and when you opt in you are making a strong statement to yourself and to your partner that you want to be together forever and that you want to keep these five promises. At the bottom of the page there is a question: "Is the Together Forever Club right for you?" Notice I am speaking to certain couples, the kind of couples I want to reach, the kind of couples who want to walk down the street holding hands.

Next, I created a membership certificate. At first the certificate was homemade using a simple word processing program. Then I had somebody who actually knew what they were doing with graphics create the certificate. When you join the Together Forever Club you print out the certificate, sign and date it, and give it to your partner. But it's not just the certificate that is so special, it's the promises that come along with it. It's one of the biggest gifts you can ever give your partner.

The Together Forever Club is a current work in progress and an example of how you can quickly create an online membership program with broad appeal to a specific niche. While it may not generate immediate income, it attracts and makes a powerful contribution to a specific group of people—in this case, people who value being a close, committed couple and want a fulfilling relationship. Using the principles and strategies in this chapter, I can easily create additional paid membership levels that meet the needs and desires of the people attracted to the free membership program. On the surface, this club might appear to be a marketing gimmick, but it's more than that. It's making a strong statement. It's offering a real service. I take great pleasure in imagining all the couples who will benefit from sharing the *Five Promises to My Beloved* with each other on their membership certificate ("suitable for framing!").

Certainly there are a lot of other people who could have come up with this type of program, but the Together Forever Club arose from a conversation with my wife that reflects my values and is my unique spin on relationships. Only I could do *this*. Only I could combine technology with relationships and personal responsibility in this way, while being equally romantic, flowery, and practical. That's me, and part of my unique contribution to promoting change in the world. With the plethora of resources available for creating a club, community, or program online, you can do the same thing with your niche, in your area of expertise, in your own special way.

What passions do you have that others may share and be willing to rally around together?

CREATING A SERVICE — GROUPS AND COACHING TEAMS

Singles love doing things as a group—something that has become abundantly clear to me over the years. But not only have I recognized that working in groups is preferred, I have also realized that it is effective. Singles like it because not only do they get to engage someone (you) that they trust, but they also have each other (their peers) for support. Group coaching is also much more affordable for the participant and much more profitable for the practitioner. Groups tend to have a long life (years!), and you get paid much more per hour for a group than an individual. Plus, I have discovered—even though I still don't fully understand it—that there is a phenomenon at work. Perhaps it's because individual services are costly or because there is a stigma associated with getting individual help. Who knows? But what's clear to me is that people are much more willing to discuss, sign up for, and refer others to group services than individual services.

Let's say you do a group for stressed-out real estate agents—one of my favorite populations to pick on in a down economy. When it becomes known that you do a group for this niche, word will spread. People think, *Hey, I know a stressed-out real estate agent* . . . and then go tell him about the program. "Guess what? There's a guy who runs a group for people just like you. You should check it out."

Creating and running groups is a no-brainer for a Million Dollar Practice for most specialties. Sure, there are some exceptions, but they are rare as far as I'm concerned. Even scenarios that are not traditionally run as groups can benefit from a little creativity to introduce a group dynamic. People benefit from mutual support and being around other like-minded people and sharing their fears, struggles, and successes.

As a therapist, I had training and experience in running groups, so when I became a coach, I immediately saw the potential of offering groups for singles. In fact, my first pilot project, the 4-week focus group that helped me launch my coaching practice in Silicon Valley, was enormously successful from the outset. As the program was launched and I started conducting classes and workshops, the graduates of those classes and workshops wanted to join my coaching groups. As I was running these groups, I started incorporating some of the things that I experienced in my men's organization where we functioned in groups. We had the larger organization, which was then broken up into groups of 10–15 men. The larger organization met monthly. The smaller groups met weekly. These groups were called "teams." My involvement allowed me to experience firsthand the different benefits of being a member of a team. The experience is much like being a part of a baseball or football team: a group of people working together and supporting each other toward a common goal. I decided to incorporate those ideas and that mind-set into my Silicon Valley singles groups. And it worked beautifully.

Coaching teams provide a powerful form of support. Clients like the format and want to be a part of it. In fact, in our case, since coaching teams were for the graduates of our classes and workshops, people were often motivated to take the class or workshop because they really wanted to be part of a coaching team after hearing about it.

Coaching teams are effective and tend to have a long life. They are tight-knit, and those who provide them find that it is far easier to retain group members than regular coaching groups. Coaching teams take group coaching to a whole other level.

A coaching team is generally facilitated by one coach, and you don't want the teams to be too big. One of the hallmarks of a coaching team that makes it work well is that everyone is expected to learn and apply coaching skills with each other. The most desirable dynamic comes when everyone acts as a coach and takes responsibility for providing positive support, not just the leader. When you check in and talk about what is going on for you, yes, you have a professional coach leading the group, but you also have the support of your fellow members of your coaching team, whose job it is to support you in a "coach-like" manner.

With a coaching team, coaching skills are taught, modeled, and expected. This is very explicit, and is even in the agreement that everybody signs upon joining the coaching team. Just like any professional service, you must have a contract or agreement to set expectations and establish a level of commitment from the outset. The coaching team has standards. And if the standards are not met, the problem is addressed. It is the leader's job to hold everybody on the team accountable to the agreed-upon standards and to follow through if they are not being met in some way. The integrity and the effectiveness of the team depends upon everyone upholding the standards.

Another hallmark of coaching teams is their nonjudgmental position. We learn and practice effective social, parenting, and management skills, and we make it a priority to alleviate the presence of ego. Over the years I have been in groups and on teams where there has been a lot of judgment. Somebody steps up and says, "Here's what's going on for me," and then they are just riddled with judgment. "You're wrong, you blew it, don't do that, you should do this." Everybody has opinions, true, and everybody tends to think their opinions are right. But a group support system with the presence of ego quickly degrades to chaos. When everybody on the team is fighting each other to insert their opinions, it becomes a competition and more of an atmosphere of winning and scarcity than support and abundance. It's dysfunctional and it doesn't work.

When everybody approaches the person being supported from a "coach-like" point of view, they are practicing nonjudgment. They ask questions and do what a coach would do: They promote a results-oriented culture of growth, safety, and respect. They ask the question "What would best support this person at this time?" Nobody wants to be in a support group where they are deemed by one or more of the members as wrong or inadequate in some way. You want your support group to yield tremendous benefit to all those involved.

Group services are an integral part of any growing business. But having a particular kind of group that has longevity and loyalty and that really provides strong, effective support brings it to the level of a Million Dollar Practice.

What areas of your practice could benefit from a structured group dynamic?

Creating a Product — Specific Solutions

If you visit my various Web sites you will notice a graphic for the Communication Map. I call it a "one-page communication system for all relationships," and it is one of Relationship Coaching Institute's most successful offerings. There is a product development story behind the Communication Map that illustrates the ability we all have to create a client-centric product that promotes change.

When I was a therapist specializing in working with couples in trouble, I felt the urgent need for an immediate communication intervention with many of my clients. They were arguing, in conflict, and generally not getting along very well. To help defuse the situation and open up some channels for progress, I needed something I could do with them right away. There are many communication models; however, my problem was that most were complicated, requiring a 6-week class just to make heads or tails of them. Sure, they were good programs, including skill-building, emotional healing, and other important tools, but my clients needed something "now." Many of my troubled couples were too dysfunctional to attend a class, and I couldn't even be sure they would return for a second session.

Faced with a need to deliver quick results to my clients, I tapped into a series of concepts, paradigms, and "rules of the road" that I had developed over the years in my work with couples, and pulled them together into something I called the Communication Map. It was a nice handout that I gave to my clients along with 20 minutes of instruction before sending them home to practice it.

The Communication Map immediately improved my clients' relationships. In fact, some of its beneficiaries swung by my office just to thank me and tell me how helpful it was to them. Over time I refined the Communication Map by adding more content, converted it to digital format, and introduced it as a coaching tool when I launched

Relationship Coaching Institute. I even gave it away on my Web site as an opt-in offer to provide value to the public while building my business. "Get your FREE downloadable copy of the Communication Map when you join our mailing list!"

For years, the Communication Map was available for free, until one day I learned from an experienced Internet marketer that while freebies are enticing, people generally don't value or use what they don't pay for. My computer desktop, which was littered with free audio programs and special reports that had caught my eye and been downloaded but never opened, gave truth to this statement. I realized that it was a bit of a waste to give the Communication Map away, because, while it was valuable and effective, it was a disservice to myself and the public to distribute it in a way that was ineffective. While it worked as a list-builder, providing it for free diminished the perceived value of this great product. So I hired a graphic designer to spruce it up, laminated it as a mini-poster, and created an audio CD tutorial of me explaining it. Eventually, I got the idea to include a wallet card so people could always have it with them as a reminder of the basic steps.

What started out as a collection of ideas, tips, and strategies that I shared with clients in my office as a couples therapist in the 1980s had developed into a free downloadable offering in the 1990s, and then a full-blown, innovative product that people buy as a part of my Million Dollar Practice.

As private practice professionals, we can all do this. We are all capable of creating products that fulfill our clients' needs on a larger scale. We are all capable of leveraging the power of innovation. But, as mentioned in Chapter 2 under the section, "You Don't Know What You Don't Know," it helps to have a roadmap. It helps to have some-body opening your eyes to the next steps. Having a roadmap helps you get an early start on things. After all, if I knew then what I know now, do you think it would have taken so long for me to generate income from the Communication Map? Instead of just making a bunch of copies and handing them out to clients in my office, I would have turned the Communication Map into a marketable product, sold it on street corners, and started making money right away. This lesson, learned early in my career, became a fundamental component of my overall philosophy for building a Million Dollar Practice.

What problems do you see over and over again in your practice that can be addressed in an effective product for purchase?

CREATING A PRODUCT — MOBILE APPS

Talky2 is an iPhone/iPad app. There is also a Web-based program that can be accessed via Talky2.com. When I first discovered it — I can't even remember how I came across it — I just thought it was the coolest thing. After a bit of research, it occurred to me that it's the world's first true relationship enhancement app — a way for people to use their computers or smart phones to get closer instead of creating more distance, as is the norm for technology.

It had been on my mind to create an iPhone app for relationships, even though I didn't have a clear idea about what that would look like — and it wasn't a priority. But after discovering Talky2, taking a look at how it worked, and realizing, *wow, what a great use of technology to enhance relationships*, I reached out to the developer, clinical psychologist Claudia Perez, PhD, who is located an hour away from me. We began with a telephone conversation, followed that up with having lunch, and developed a co-marketing partnership. Dr. Perez now markets the Communication Map and RCI to people who sign up for Talky2 or go to her Web site, and I market Talky2.

Dr. Perez works exclusively with clients in her office as a solo practitioner. She has no infrastructure, no staff, no Internet marketing experience of any kind. She just had an idea for an online communication program many years ago, and when the technology caught up with her idea, a 15-year-old neighbor created the app for her. And while it was well done, Dr. Perez had no idea how to leverage or monetize it. Taking the reverse approach of the Communication Map, she initially charged for it, then decided to make it free after having few takers.

Talky2 serves as both a "what-to-do" story and a "what-not-to-do" story. The what-to-do story is thinking about how you can create a product and leverage your expertise to help people in different ways — in this case, by using smartphone apps. There is a whole world of possibilities out there. Just as there was nothing like the Communication Map on the market before I identified the need for it, created it, and evolved the product over time, the same is true with Talky2. Dr. Perez identified a need based upon working with her clients, put her expertise to use, and created a product. And because when people choose Talky2 they are expressing a general interest in enhancing their communication, it can be used as an entry into additional services, products, and programs— for example, the Communication Map, online classes, or home-study courses.

That's the thing about marketing: When you put stuff out there that is valuable, you are more readily able to identify people that have raised their hands and said, "Yes, I'm attracted to that. What else you got?" They have come forward in response to your offerings, you know who they are, you know what their problems, needs, goals, and challenges are, and you know that they are candidates for your other services, products, and programs.

The what-not-to-do side of the equation is that Dr. Perez had no idea how to monetize her creation, no idea how to leverage it. In fact, as I did when I first created the Communication Map, she offered it for free. In my case, this method at least worked as a way to incentivize people to sign up for my network and become part of my system. But hindsight makes it clear that it was much too valuable to give away. It wasn't until I turned the Communication Map into a product for purchase that it became truly successful, not only in terms of better building my business, but in better serving the public. Remember: When people purchase something, not only are they more likely to value it, but they are also more likely to use it. And when it comes to the Communication Map and Talky2, both designed for enhancing relationships, that's a good thing.

Speaking of apps, mobile devices have changed consumer technology and habits tremendously, to the point that (at this writing) mobile device use exceeds TV and computer use at a rate of 5:1. People with mobile devices spend much more time in apps than on Web sites, and 25% use their mobile devices only to access the Internet, so to reach this huge segment of the population, your Web site must be compatible with mobile devices and you might consider publishing an app.

Here are my top four app ideas for helping professionals:

1. Turn your book or e-book into an app.
   This can be free or paid and can include other content (audio, video, etc.), features (messaging, wall, social media, etc.), upsells, and the like.
2. Create a mobile portal for your practice.
   Make it easy for prospects and clients to learn about you, contact you, make an appointment, get directions to your office, and get valuable tips and other content from you.
3. Create a mobile portal for your content.
   This can be free or paid and can include audio, video, articles, e-courses, upsells, social media, quizzes, messaging, contact forms, and the like.
4. Create a mobile portal for your program.
   Any multimedia, multistep program can be converted to an app and engaged much more conveniently in an app than on a Web site or computer.

For more information about creating apps for your practice, visit www.easyproapps.com. For more information about leveraging mobile media to build your business, visit www.mobilemediamarket ingrevolution.com.

What client needs can you address through innovation and technology?

Creating a Product — From Workshops to Home-Study Courses

Let's contrast the Fatherhood-in-the-90s fiasco I mentioned earlier with a 1-day relationship coach–training workshop I conducted several years ago. I had it professionally recorded with the intention of creating a home-study product. The same manual that I created for the workshop became the home-study workbook. The recording became a six-CD set. This 1-day workshop, which I created and conducted to meet the needs of the people in my niche, afterward became an enduring home-study program. You, too, can do this.

Every private practice professional should have a signature presentation, a 20-minute to 1-hour talk for the people in your niche that really struts your stuff, demonstrates that you understand them, and shows them a paradigm for how they can solve their problems or achieve their goals. This signature program can be turned into a workshop or class. It's the first exposure that people in your niche would have to you. But then don't forget, *"What's next?"*

What would you want the participants to do after that? You might want them to hire you, but that could be a stretch for some folks. You skirt this issue by remaining focused on your niche. Take an effective solution and offer that as the next step toward working with you. In my case, I turned a 1-day relationship coach–training workshop into a home-study program. Any time you have content, think about the many different ways you can package that content — audio, video, e-book, Web-based interactive, smartphone app — as a way to give your niche more access, more value, and more results. A 1-day workshop can be created and expanded upon to meet the needs of any niche on any topic.

Based upon your niche and your market research, what could be your first product offering? How could you leverage that into something that provides additional value?

CREATING A PROGRAM — ECOSYSTEMS

The Conscious Dating program (consciousdating.com) is not an empirically proven and researched program. And yet it is used by a great number of singles every day to find the love of their life. Why? It works.

As mentioned earlier in this book, I built a successful coaching practice very quickly. In 1997, I went from a blank slate, not knowing anything about working with singles, to a full practice in 3 months. And things just grew from there. Originally focusing on a need to serve singles in my area, over time I created an entire program, complete with licensed Conscious Dating coaches all over the world.

Conscious Dating has its origins in my initial research and work with individual singles. When I had the idea to put together a workshop for singles, I started by making a list of ideas on a legal pad and then put them together into a class. The graduates of the class joined a coaching team. Then came speaking engagements, then came the *Conscious Dating* book, then came Conscious Dating workbooks and professional manuals, then came training and licensing Conscious Dating coaches, then came Conscious Dating tele-seminars and tele-clinics, then came an online Conscious Dating Virtual Coaching Program, then came Conscious Dating mobile apps, and on and on. It developed into a whole ecosystem. And people respond to it.

What ideas can you transform into a comprehensive program that effectively serves your niche?

CREATING A PROGRAM — NICHE COMMUNITIES

Ever since I was able to fill my practice — and the practices of four other coaches — by building a community for singles in Silicon Valley, I have wanted to see similar communities all over the world. Fifteen years later, Relationship Coaching Institute has reached the critical mass necessary to make it possible.

RCI now has large groups of coaches worldwide, and we are empowering those coaches to come together and create teams that will host and sponsor Conscious Relationship Communities, or as we also like to call it, Club Relate®, for which the description and manifesto can be found at clubrelate.org.

Relationships are important. They pervade every aspect of our lives and are among our highest values and goals. Still, even though nobody can argue with the necessity of cultivating relationships, it doesn't necessarily make it easy to get clients as a relationship coach. You still must have tangible services, products, and programs. You still must have credibility, and you still have to market — which is fairly easy to do. But you know what? *All* practitioners focus on an area that is important to people. The people that you want to target do flock together. There are underserved niches all around you. And anywhere there is an underserved niche is fertile ground for a niche community.

118

Hosting a niche community provides people the opportunity to get together, feel safe, learn, support each other, and have fun. Hosting a niche community gives you a room full of genuine, potential clients. They will drive traffic to you. That is all the marketing you will need to do. While my specific area of expertise is relationships, professionals practicing across the full spectrum of specialties can benefit from niche communities.

At RCI we took to the next level what I did in building my own Million Dollar Practice by helping our members do the same. The Conscious Relationship Communities Project effectively answered the questions, *"What works?"* and *"What's next?"* The specific focus has been on building a Million Dollar Relationship Coaching Practice through the development of conscious relationship communities.

Additionally, this project ties into owning a niche, which is nice because, as you know from Chapter 3, there is a lot of job security in that. RCI is ranked number one in most search engine queries for "relationship coaching" because we own the niche of relationship coach training. We are not going anywhere. Even if there were 50 other relationship coach–training organizations out there, we would still stand out. It would take other organizations *years* to catch up with us — that is, if we were standing still, which we are not. Even then, other organizations would not be doing it our way. We have a unique value proposition among training organizations and our emphasis is on practice building, marketing support, and being a membership organization committed to helping its members have successful practices — and making it affordable for them. This is not a franchise people need to plunk down $50,000 to buy into. It's a value-based organization that provides results — again and again. There is simply no other relationship coach training organization doing anything like it. You can create a niche community that effectively serves your niche in the same way.

What needs related to your niche in your community can you identify that are not being met?

All of the preceding examples serve as practical, real-life examples of things you can do to create services, products, and programs that promote change. The idea is to always have something new, exciting, and intriguing that engages potential clients in a conversation about how you can best serve them. Don't stand still. Leverage the power of the Platinum Rule of Marketing and the organic approach, and constantly ask yourself "What works?" and "What's next?" in response to your work with your clients—and watch your business grow into a Million Dollar Practice.

Million Dollar Questions for Chapter 4

1. Assuming you have a program (or an idea for one), what ideas occur to you for packaging your program into a workshop, class, book, workbook, app, membership program, and niche community?

2. What product ideas (home-study course, book, CD/DVD set, etc.) occur to you for providing value to your niche?

3. What kind of groups and group programs could you implement in serving your niche?

CHAPTER FIVE

Creative Business Models and Service Delivery Systems

It's one thing to have a stable of well-defined services, products, and programs you wish to present to your clients. It's something entirely different to have a well-thought-out plan of distribution with multiple entry points to your practice that all tie together into a cohesive system and profitable business model. This chapter focuses on leveraging the organic business development process to make the most of your market research, expertise, and hard work in pursuit of a Million Dollar Practice.

CREATING A SYSTEM

Things that are systemized tend to operate more smoothly and be more effective than things that are not systemized. When you have a system, you can remove yourself from the equation by training others to step in and take ownership of certain tasks. Despite its benefits, however, creating a system is not always an easy concept for people to wrap their minds around. When it comes to helping professionals, it can be downright hard. It's the classic entrepreneurial struggle:

transitioning from a business that you created and ran by yourself to putting systems in place so that it can run more efficiently and without your direct involvement.

Many private practices you encounter on a daily basis—from chiropractors to physicians to dentists—have a system. They have ways of conducting intakes, assessments, and treatment plans, and they have procedures in place to cover contingencies. But despite the number of businesses and organizations that have systems, a significant number of private practice professionals still have no systems of any kind.

Psychotherapists are notorious for not having standardized systems. We may have general operating procedures, intakes, billing forms, and appointments. But with every new client and with every new problem or challenge, we go about things a little differently. We weren't trained to treat our clients one particular way; we were trained to focus on uniqueness: "Okay, with this kind of client you are looking for this, and you want to do these kinds of things."

While it is true that each client is unique, it is also true that there is a degree of crossover that can be applied in treating each unique client based on a set of proven successful methods and procedures. This general consistency and effectiveness of approach can be lost on our clients if we don't have service delivery systems. This not only helps serve your clients, it can create multiple streams of revenue that form the basis of your creative business model.

Building a Million Dollar Practice and making a bigger difference in the world hinges on your willingness and ability to systemize *everything*, from your administrative procedures to the way you deliver your services, products, and programs, so that at any one point in time somebody else can step in and effectively serve your niche, and you can continue earning the living you deserve.

SYSTEMS IN ACTION

One of the coach trainings that I participated in conducted a fun exercise that I have since seen in other situations. It's called serial coaching. Each coach has 1 minute to coach a client without any preparation or prior knowledge of the case. Each subsequent coach comes along, sits in the chair, and takes over from the coach who was just ahead of him. It's a great example of the benefits of a system. In this scenario, when you have a system, anybody trained can sit in that chair and effectively take over the case.

My dentist's office, mentioned in Chapter 2, is another example of effective use of a system. Not only is it a great service provider, but it is also highly systemized. During any given visit, anybody who looks in my mouth says the same thing. The hygienist: "Oh, well, you have that going on, but we're going to be watching it for a while." The dentist: "Hi, David. Let's see what we have here: Well, you have that going on, but we're going to be watching it for a while." The dental assistant: "Hmmm . . . let's see . . . well, you have that going on, but we're going to be watching it for a while." The hygienist, the dentist, and the dental assistant could all be the same person. They are all on the same page. They are very much a team, and they have a system. And it works beautifully.

The more variation in delivering professional services, the more risk that clients will not get quality or effective service. When you treat clients as unique, you are approaching each case as if it were the first time that you have ever come across a given situation—every time. And you run the risk of treating each individual case in a different way than the last time you encountered it. An effective service, just like an effective anything, requires a systematic approach based on experience of what works and what doesn't work. Still, many private practice professionals tend to function without service delivery systems.

THE ALLURE OF THE MYSTERY NOVEL

As a therapist who once owned his own private practice, I clearly remember how interesting, fresh, and exciting it was to meet with a new client: "Who is this person? What's going on with him? Where will this lead?"

It's sort of like picking up a new mystery novel—every time you do it, you enter a whole new world.

And even if the book is by the same author who has written 20 others, you still never know what to expect with this one. So I understand and relate to those who resist giving up some of the mystique, those who believe they must treat every client with a new approach, those who feel they must apply their full scope of experience and training with each new client and look at them with fresh eyes.

Many, if not most "soft topic" practitioners (psychotherapists, coaches, counselors, social workers, etc.) tend to welcome the blank slate and don't want to be constrained by rigid treatment protocols. We want to do things in our own special ways. We want to make up our own minds and clear the pathways for our adaptive talents to take effect. This approach, while exciting for the practitioner, is not in the best interests of the client and, therefore, not the path to a Million Dollar Practice.

Think of it this way: Would you want to be in the client's situation, hiring somebody to help you who is making it up on the fly? Let's say you want to decorate your home or your office, and you hire an interior designer because you know nothing about interior design. Would you feel comfortable with a person who relied totally on creative instincts or idiosyncratic version of feng shui? "In this space I'm seeing that we could do this and we could do that." That may be fun for the interior designer, but would you want to be the client on the receiving end of somebody's arbitrary inspiration? Perhaps, if you truly believe in and trust that interior designer—he or she is tops in the field, comes with all sorts of high recommendations, and all of his/her clients have been happy with the work. If that were the case, you may be more inclined to give that person some latitude. Short of that, you might be shopping for another interior designer, one with more of a system or clear rationale for how they approach helping you.

As is the case with most of my provider relationships, I have been dealing with the same real estate agent/mortgage broker for 20 years. He is brilliant and I trust him without a doubt. I know he is looking out for me and that he invariably figures out the best way to go. When he says, "David, I think in this situation you should do this," I am 99% inclined to do it without thinking about it too much, because he is diligent and already has done all of the thinking for me. If your clients have that kind of trust in you, if you have established that kind of credibility, you can probably get away with not having a system. Otherwise, you might want to think about changing tactics.

Consumers are much more inclined to trust providers with a system than those who are making it up as they go along. Whimsically approaching each new client leads to uncertainty, inconsistency, and error. So if you want to make a bigger difference in the world by sufficiently serving your clients, everything you do as a private practice professional needs to be systemized, which is certainly within the realm of possibility. A real estate agent and mortgage broker can do it; so can an interior designer. And so can you.

Your private practice does not have to be — nor should it be — freeform. The creativity and ability to improvise in any given situation or environment can still exist, even as the system ensures a standard of quality and provides added benefits.

HAVING A SYSTEM — BENEFITS TO THE CLIENT

When you have a system, clients immediately feel more comfortable and are willing to put themselves in your hands. They know what to expect and have the sense that the steward of their affairs has some experience. They feel that there is a rationale for what is being done — and how, when, and the way it is being done — that makes sense. Clients are assured that the professional is not just winging it. As consumers, we are comfortable when we know what to expect. We are able to relax, to go with it, to experience it fully, and to reap the entire benefit. When we don't know what to expect, we feel anxious and don't quite trust the situation or the practitioner. Having a system helps minimize this fear.

HAVING A SYSTEM — BENEFITS TO THE PRACTITIONER

While having a system benefits the client in many ways, it also benefits the practitioner. And it starts with getting clients. Clients are much more willing to hire you if they see that you have a service delivery system that makes sense and that they can buy into. "Wow, you've really got it set up here. You must know what you're doing. Where do I sign up?"

Another benefit to the practitioner comes in the form of efficiency. Re-creating the wheel takes a lot of time and energy, and it also leaves more room for error. With a system, you don't have to re-create the wheel with every client, and you can leverage your past experience to help future clients.

To the technicians among us, this next benefit of having a system may seem counterintuitive. But entrepreneurial practitioners see the value in becoming *dispensable*. This concept is often difficult for technicians to grasp at first, because when you are a technician, you don't want to make yourself dispensable—quite the opposite. If you create a system and become dispensable, you put yourself out of a job. "I have this down to a science. Anybody can now come in and do what I do. They don't need me anymore . . . uh, oh." This is not good if you are a technician. But for an entrepreneur, that is the whole point. You want to become dispensable in your system so you can take yourself out of the equation, plug in other individuals, and free yourself to focus on the things only you can do.

If a service lacks systemization and depends entirely upon you, your creativity, your experience and training, and your unique approach to the client, then only you can perform that service. And you are stuck. But if you have a system and you make yourself dispensable and replaceable, then you can train and hire somebody else to implement that system and effectively and seamlessly serve the client.

SYSTEMIZING YOUR BUSINESS

Accountants, most medical professionals, and many other private practice professions lend themselves to systemizing. It's easy to identify a need and figure out a system to deliver the solution—and you simply cannot build a Million Dollar Practice unless you do—but even if you have a system at the professional level, you also need to incorporate it at the specialty level.

As mentioned earlier, most of us are not trained in one specific system. Coaches, psychotherapists, and other practitioners are trained in different approaches, and we are expected to use our judgment with each unique client situation. We have a number of different approaches we can take, which is part of the problem: too many choices. However, there are a host of individual practitioners who generally tend to approach certain clients and certain client situations in systematic, predictable ways. And their clients are better off because of it.

If you habitually choose one treatment modality or way of working with a client, you will likely fall back to that method time and again. Despite the vast number of possible therapeutic options from which to choose, most of us use only a fraction of them. Most of us have a "theoretical orientation" and stay in a groove or a narrow band of what we believe to be effective or what is congruent with our individual style. In doing this, we often fail to remain focused on the approaches that would best serve our clients.

If you are looking to hire an artist to do a painting, you will readily see that each artist has her own style. You are absolutely not going to get the same result with one artist that you would with another. The same can be said of photographers. Each photographer has his own orientation and way of working. It's a similar situation with chefs. No two chefs cook the same way. You may have the same basic ingredients, but you won't get a dish that looks and tastes *exactly* the same way from two different cooks, even in a chain restaurant.

Private practice professionals are in a similar boat. While it may be hard because we have so many options about how we can work with a client, we have to choose. Sure, we prefer some styles over others. But that's the beauty of it. We can select the methods that best serve our clients and then create our own systems around them to deliver consistent results.

In my case, as a helping professional, I have a fairly unique ability and spin on things. I'm pragmatic. I understand the feeling world, but I'm not a feeling person. I can work with people who would have other practitioners shaking in their boots and maintain my composure. I am also linear. I create systems that make sense, that have a step one, step two, and step three. I am good at taking complicated things and simplifying them. Who I am as a person, as a man, as a professional—with my particular intellect and way of looking at things and expressing them—resonates with certain people. They "get it" better and more easily from me than from anybody else. I have heard it over and over and over again: "You make so much sense to me, David." And yet there are other people with whom I don't resonate—particularly the feeling types. They don't get their need for nurturing and empathy met from me. There are other practitioners who are a better fit for them.

We all have our unique abilities, and we all have people whom we are able to reach and help best. We all have a sweet spot. There is a wonderful opportunity for us to identify our ideal client, the one we help best, and the one we can help in our sleep—literally, if we design the right product, program, or system. It is fun for us. It is easy for us. And what's easy for us may be hard for other people. Our gift to the world—to our profession, clients, and ourselves—is to be able to systemize that.

THE IMPORTANCE OF CREATING A SYSTEM

Over the years I have learned a lot about relationships, both through study and practice. That knowledge—about being single, about the process of finding a partner and making good partner choices, and about having a great life—has now been simplified into a step-by-step program called Conscious Dating. It is a tremendous gift—to the world, to singles, to myself, and to future generations— and it was something that nobody else had done before, though there have been a lot of people since who have tried, each with their own spin. That's the beauty of ideas. Your particular program may not res- onate with some, but it will resonate with others. There is room in the market for everybody.

There is, however, a bit of a downside. And it is a very little known and little understood problem having to do with how hard it is for people to ask for and get help. When they finally make the leap and give it a try, if it doesn't work or they don't have a positive experience, they tend to dismiss the entire profession or service. If, for example, a person considered working with a life coach (or therapist, or energy healer, etc.), gave life coaching a try with a "sample session," and the approach of that particular coach didn't resonate, the person might reach the conclusion that "Coaching isn't for me." That's one of the reasons we don't recommend selling "sessions" and instead advocate creating services, products, and programs that can be incorporated into a service delivery system. Your program might resonate with people who are turned off by another practitioner's program, and they might be willing to give yours a try.

Because people might not understand what we do and that all practitioners are different, they might generalize and figure a bad experience with one therapist foreshadows a bad experience with all. As practitioners, it's up to us to be unique and to communicate our uniqueness in concrete, tangible ways. It's incumbent upon us to systemize, package, and deliver our services, products, and programs effectively and point out the differences among providers.

GETTING TO "YES"

Systemizing your offerings isn't merely an act of guesswork. There is a behavioral principle at work that has to do with practicing mistakes.

In training, you want to promote success by intervening to minimize practicing mistakes when they occur. If you don't, those mistakes become habits that interfere with success, and changing them becomes hard. This results in the student becoming discouraged.

The way to have a positive training experience is to show people the right way and immediately correct their mistakes before they get too far off course. The people who need your help have already gone down a path that doesn't work. There is a tremendous amount of change that needs to happen and a tremendous amount of inertia that needs to be overcome, which amounts to a huge hurdle.

When clients make the decision to trust you and throw their hat in the ring with you, you want to ensure that they have been set up for success. It has to be the right fit. It has to meet their needs. They have to be happy with what you are providing. It has to make sense to them. It has to have a name that speaks to them. Any negative experiences will likely turn them off, not just toward you or your services, but toward getting help for their problems in general. Having an effective system that clearly lays out the benefits and removes guesswork is a recipe for alleviating a barrier to entry, necessary for clients if they are to benefit from your services, products, and programs.

When we reach potential clients we have their attention for a very short amount of time. By making our offers compelling, we raise the opportunity for them to take action, for them to make a choice that will change their lives. Our job is to help them make that choice. If they don't make that choice, in that moment, then their problems and opportunities go back on the shelf and nothing changes. Who knows when they are going to come down off that shelf again—a year, 2 years, 5 years? The problems and opportunities will come back down when they are sick and tired of them, when they are in enough pain to take a look at them again. In the meantime, they're stuck living with a problem they wish they could solve, unhappy with their situation.

There is a bit of urgency here, because this is an area people tend to avoid. They don't really want to do it. Getting help isn't their first choice of how to spend their time and their money. The rare situation when people are in conversation with you about their biggest problem is the time for them to say "Yes." If they are not going to say "Yes," they are going to lose, because their lives are not going to change.

That's why it is incredibly important that when we do reach members of our niche, we have a tangible, properly packaged system for them to sink their teeth into.

Getting people to say "Yes" is an important topic for a future chapter on sales and enrollment. But first, we must develop something powerful and compelling to which they can say "Yes."

When you look at your business as a system, and you create systems for your business, and you choose your audience, you're clear about who you want to help and how you want to help them, and you're constantly on the lookout, you're constantly responsive to their needs, and you put stuff together for them, big and small, that builds and evolves your system.

I'm a lot more comfortable with this process now than I used to be. It's all a building process. But if you understand the process, and you recognize the path . . . I mean, I know my path, I know exactly what path I'm on. I know exactly what direction I'm going on that path. I know exactly what I'm going to encounter and what pieces I'm going to put in place along that path. Where the path ends, I don't know, but it's my desire that, as practitioners, we all know our path, we recognize it, we're on it, we're progressing along it, we're putting the pieces in place along it, and along the way we're building something substantial that will make a difference in the world.

BUILDING YOUR SERVICE DELIVERY SYSTEM/ CREATIVE BUSINESS MODEL

Your service delivery system is simply how you deliver your services. But it also serves as a creative business model that provides multiple streams of income from your efforts. Ideally, it is created in response to your market research and tailored for the needs of your niche.

As we discussed in Chapter 4, it might be tempting to build a service delivery system around what "sounds good" or "seems right" to you. Regardless of how good your hunches are, my unwavering advice to you is always to do your market research first, and then base your service delivery on the hard data that you generate. If this merely verifies what you already guessed, then more power to you, but more times than not, your market research will reshape your hypothesis of what your niche wants and needs.

Another way of putting this is: Market to your target audience, not to yourself. And make no mistake, you are not your target market. This is one of the biggest flaws in all marketing—by no means limited to private practice professionals. Often, businesses of all sizes forget that they aren't their own target markets. Or, to put it differently, they assume that they are their own target markets. They simply say to themselves, "Hey, this makes sense to me, so it must make sense to the people I'm trying to reach." This is patently false.

Remember the Platinum Rule of Marketing? "Do unto others as they want to be done to." This rule surfaces again and again in creating your Million Dollar Practice and is critical in building a service delivery system. Still, many practitioners ignore it, and their businesses—and their clients—suffer as a result. There are a couple of reasons for this.

1. Your Target Market Doesn't Define What You Do in Your Terms

You live and breathe this stuff. You (naturally) take mental shortcuts. You know what your subject looks like from the "inside." You know the details. Your target market, however, does not. They have some understanding, but not at your depth or breadth. And this difference is far, far more than just a matter of simplifying and avoiding deadly jargon. It's a fundamental shift in *what* you communicate, not just *how*.

For example, you may think that coaching is a "service that helps people achieve goals and move forward in their lives." Sure, that sounds reasonable—to you. But if you ask 100 people out there what coaching means, probably less than 5% will come even close to that definition. They will more likely say something like, "Coaching is a way for me to overcome problems and be happy." The two versions—yours and theirs—may look similar, but the differences speak volumes. You are looking at something from a feature-driven perspective. They are looking at things from a benefit-driven perspective. You are looking at something in terms of what it does, which is logical and factual. They are looking at something in terms of how it promises to achieve a satisfying outcome, which is emotional and abstract.

And keep in mind that this is just an example. If you go one step further and imagine what a targeted niche will say about coaching, the differences between your initial assumptions and their black-and-white responses will be even bigger. This is because your target market has their own language and will interpret and define coaching as it relates to their worlds, that is, to their niches. In doing this, they will do more than just change your (expected) words around. They will change the nuance and even the direction. What struck you as so obvious will reveal itself to be quite different. And you don't have to wait long to see the evidence. The moment you start generating market research data, the proof will be right there in front of you: What you thought they wanted isn't what they actually want. Remember the success of Shannon Silva's "Unstoppable Women" rebranding from Chapter 3?

Another example of how you view things differently than others is in the concept of therapy itself. I would argue that you believe, rationally, that pretty much everyone out there in the world would benefit from therapy and enjoy personal growth. But guess what? Most people out there will disagree! Instead, they figure that someone has to be "pretty messed up" to need therapy and that working with a therapist is a choice of last resort.

As an aside, yes, this stigma about therapy pains many therapists, as it did me. And worse than that, it prevents therapists from reaching many of the people whom they would like to help. In fact, this dynamic may be one of the reasons why many practitioners look to bring coaching into their professional worlds. If you find yourself in that category, then be assured: You are not alone. Welcome to the club!

2. You Don't Buy Your Own Services

As obvious as it may sound, it is worth stating: While you may have some powerful—and ultimately correct—insights about your target market, you truly cannot see their world as clearly as they can because you don't buy your own services.

To put it another way: You are already sold on your services. Whether you are consciously aware of it or not, your intuition and subconscious are working overtime, behind the scenes, to create the reality that you want to experience—that is, one where everyone loves your services, products, and programs and would buy them simply because, well, who wouldn't?

Remember: People don't always (some cynics might argue often) buy things that "make sense." How many people smoke, even though they know it's doing severe damage to them? How many people crave losing weight but drive to restaurants where even the water has 1,000 calories? These people are not insane. Their mind is enabling them to do something insensible, so that decisions like smoking or speeding dangerously in a car or eating that hot sauce that they know will have them crawling helplessly to the bathroom at 3:00 a.m., all, somehow, make sense.

The same unreasonable "logic" applies when creating your service delivery system. You cannot simply assume that people will come to you because they have problems and you have solutions. Again, that may be why *you* would buy your services. But as we pointed out, *you* don't buy your services. You need to understand both the problems and the solutions of prospective clients in their terms. And those terms will be different in obviously small and surprisingly big ways.

A related phenomenon that drives me crazy is that people will much more readily spend their money on what they *want* than on what they *need*. This is one reason (in addition to stigma, etc.) why they are reluctant to pay out of pocket for therapy. Coaches don't have this problem, though, as they are (supposedly) focusing their services on helping people get what they *want*.

If you ignore—or don't conduct—your market research and simply put together what you want to do or what you assume is going to work, then you risk failure. If you listen and respond to what your niche wants, you are almost guaranteed success.

YOUR SERVICE DELIVERY SYSTEM AS A CLIENT CREATION FUNNEL

As a private practice professional you have likely come across the term "marketing funnel," which is a way to easily represent a system of reaching out to a target market and bringing them into your sales cycle. In terms of building a Million Dollar Practice, I call it a Client Creation Funnel. It's a way of reaching out to the people in your niche, systematically introducing them to the services, products, and programs that you have organically created, and then ushering them into your practice, ultimately turning them into paying, satisfied clients.

On the next page is a snapshot of a three-tier client creation funnel. Don't worry if these terms at first make little or no sense. As I explore each tier, you will see how they all fit together. For now, just become comfortable—or as comfortable as you can—with the shape of the client creation funnel: The widest part is on top, and the narrowest is down at the bottom. The top tier of the funnel comprises your marketing activities designed to create prospects. The middle tier contains low-to-moderate-cost products and group services designed to provide value and create clients. The bottom tier is where your client services live.

Top of Funnel: Your Marketing Activities

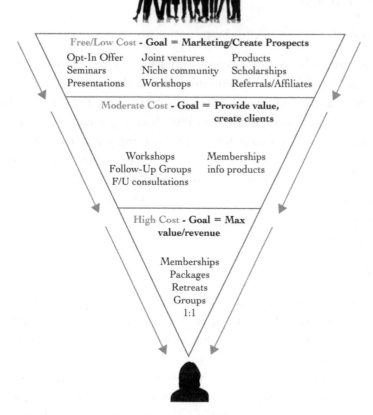

Service Delivery System/Client Creation Funnel

TOP OF FUNNEL: YOUR MARKETING ACTIVITIES

One of the wonders of marketing is that it allows you to communicate with people you don't even know—people who, potentially, are searching for precisely what you have to offer. And it's the mission of your marketing activities—or the top of your funnel—to reach out to these good people and say: "Hi there. I'm here for you."

While there are many ways to do this, the strategy that I use, and hence endorse, is one where you "market by providing value"—that is, where you share valuable information and resources with your niche in a way that encourages them to want more.

There are three things to note about "marketing by providing value" activities.

1. They're Free

If you must charge something—and I have a hard time imagining that you must, but maybe you do—then it should offset your costs, not be a source of profit. Remember: These activities are about reaching out to your niche and introducing yourself. Just as you wouldn't charge someone for simply meeting you for the first time on the street, at a conference, or even in your office, you shouldn't charge for these kinds of marketing activities. Frankly, most people won't pay, and even a nominal fee will turn away far more people than it will attract. In the long run, you will undermine your marketing and lose money.

2. They're Valuable

This second point, as apparent as it may be, has to be mentioned. The resources you offer must be perceived as *valuable* to your niche. The offer can't be thinly veiled advertising where you just self-promote and pitch your services. It has to be something that your niche finds interesting, informative, and helpful. Your market research should help you identify your niche's top needs, challenges, goals, and questions, which you can use to organically create free services, products, and programs of high perceived value that will attract prospective clients.

3. They're Designed to Build a Relationship

What you offer at this stage is not the "be all and end all" of how you hope to connect with your niche; rather, it's the beginning of a naturally evolving process. That is why you must create your resources with a vision toward encouraging prospective clients to deepen their relationship with you—and move further down the client creation funnel. One of the most powerful ways to do this is to simply plan and create your clients' next steps and place strong, focused calls to action for those next steps at the end of each valuable service, product, and program.

TOP-OF-FUNNEL ACTIVITIES: PROSPECT GENERATION

You have likely come across some or all of these types of top-of-funnel resources in your own travels. They include newsletters, reports, e-books, seminars, tele-classes, audio programs, and other offerings. In addition, there are what I call *primary forms* of top-of-funnel marketing activities, which simply communicate what you do. These primary forms are speaking, writing, and networking.

Here are some examples of top-of-funnel activities.

Speaking

Speaking refers to giving presentations to groups, either in person or via conference call (tele-seminar or webinar). Speaking is effective, as it gives listeners an experience of your presence and voice that approximates your actual service. Listeners connect with your message and become attracted to the idea of working with you. The listening experience is also "safe" for your listeners, because they are anonymous or part of a group and are thus not on the hot seat in a one-to-one conversation. This allows potential clients to experience you from a distance and become comfortable with you.

As a nice residual benefit, your speaking engagements can be recorded (audio or video) and repurposed into programs available on your Web site. You can then offer these programs to Web site visitors in exchange for their contact information. And even better, you can set up the exchange so that it's automatic—you don't have to manually send your Web site visitors anything. They simply self-identify that they want to "opt-in" to get your audio or video program, and they automatically receive the material.

Writing

Writing includes all of the content on your Web site and blog and in your published articles (in print and online), books or e-books, e-programs (a series of lessons delivered automatically by what is called an "autoresponder"), and so on. Through your writing, you can provide valuable information to engage, inform, and help the people in your niche see that you are a credible expert who understands their needs.

Also, when writing—and this applies to speaking, too—don't worry about giving too much information away and, ironically, not positioning yourself to actually help the people in your niche. Information in today's world is freely and easily available. The information you provide will motivate and inspire, but by itself won't typically create lasting change, which is why they need you, which by all means you can convey in clear, honest terms in your material.

If you're willing and able, I recommend you consider writing a book. You have information and wisdom to share, and if you write a book that targets your niche it will be your best door opener and marketing tool. I resisted the call to write a book for a long time, but in retrospect, I wish I hadn't waited. Don't worry—as I did—that you might not have anything unique to say. Just write from your experience and perspective. In doing so you will provide value to people in your niche.

Networking

Networking includes building your referral relationships and joint-venture partnerships. It also includes participating in groups and organizations that fit your niche—online and offline. Research shows that, by far, the most effective way private practice professionals find new clients is by word-of-mouth referral. As such, networking and building your referral relationships is the single most effective way to fill your practice.

Free Information Products

Both free and low-cost products are valuable marketing tools at the top of your funnel. These include audio and video programs, mobile apps, e-books and e-programs, and printed materials such as books, pamphlets, mini-posters and wallet cards. All of these products can be produced digitally and offered online at minimal cost to you. Hard copies can be produced in bulk at very low cost to be distributed in person or by mail.

Don't be afraid to invest some money in creating great promotional products, as most of them are far less costly than color brochures—and they are more effective! For example, the last time I used brochures (four-color trifold on glossy card stock), I paid close to $2.50 each. But promotional CDs cost me $0.40 each, and CDs are far more effective at providing value, attracting prospects, and delivering my message and promotional information.

Workshops and Seminars

Workshops and seminars are effective for attracting prospective clients. While you could provide these at a low cost to cover your expenses, I recommend offering them for free—provided that attendees register in advance on your Web site. Again, you can use an autoresponder system to make this fast and easy for everyone, including you. Don't balk at the idea of offering something for free. Many successful personal-growth gurus conduct free seminars and workshops as their primary marketing activity. Until people get to know you, a fee can be an impenetrable barrier. Remember: You are not at the bottom of your client creation funnel yet. You don't need to—nor should you expect to—profit from these top-of-funnel activities. This is all about generating prospects by reaching out and saying "Hello." It's not about generating revenues—yet!

Niche Communities

We covered this topic at length in Chapter 3 (so if you skipped it, you know what your homework is). Frankly, niche communities are my favorite top-of-funnel marketing activities. They are a gift that keeps on giving and they have worked well for me, which means they can work for you, too.

MIDDLE-OF-FUNNEL ACTIVITIES: CLIENT ENROLLMENT

Middle-of-funnel activities allow you to connect with many potential clients so that you can engage them individually and identify needs, goals, and challenges that require more focused, personalized support. Your middle-of-funnel market is fed by your top-of-funnel activities.

Middle-of-funnel activities are low-to-moderate-cost products, services, and programs designed to provide value, generate revenue, and, most important, create clients. Here is where you do more than just say "Hello." It's where you say "I can help you, here's how, and here's what it will cost." As with your top-of-funnel activities, middle-of-funnel activities address the needs of your niche that you identified in your market research.

Here are some examples of middle-of-funnel activities.

Workshops, Seminars, and Classes

Workshops, seminars, and classes are time-limited group programs that give participants (i.e., your potential clients), an extensive experience of you so that when those activities are finished, there is a reasonable expectation that some or all of the participants will want to purchase your services and become clients.

Unlike the top-of-funnel workshops and seminars we just considered, here in the middle-of-funnel stage you are more direct and explicit about how your services are going to help participants. At this stage of the funnel, it's very easy and natural (i.e., not "sales-y") to discuss your offerings and explain that by working closely with you, participants can apply what they are learning instead of struggling to do that on their own. Your participants have qualified themselves as "interested" (AKA "hot prospects" in marketing lingo). They have paid real money and invested a significant chunk of time to participate in your workshop, seminar, or class. In other words, you know they are not "looky-loos" like some of the top-of-funnel folks. These people seriously want the results and benefits that you have made available and have proven they are willing to pay for them.

Paid Information Products

Information products such as books, CDs, DVDs, and e-books can be packaged into a "Home Study Program," which includes a workbook. What distinguishes these from the top-of-funnel products is that there should be a fee associated with them. These products can be digitized and offered as downloadable products from your Web site, which is good for immediate delivery and keeps your costs down. If you aren't sure what to put into your program, simply record the seminars, workshops, and other programs discussed earlier.

The great thing about information products is that folks on the receiving end are telling you, clearly, that they are motivated to learn more about your services. You definitely want to follow up by calling or e-mailing them. You can do this in a pleasant and acceptable way by simply thanking them for their order and letting them know that you are available for questions. You can also send them a gift certificate for a free consultation with you or some other valuable incentive.

Also, it's a good idea to follow up a couple of weeks after the information product has been downloaded or shipped. Most purchasers of informational products don't get around to actually using them—at least not for a while. In my experience, when you contact folks and remind them of the value of "consuming" what they have already purchased, they respond favorably and are very impressed by your caring customer service. As your business grows, I recommend that you add staff who can perform this important follow-up function.

Paid Memberships

Memberships include telephone and Web-based niche communities and both virtual and in-person group programs. The difference between the top-of-funnel niche communities and middle-of-funnel niche communities is that here you provide more focused and personal support, coaching, and mentoring at a group level—and you will charge enough to obtain participant commitment and investment. Also, a top-of-funnel niche community might have a casual "show up when you want" attitude, while a middle-of-funnel membership program expects regular participation, is ongoing, and uses recurring billing to charge by the month—or year—until the participant cancels.

A straightforward way to set up a membership program in the middle funnel looks like this:

- Market the program with a promotional seminar or tele-seminar.
- Begin the program with a 6-week class to cover the information members need to learn and help them get started.

- Meet by telephone for ongoing support once or twice a month.
- Supplement the program with a dedicated Web site, online community for group interaction, and regular tele-clinics for more focused support and problem-solving.
- Offer "bonus" seminars for more advanced information.

If you decide to run this kind of membership program virtually (i.e., online), you can potentially serve hundreds—even thousands—of participants at the same time!

BOTTOM-OF-FUNNEL ACTIVITIES: YOUR CLIENT SERVICES

The ultimate goal of your funnel is to create a regular stream of clients. As a private practice professional, you know that growth and change is hard and that the vast majority of people need personal support to achieve their goals. Change is tough, but you can help. Your top- and middle-of-funnel activities introduce and convince your prospective clients of this fact, and your bottom-of-funnel activities focus on carrying it out.

Here are some examples of bottom-of-funnel activities.

Individual Services

Individual services might be the ultimate goal of your funnel system. However, if you successfully target your niche and develop a solid top and middle funnel using the preceding strategies and ideas, you might encounter one of those "nice problems to have": You don't have time to meet with individual clients! To remedy this, you can leverage your time with group programs, discussed next. You can also bring associates into your organization, whom you train and mentor. You then choose the clients whom you want to serve and refer the rest to your associates.

Groups

Groups are a great bottom-of-funnel activity, especially a small group of five to ten people. It's affordable for participants, profitable for you, and achieves measurable results. As mentioned in Chapter 4, participants benefit from multiple sources of input and support through brainstorming, masterminding, and supporting each other—provided that a good group leader is there to encourage and facilitate this. And as an added benefit, a good, ongoing group becomes very tight-knit, which in turn functions as a powerful support system for participants and promotes longevity and retention. I've seen coaching and therapy groups stay together for years.

Retreats

Retreats are like workshops, though typically longer, more personalized and intimate, held in a beautiful vacation-like setting, and often involve recreation and play in addition to "work." Imagine the great transformational experiences you could provide with a small group in Hawaii or on a cruise ship or in a cabin in the mountains for a weekend or even a week or more!

Packages

Packages involve grouping your services, products, and programs into a package tailored to meet the needs of your niche. All of the bottom-of-funnel activities explored so far can be packaged and further grouped into tiers, such as "Silver," "Gold," and "Platinum" packages. To figure out how to do this, once you have designed your service-delivery system and all of its components, ask yourself this question: *If a client were to pay top dollar for my best and most effective program, what would that program look like and how much would it cost?* Include all of your organically created services, products, and programs, and provide numerous bonus items for added value, such as an iPod or MP3 player loaded with your audio programs, additional coaching/consulting time with partners or associates, and free airfare and lodging for your retreats. To make smaller or less expensive packages, simply start removing some of the pieces of the "premium package" and reprice accordingly.

Remember: Although creating, packaging, marketing, and delivering free and low-cost services, products, and programs in your top and middle funnels might seem like a lot of effort, time, and even some costs, the rewards are immense. You will identify and connect with many highly qualified prospective clients—people whom you could not have reached otherwise. Maintaining your organic approach to creation and then structuring your offerings into a seamless service-delivery system and creative business model makes for ease of entry and maximum benefit for your clients. If you do this, you will be making a broader difference in the world, and you will be well on your way to a Million Dollar Practice.

Million Dollar Questions for Chapter 5

1. What are the typical stages or steps that clients in your niche experience?

2. What are the top-of-funnel activities that would be most effective to reach your prospective clients when they are most motivated to act on their goal or problem?

3. What are the middle-of-funnel ways to serve your niche that would be attractive and affordable for them?

4. What are the bottom-of-funnel ways to serve your clients that would be most effective for them and most profitable and enjoyable for you?

CHAPTER SIX

Creative Marketing

When you think about your niche—when you live and breathe it—
it becomes very real to you. The people in your niche become your
people, like your children, whom every day you hold in your heart,
mind, and spirit. Maintaining your focus on them helps stimulate
your creativity. It challenges you to figure out how you can better
serve them and, by extension, how you can better inform them of
your ability to serve them. But how do you do this? How do you leverage your experience and expertise and stand out from an already
crowded field?

We see it all over the place—on television, in the newspaper, and on
the Internet. We see what other people are doing for marketing, and
we have our own experiences as well. We see the way marketing is
supposed to be done. But automatically accepting an existing philosophy clouds our judgment and lumps us in with everyone else. Highly
effective marketing requires you to blaze your own trail. You have to
clear the decks, leave no option off the table, and start from scratch
with no preconceived notions or prescribed formulas. You have to
pose and stay in the questions that will ultimately help you define and
deliver for your niche. This approach, which I call "creative marketing," requires an anything-is-possible point of view and is crucial for
breaking away from the pack and putting you on the path to a Million
Dollar Practice.

GOOD NEWS, BAD NEWS

Like most of the concepts in this book, creative marketing doesn't come without its challenges. It has both good news and bad news. The good news is that when approached with a truly open mind, solutions organically arise. You don't need to force them. The bad news is that you *can't* force them, no matter how hard you try.

Creative marketing requires you to patiently engage in the creative process. You can't just sit down and think, *Okay, I'm going to come up with an idea now*, and have it magically appear. It doesn't work that way. Creativity tends to be a messy process. But the benefits to your clients, and to your business, are endless.

INCREMENTAL PROGRESS

I've tried many things over the years that I thought were great ideas and was excited about. Some of them even had me thinking, *This is going to propel me to the stratosphere. This can't miss.* I've had mixed results. Some of my ideas worked, some of them didn't. But all of them brought me incremental progress.

Let's take my big, flaming direct-mail campaign disaster—the one where I shelled out $8,000 and received not a single client in return. One way of thinking about that experience is, *Wow, that was a stupid thing to do.* Another way to think of it is, *Wow, that was $8,000 well invested.* That move, while naïve at the time, put me on a path to reexamining how to improve as a professional, how to market myself and my business, and how to better reach my desired audience. This "failure" actually set me straight and taught me some important lessons.

For starters, if I had it to do over again I wouldn't risk that much money up front. Instead, I would do a test, though I must admit the unknown is part of the fun and excitement that comes with having my own business. While I often build on the efforts of myself and others, I am naturally drawn to the thrill of charting a new course. Still, while I remain an optimist and always hope for the big win, I know it is best to do your market research to increase your chances. I also know there are no guarantees of success. But that's okay—even the failures have value and lead to incremental progress.

BLANK SLATE

When I became a relationship coach in 1997, I was excited about my new direction, but I had no idea how to get clients. Trained and successful as a therapist, I knew how to sell pain relief, but I didn't know how to sell prevention. I didn't know how to sell personal growth and be proactive in life. Anthony Robbins and other personal-growth gurus, while inspirational and pioneers in their fields, weren't doing what I wanted to do and were much further down their practice-building paths. I was helpless and innocent — the question for me was, *What am I going to do to market and get clients?*

It wasn't until I wiped the slate clean, removing every preconceived notion and every adapted marketing strategy from my previous life as a therapist, that the answer, the single most powerful epiphany of my life — "singles become couples" — came down from the sky.

Prior to that point, couples were all I knew and all I thought about. I had tunnel vision. Clearing the decks and looking at my situation with fresh eyes made the answer glaringly obvious. Who wants successful relationships? Everybody. And a significant percentage of that population is single.

Clearing the decks opens pathways for creativity. But you must keep those pathways open to get where you want to go. As exciting as it was to have identified a new target market, my problem wasn't solved by that alone. I still had no idea how to help them or what to do with them. My willingness to keep an open mind, my quest to serve, and a shift in mind-set eventually led me to a Million Dollar Practice. These elements helped me write a groundbreaking book, develop a pioneering coaching program — complete with professional manuals and workbooks — and train thousands of other helping professionals in how to work with singles.

Even though I knew nothing about coaching singles when I started, I knew enough not to make up the programs off the top of my head or rely on what others were doing in other areas. That's the downfall of many private practitioners. They (unconsciously) think, *I'm going to impose my beliefs and the accepted-as-standard strategies that I've acquired along the way, and I'm going to develop a program for these people. And it's going to rock their worlds. And I'm going to charge them a lot of money for it.* This is not the way to a Million Dollar Practice.

Theoretical orientation, professionalism, and ethics were drummed into me while training to be a therapist. I went through statistics and research classes learning about reliability and validity. As a result, I wanted to be responsible in developing my coaching practice and my singles program. Yes, I had been single, but this venture was not about me, so it couldn't rely on my own experiences. And since I was pioneering a new field, there were no examples to model, even if I wanted to. The only way to succeed was to learn about the singles I wanted to serve.

My first step was putting together a pilot project where I invited 12 singles to join me in my office for 4 weeks. Spending time with my target audience, I really got it—who they were, what they needed and wanted, and what would and wouldn't work for them. I launched a weekly singles event designed around what they told me, and it was rapidly and wildly successful.

Admittedly, the first couple of meetings were scary. They started out with 15 people, then 18, then took off quickly, to the point that I needed to bring in partners and associates to help me manage the load. The fact that I grew and filled my coaching practice within 90 days may sound like hype that I made up—sometimes it's even hard for me to believe, partially because it was so long ago now. But it's a true story. And I owe it in large part to creative marketing, an approach that stems from raising questions, not expecting to have all the answers, and making a shift to a new point of view.

CREATIVE MARKETING AND THE COACHING POINT OF VIEW

There are several great things about being a coach that relate directly to creative marketing. One is that coaches are not considered or expected to be experts whose job is to tell their clients what to do. As coaches, we are taught to partner with our clients and help them discover things within themselves. We don't have to be gurus. We don't have to know all the answers.

For someone trained as a therapist, not being expected to be the authority on all things related to my niche was quite a revelation. In fact, it made for a downright difficult transition into the world of coaching. I had lots of ideas and advice to give, and this new mind-set meant I wasn't going to be able to give any of it. But as a coach interested in best serving my niche, I learned to not only accept this fact but learned to relish it. I realized that true coaches are more interested in doing what is best for their clients than in imposing their own views.

Another cool thing about being a coach is the emphasis placed on curiosity and inquisitiveness. Coaches are taught to ask questions as a way of tapping into creativity. As a new coach looking to help singles, I had no idea how to proceed. I read a bunch of books for singles — how to get the guy, how to get the girl, how to flirt — but they were useless. Yet I was determined to find a way forward. My principal question became, *How do I help singles find and have successful, lasting relationships, and not just "hook up?"* This question became a driving force on my road to a Million Dollar Practice.

Vision and purpose also play a big role in the coaching profession. As a relationship therapist, I spent many years working with couples who had chosen their partners despite some basic incompatibilities. Many of them, despite my best efforts, got divorced anyway. I discovered there was an immovable force preventing many of them from making their relationships work. Continually witnessing — and experiencing in my own life — the process of breaking up due to irreconcilable differences prompted me to come up with the idea of requirements. I laid out a set of commonly held requirements and worked with people on identifying their own. Requirements in relationships are similar to the concepts of vision and purpose in your life and in your business, essential ingredients to staying on track and getting creative with your marketing.

Approaching singles with fresh eyes and from the point of view of a coach, combined with the epiphany that singles become couples, helped me develop my coaching program for singles. It also caused me to look at the progression of how people go through stages in a relationship — from being single to being in a fulfilling relationship. The five stages I developed were different from other developmental relationship models out there and led me to wonder how I could help people in each of those stages. This question eventually led to the development of my five-stage model of relationship coaching, which ended up forming the curriculum at Relationship Coaching Institute.

This sequence of events all started because I had no clue how to coach relationships or how to market coaching for relationships. The answers formed the basis of my creative marketing campaign and led me on the path to where I am today.

Again, the creative marketing approach requires you to approach questions with fresh eyes, leave nothing off the table, start with a blank slate, and take a coach-like point of view toward your audience, even if you're not a coach. Creative marketing requires you to look at your specialty and the people you want to serve as though you're seeing them for the first time.

PUTTING YOUR TARGET AUDIENCE IN THE DRIVER'S SEAT

Looking at my niche with fresh eyes enabled me to clearly understand and serve them on a consistent basis. I took good care of the people who showed up at my weekly events. I showed them a good time. I was responsive to their wants and needs. I was there for them. And they came back. In creating and delivering my programs, I continually asked myself: *What do they want? What do they need? What would they want to attend? What would make them want to return?* This is the Platinum Rule of Marketing. I couldn't have been half as successful trying to market my own version of things. "Here's what I want to do for you. You want it, don't you?" No, my singles program was totally focused on them. And it originated from a blank slate.

I liken it to being removed from your familiar, comfortable home and community and being put in another country. Everything is new. The people speak a different language. All of your preconceived notions and all of your assumptions about how society works are out the window. You have to open yourself up and listen hard to adopt their culture and customs and learn how to communicate in your new surroundings. That's the essence of marketing. It's also the key to the creative mind-set: Let go of everything you think you know. Let go of your agenda and what you want to do. Let your audience drive it.

When I mentor other professionals conducting singles events, one of the most common problems I am presented with is the gender imbalance at their events. They complain that there are always more single women than single men and ask, "How can I get more single men to my events?"

Number one, they are assuming that they must have an equal gender balance, which I believe is a false assumption. Unless it's speed dating, the purpose of creating these events is not primarily to create a meet market for singles. The proportion of single men and single women doesn't have to matter. So my response to complaints about the presence of more single women than single men is, "We are here to create a community that supports each other and to learn about relationships. While we certainly would love it if you found the love of your life, that's not what we are expecting here or what this environment is about."

But from a creative marketing perspective, if you are promoting a program that *does* require a gender balance, the answer is simple: If you want more single men at your events, you have to tell them only one thing, "Hey, here's where the women are." In other words, pose the question your audience needs answered and step up your marketing to answer it. In this case, your audience is men. And what do single men want? They want to meet single women. So go ahead and communicate that and market it in whatever way feels good to you as aligned with your ethics, values, mission, and message.

When you are designing your business for the people in your niche, and it is truly about them, and their needs and wants are driving your business — and if you are not approaching it with preconceived notions — then your principal objective is clear: You need to be creative in how to solve problems for people and how to communicate your solutions to them. But sometimes, as in the case of being a parent, the best way you can help your niche is — as we mentioned earlier — to serve as a coach, whether it's in your job title or not. One of the most freeing and effective approaches you can take in communicating your message to your niche is to realize that it's not always your job to solve their problems; rather, it is to support them as they arrive at the answers themselves.

As an example, right now one of my boys is struggling because he doesn't have anything that fuels his passion. We are trying to get him plugged into something that might excite him, and it's a challenge. The question for him is, "What can I do with my time that would be productive, fun, and exciting?" I wish I had the answer for my son. But it's up to him to figure it out. Kids have lots of wants and needs, and our job as parents is to determine which of those wants and needs should be left for them to tackle on their own and which ones we need to do something about.

As helping professionals, we face similar scenarios with our clients. We often pose questions like these: *How can I best help my client do X or overcome Y? How can I best get their attention about this or that?* It's a healthy thing to acknowledge that we don't always have the answer, nor are we expected to. While those practicing the Golden Rule think they must have the answers and impose lessons from their own journeys on their target audiences, those practicing the Platinum Rule know that the best solutions often truly lie with those they are seeking to help. Your job is not to impose your ideas but to formulate each challenge in the form of a question, stay with that question, and listen to what the members of your niche tell you they want and need. From there, you can figure out how it can best be provided, test for effectiveness, and then communicate that you can provide a proven solution.

NATURE ABHORS A VACUUM

Practitioners often become frustrated and stuck, and they fail when they continue to fall back on "what sounds good to me" or "what I want to do." As I have already discussed, in my mind the secret of success in serving your niche is to keep your eye on the ball of the Platinum Rule—that is, what works for *them* and what *they* want. This is the value of starting with a blank slate and wiping away every preconceived notion of what you thought might work or what you might do. No option is off the table.

Nature abhors a vacuum. Every question wants an answer. This principle is the power behind asking questions: *What would work in this situation? What would work to reach these people? What would work to help these people? What would work to get them to sign up and take the next step?*

When you ask questions, a variety of answers will come to you to fill the vacuum. And not every answer is the best one. But staying with the question helps you find the best answer in any given situation. And this is the essence of creative marketing. Stay in the question, keep asking it, and don't ever become complacent. Don't think, *Oh, well, I answered the question once, now all I have to do is implement this proven solution.* No, stay with the question and more answers will come.

CASE STUDY: STAYING IN THE QUESTION AND CREATIVE MARKETING — THE INSPIRATIONAL RELATIONSHIPS VIDEO PROJECT

YouTube is the Library of Congress of online videos. If you don't find it there, it likely doesn't exist. Online videos are insanely popular with young and old, and rank high in search engine results. Recently, I posed a series of questions that prompted me to scour YouTube's catalogue of relationship videos. I found there were two primary categories: people ranting about their exes and "relationship experts" giving advice.

But YouTube is full of homemade videos by real people sharing their story with the world. Where are all the videos of real people sharing their relationship stories, giving hope and inspiration to motivate others to get into action and join the world of happy and healthy relationships? My market research told me that when the people in my niche were struggling with relationships and searched the Internet, they were looking for hope and inspiration — not advice, information, or rants. After all, to benefit from information or to want to seek help, you have to believe success is possible, which is hard when you're feeling hopeless.

This realization was triggered by a series of questions: *What do the people in my niche need in their darkest hours when they are searching on the Internet? How can I be of service? How can I help them? How can I reach them?*

How can I communicate with people who need and want relationship support and resources and who can benefit from RCI and RCI coaches? How can I bring them into my fold?

It was posing and staying with these questions that helped me identify a need and create a new genre of online videos: people sharing authentically about their relationship journeys, describing their struggles and challenges and how they overcame them. These videos would inspire struggling singles and couples, give them hope, and form the basis of my next creative marketing campaign.

The Inspirational Relationships Video Project started off with just a few entries. Darlene and I invited a handful of couples, friends, over to our house. Although you can create decent videos from most cell phones these days, we purchased some high-quality equipment and created a little video studio in our home (complete with high-powered lights and green screen). We shot and edited the videos—most of which are only 5 to 10 minutes long—and then put them on YouTube and on a new Web site created just for this project. Then we went to a couples' conference, expecting a gold mine for more inspirational videos. The conference didn't disappoint. We had partnered with the host organization, BetterMarriages.org, as the executive director and I know each other and get along well. She loved the idea of inspirational relationship videos and helped promote it at the conference. Darlene and I were invited to take the stage during one of the prime-time gatherings to talk about our project and show one of our videos to the group.

With the exception of my studio lights and green screen, I brought all of my high-quality video equipment, including my best camera (the one I usually don't let out of the house). Darlene played director and I played cameraman. We both prepped the couples and then shot the videos. And we came home with our memory cards full of videos, one of which I absolutely love. It's this couple talking about their sex life so authentically, so honestly, so candidly—also cleanly—in a way that I have never seen anybody talk about their sex life before. It is wonderful. People will fall in love with this video and with this couple. This video should go viral. You can see it ("Paul and Beth") at consciousrelationshipvideo.com.

We used the same general format for all of the videos. We made couples comfortable by letting them know the videos didn't have to be perfect; in fact, imperfect was better. We wanted them to be themselves. We also let them know that we would edit the videos, so they should not worry about saying things they didn't want on them. We let the couples know that if they made a mistake, they could just stop and start over. We had them sign a release and made sure they knew we were going to give them first right of refusal. If they didn't like the videos and didn't want them up on the Web for the world to see, all they had to do was let us know. This formula led to a wealth of great material that we can use to inspire others and attract more people into the fold of RCI. But it also presented a problem, which brought up another question.

The problem is that I now had all of these videos that required careful editing to prepare for the Web site. And because what to leave in and what to take out required judgment from somebody who clearly understood the mission and message, I preferred to do it myself. But I'm a busy guy. Then as now, I had lots of other projects going on and simply didn't have time to get to all these videos. As a result, to this day, the videos are going up on the Web site more slowly than I would like.

So the question is, *How can I get quality, properly edited inspirational videos up in quantity—especially if I get more submissions—when I don't have the time and I only trust myself to do it?* I don't know the answer. But the question is out there. And because nature abhors a vacuum, I'm sure the answer will eventually appear.

This all came about from asking myself what my niche wanted and needed in their darkest hours. My answer was The Inspirational Relationships Video Project, and it is one that is very much aligned with my mission and message. Nobody else was doing this. It was a need that I identified. People feeling stuck and hopeless in their relationships don't go to therapy. They don't get counseling. They don't sign up for coaching programs. Sure, they might buy a book, but they are generally feeling stuck and hopeless. They are experiencing a common theme among people: If you don't believe that anything is going to change, then you won't take action. This belief becomes self-fulfilling. Nothing changes because you don't believe it's going to change.

Over the years, I've learned that people need hope and inspiration to benefit from all the solutions out there—workshops, coaching, counseling, whatever it might be. And being on the Web and in the world, studying Internet marketing and the role of the Internet in reaching large audiences, I identified what to do with it. Nowadays, video is the way to go. So I looked for relationship videos, and what did I find? Nobody was inspiring people with stories of their relationships. So I stepped in and filled the void. And this creative marketing process began with a question.

Now there is nothing inherently wrong with the two other existing categories of relationship videos that I found. But they didn't meet the need that I identified: people feeling stuck in their relationships and searching on the Internet for information. As relationship experts, we want them to find us at this moment, right? That's when they are ready for solutions. That instant is when they are ready to buy something or to take some action.

It's a powerful, pivotal moment when somebody chooses to go on the Internet and search for a resource. It could be information; it could be a Web site; it could be a video; it could be a product, service, or program. The point is that they are looking for something. They have a problem. They are in pain. And these days, they go on the Internet (or, increasingly, the mobile app store) and they search. As experts, we want them to find us. Your job is to help your target audience to find you.

But remember: If we practice the Golden Rule, we are going to put out what we think they should want or need and what *we* would sign up for. We are going to have a Web site about ourselves—here I am and I'm an expert and I'm great and please buy my book, service, product, or program. However, if we practice the Platinum Rule, we are going to think about the needs and wants of the people whom we want to help in their darkest hours and seek to learn what *they* would buy or join. And we will have a much better chance of reaching them.

Picture this: Members of your target audience are out there right now, in their darkest hours, thinking, *I'm so stuck and frustrated. I'm in so much pain. I want the pain to go away. I have to do something.* And right in front of them are their computers or iPads or iPhones. What are they searching for? What keywords are they using? That's important market research. Since videos show up so high in search engine results, it makes sense to have videos out there, but you want to have videos that provide inspiration and hope and that prompt viewers to take action. They are not ready to be sold anything yet. They are not ready to be given advice, and they don't want to be told what to do. Think about it: If you were in your darkest hour, thinking things were hopeless and you were feeling stuck—even though some part of you didn't want to give up—and you were going to reach out for some form of support, would you want that support to be somebody telling you what you should do? Perhaps some people might. But that approach really doesn't work. And as we mentioned earlier in this book, if the advice doesn't work, you may feel worse about yourself and the person who gave you the advice.

Creative marketing is not about how many potential clients are out there. It's not about the demographics. It's not about the economy. It's not about whether people are going to be able to afford you. It's not about the competition. All of the barriers and obstacles encountered in marketing and practice building are inside us—all of them.

Ask yourself the question, *What are the members of my niche searching for in their darkest hours and how can I best serve them with my services, products, and programs?* I don't have the answers for you, but staying with the question feeds off the principle that nature abhors a vacuum. The answers will appear. Not all of them will be good ideas. But staying in the question ensures that a good idea will eventually appear. This is the foundation of creative marketing for building a Million Dollar Practice.

CASE STUDY: STAYING IN THE QUESTION AND CREATIVE MARKETING—CAMPBELL WORKING TOGETHER

"WOOOO-HOOOO!" the resident screamed into the microphone. He then turned and directly addressed the five city councilmen sitting on the dais: "That's what I hear every weekend at three o'clock in the morning."

Campbell, California, the town where I live, has a small, compact downtown area spanning about four blocks, surrounded by residential neighborhoods. Within that span is an even smaller space, about two blocks, that has become the center of a big, divisive issue.

The two-block area to which I'm referring has a concentrated number of alcohol-serving establishments. This by itself wouldn't be a problem if it weren't for the fact that the alcohol-related headaches have extended beyond the patrons and into the surrounding area.

After leaving the local bars and restaurants, people are going to their cars, often stopping and vomiting or urinating in people's yards, and engaging in vandalism, rowdiness, and drunk driving. Things have gotten out of control, and the residents don't like it. And while policies have been put in place just 2 years ago to mitigate the effects, the city council, in an effort to boost downtown activity and revenue, has proposed relaxing restrictions on alcohol-serving establishments. This has Campbell residents and officials up in arms.

Residents want the city council to fix the problem. But the city council doesn't have the power to fix it. The city council relies on the police department to enforce the laws. But the police department doesn't have enough officers, because the city lacks the financial resources. The bar and restaurant owners attract business to downtown and pay taxes, which generates revenue, but their patrons, whose behavior they can't control once they leave their establishments, are wreaking havoc on the community. All of this comes back to the residents feeling like their needs are not being met. It's one big, dysfunctional mess.

Now most people who find out about the existing alcohol policies, myself included, think they are great. Darlene and I were curious about the call for change, so we went to a few city council meetings to learn more. There we found residents expressing serious concerns and telling horror stories about alcohol-related behavior. We live in the downtown area, but we live a few blocks away from where all of this is happening, so we don't really see it or hear it. We were shocked when we heard about it. But rather than blast the city council's decision to raise the specter of changing the policies, Darlene and I posed a question: *How can we leverage our expertise to make a difference on this issue?*

As a result, we started making phone calls and setting up meetings with city council members and community leaders. We were genuinely confused and wanted to understand what was going on so that we could see if there was anything we could do to help.

The first thing that became abundantly clear was that the city council members are good people. They are doing the best they can. And who would want to be in their position, anyway? And who else, given their position under the current circumstances, could do any better, including those doing all the complaining?

After our meetings, Darlene and I understood the various officials' perspectives and their current predicament. But we also understood that the rest of the community was still in the dark. So the second revelation that came from our meetings was that there was a tremendous lack of communication and shared sense of purpose in the community. We uncovered a crying need for all the parties to work together to create partnerships to come up with creative solutions and work together in implementing those solutions. There was a tremendous relationship issue pervading the community, and, given our background in relationship coaching—and our strong belief in the power of taking personal responsibility, working together, and getting *creative* to solve problems—Darlene and I found a way that we could address it. During a meeting with one particular city councilman, we volunteered to put together a town hall meeting for that express purpose. He took us up on it. So that's what we did—with an added twist.

LEVERAGING YOUR EXPERIENCE AND EXPERTISE—CREATIVELY

Just as in private practice, as I learned from my *Fatherhood in the 90s* event, you don't want to ever just do something once. You want to fit it into your business plan. You want to leverage it. So, rather than a one-shot effort, a town hall meeting, we took it to the next level and created a public service organization. We called it Campbell Working Together.

Our thinking was, *"Let's leverage the need for a town hall by creating an organization that will not only host a town hall, but will have other activities to promote working together, partnerships, and creativity."* In addition to the alcohol-related problems, like other communities, Campbell faces many issues that, if the community were to get together on them, could be addressed far more effectively than divisive finger-pointing and expecting somebody else to take care of them. This creates a positive environment for an organization—and community relationships—to grow and become more effective over time.

With an approach committed to promoting a safe, clean, pleasant community, we developed a four-pillar philosophy for Campbell Working Together that looks like this:

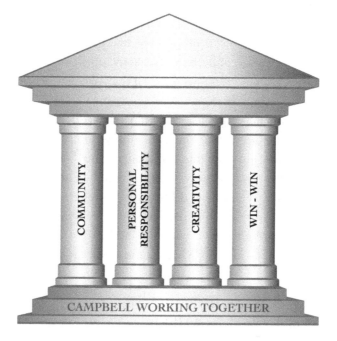

1. *Community*—"All for one and one for all." The future of Campbell depends upon all parties (residents, business owners, city staff, elected officials, police, etc.) being on the same team. "Us versus them" doesn't work. We assume positive intent and that we all want the same thing—a safe, clean, pleasant community.

2. *Personal Responsibility*—"If it is to be, it is up to me." Holding others responsible for the problem and solution just doesn't work. A related principle is that "people support what they

help create," meaning that grassroots, bottom-up solutions that meet the needs of the parties involved work better than those imposed from the top down.

3. *Creativity*—The best solutions to seemingly unsolvable problems are often situational and individualized and are almost never readily apparent. We assume the solution exists and is best discovered and implemented together as a community.

4. *Everybody Wins*—We assume that all parties have valid needs and issues, and the only workable solution is one that meets the needs of all involved. Fear that one party will win and the other will lose creates competition and conflict. This is the biggest threat to our community, as fear and competitiveness are often our knee-jerk responses—and the source of wars, conflict, violence, mistrust, and other negative outcomes. Accepting each other's right to exist and committing to finding win-win solutions to problems is crucial to the future of Campbell—and our planet.

With this philosophy, and with our experience and expertise, we set about strengthening relationships in the community and making a bigger difference. And even better, we invented a new specialty—Community Relationship Coach!

CREATIVE MARKETING AND YOUR RELATIONSHIPS

Throughout this book, I have stressed the importance of doing your market research and then developing your services, products, and programs to suit the wants and needs of your niche. But you can't stop there. Even the best and most helpful and innovative offerings won't help a soul if no one knows they exist. You have to market, and you have to be creative about it.

You are in a relationship business. You are in a people business. The fact that you are reading this book means you want to help people change their lives and make a difference in the world. And since that has to come from your passion, you must ask, "What increases passion? What helps passion flow freely and powerfully?" The answer is being creative. And being creative means starting with a blank slate and asking questions. You must then stay in those questions until answers emerge that seem to be a good fit. This will put you on the path to strengthening your relationship with those you want to help, which in turn leads you toward a Million Dollar Practice, because the beneficiaries of your services, products, and programs will spread the word and broaden your circle of influence. But this doesn't happen on its own. You have to put in your time.

It is well-documented that the most effective forms of marketing for private practice professionals are word-of-mouth referral and social proof. Word-of-mouth referral is people telling other people about you, and social proof is people being willing to tell the world about you. So, how do you get people to do that? It all starts with relationships.

In looking to shore up your relationships, look no further than the people you have already served. In the process of doing your market research and developing and testing your services, products, and programs, you have already developed a base—a foundation of people who already know you, with whom you are already connected, and who are already in your target audience. You need to ensure that your relationships with these people are strong. Once you have a base to operate from, you can build from there.

When I launched my market research–based weekly singles events, the primary audience consisted of the 12 people I recruited for my pilot project. They spread the word and brought their friends to the next event. Those people told other people, those other people told more people, and before I knew it, therapists were referring clients to me. No matter what private practice we are in, no matter what specialty and niche we have, it remains a relationship business. So the question in marketing is, "How do I leverage my relationships, creatively, in a win-win fashion, to reach and serve the people in my niche?" It's a question that, when answered, will have clients flocking, putting you well on your way to a Million Dollar Practice.

Campbell Working Together is an example that shows just how much relationships matter, and how you can potentially leverage them on a community-wide level.

GOING LIVE

Campbell Working Together's launch event was conducted pretty much as I would launch any top-of-funnel workshop, complete with all the tricks and strategies of putting on an effective marketing event. Prior to the event, we built a Web site and had signs and banners made. Immediately leading up to the town hall, we deliberately kept the doors closed because we wanted people talking to each other and milling around with anticipation. And when the doors finally opened, we had heart-pounding music to welcome them.

I then employed all of the speaking skills I have been taught to engage the audience and to set the tone. Darlene and I started the event not by directly addressing the audience, but with us holding hands and having a little, intimate conversation in front of them, drawing them into our world. Throughout the event we did our best to apply some effective strategies to get people to shift their functioning and their thinking to help them accomplish what they wanted.

The event generated lots of media attention, and it was successful in terms of a marketing event. But we had to work for it. For starters, the media didn't just get wind of what was going on and come find us. We had to pitch them. We sent them e-mails and let them know what we were doing. We gave them story angles. And since our launch event was going to be a town hall featuring a city councilman—the same city councilman at the center of all the controversy for putting the alcohol policies back on the agenda—Campbell Working Together gained traction.

The event also gained traction because we were getting into action and doing something to solve a problem. My professional background also played a role. The media checked me out on the Web to find out who was behind the effort. Because of my various Web sites and endeavors, they were able to determine that we were substantial enough and real enough. In essence, the media found it easy to look at us as credible, serious players. They knew we were not just making things up off the top of our heads. They could see that Campbell Working Together was a potentially significant new force in the area and at the very least was making an effort to pull citizens together to contribute to the solution. That, by itself, is a feature story. But again, it was up to us to make them aware of it.

REACHING THE MEDIA

One of the things I always recommend regarding the media is to make it easy for them to figure out what the story is. And the story is not how great you are. You have to figure out what the story angle is and communicate it to the media. The media needs stories. The media wants to promote you if you are providing value, but it won't promote you for your agenda. It has to be something of interest to their audience.

The secret to getting media exposure is to come up with a product, service, or program, and a story angle related to your niche and your expertise that will get their attention and cause them to want to publish it. You need to convince them that it is of general interest and that people would want to know about it. In other words, "What can you communicate related to your mission and message that is cool?" In Chapter 5, we talked about top-of-funnel activities. In this case, we created Campbell Working Together.

While it was not the intent in this instance (I don't have a local practice and am not seeking local clients), if I were a local relationship coach looking to build a Million Dollar Practice, creating a public service organization like Campbell Working Together would be a good place to start. We opened a dialogue about how we all need to work together and about how the way to get along better is to shift from an "us versus them" mentality to being on the same side — realizing that we all more or less want the same thing — and to communicate effectively by following a series of proven guidelines.

If we look at Brian Whetten's *Seven Stages of Practice Building*, the higher levels involve teaching others, creating your own organization and running it, and then having other people run the organization for you. In terms of creative marketing, there is tremendous potential for lending our expertise at a community-wide level, providing a public service.

Once we decided on the "what" we moved into the "how." In launching Campbell Working Together, I put together an e-mail pitching the media, giving them background, introducing Darlene and me, providing a bit about the alcohol policy and what we saw needed to happen, and what we planned to do about it. We also gave them the link to the Web site we had created so they could check us out. I sent the same e-mail to every media contact whose column and writing I thought were a good fit for this kind of story. Eventually it got into the right hands. But I had to spend the necessary effort figuring out who the right hands were. One prominent columnist interviewed Darlene and me and wrote a feature article about our efforts, and our story and photo filled the front page of the local section of our largest daily newspaper. My kids were surprised when their teacher at school showed them the article!

Doing your due diligence is critical when you want to leverage the media. You must take the time to look at television stations and seek out the appropriate producers or hosts whose beat it is to cover stories like the one you are proposing. It's the same with radio. Ask yourself these questions: *Which local radio stations do I want publicity from? Which radio hosts and producers would most likely be interested in this?* And then find them and pitch them. But don't stop there. Don't just pitch them once—follow up and build relationships with them. Remember, it all comes back to relationships.

As a result of our efforts at Campbell Working Together, we now have relationships with local media that we didn't have before. So the next time we have something to say or a message to broadcast, we have a go-to group to help us spread that information. Our contacts know we are interested in solving problems that relate to their audiences. They know that we are media-friendly and that we make it easy for them to figure out how to approach their readers and viewers with our stories.

In my case, I lent my expertise and resources to Campbell Working Together. As a result of our efforts, we received invaluable media coverage and established key connections with reporters and community leaders who wouldn't give me the time of day if I were doing this to promote my own business.

But by lending my expertise and my resources to my community, by identifying a need that my community had, and stepping up to it,

I'm plugged in now like you wouldn't believe. If I were to contact the mayor, or any of the city council members, or the executive director of the chamber of commerce, or the guy who owns the biggest and most successful restaurant in town, chances are they would take my call. Only a month before, we were just David and Darlene Steele, local Campbell residents who happened to be members of the local neighborhood association. Now, because of a big issue that has come up in our town and because we decided to get involved, everybody knows who we are.

Here's an example: Darlene and I had meetings with most of the city council members, and we were invited to join a local leadership organization. This group wanted to conduct a community survey on the alcohol policies, and Darlene volunteered to lead the effort. She compiled the results, put them together in a format that could be interpreted and read, distributed it, and followed up on it. The survey results are available at CampbellWorkingTogether.org.

The results were also distributed to the city council members before a city council meeting where they reviewed and discussed Darlene's survey. During a break, the mayor came up to Darlene and said, "Hello, Tinker Bell," to which Darlene smiled broadly and did her trademark curtsy.

A month ago we were just David and Darlene, Campbell residents. And now the mayor is coming up to Darlene and playfully calling her "Tinker Bell." If you want to have a Million Dollar Practice, wouldn't it be nice to have the leaders in your community know who you are and appreciate your contributions? All of the connections we established stemmed from posing a question about how we could lend a hand to our community.

CREATIVE MARKETING ALIGNMENT

In addition to having the presence of mind to know when to wipe the slate clean, creative marketing relies upon leveraging your experience and expertise. I wouldn't be getting involved in the city's budget problems. I'm not a money guy. My experience and expertise is in relationships. I saw and acted on a community problem that touched my passion and the way that I wanted to make a difference in the world. I didn't do it to promote my own business, although I have no problem with enlightened self-interest, which basically means that you can fully expect to benefit by making a positive contribution to the world.

There are needs all around you. And if you have an entrepreneurial mind-set, you will watch for needs that align with your passion and where your energy wants to go. If you are a social entrepreneur, your alignment will include your desire to make a difference in the world. I'm not saying you should create a business around every single need. But when something comes along that looks like a good fit for your business model or for what you feel would be good for your business, go ahead and jump in.

I don't know where Campbell Working Together is going to go. I don't know if the model will be outrageously successful, become the norm, and catch on like wildfire all over the country—Enter-Your-City-Name-Here Working Together—or if it will fizzle. It doesn't matter. Campbell Working Together arose from a local need, and as somebody who wants to make a difference in the world of relationships in my community, I stepped up to do what I could to address that need and be of service. The rest will take care of itself.

Campbell Working Together is an example of what you as a private practitioner can do to build a Million Dollar Practice. Your community needs you. You just need to identify how they need you, where to step in, and with whom to partner. Remember: You don't need to do it all yourself. Darlene and I have always wanted a way to be more involved in our community, making change where change is wanted, and this gives us an opportunity to do so. If you see a need and there is no existing way for you to do something about it, you can create the way. There was no relationship coach training organization when I wanted to become a relationship coach, so I created Relationship Coaching Institute. And before that, there was no standardized relationship coaching model—everybody was doing their own thing—so I came up with my own standardized model. You can do that, too, in the areas that are most meaningful to you.

Take advantage of any way you can align a potential need with the pursuit of your mission and message and make the difference in the world that you feel called to make, whether you get paid for it or not. In fact, when you don't get paid for it is when people tend to consider you a hero, which is the best form of marketing.

THE HERO'S JOURNEY CONTINUES

If people take a look at what you are doing and say, "Wow, that's cool. That's heroic. That's unusual. Hey, I've never seen that before," then you have differentiated yourself, which is a good thing. That's how you get people's attention. That's how you get press attention. Unfortunately, many private practitioners put limits on what they do based on short-term monetary gain, which puts them in the "average" category.

Million Dollar Practitioners, however, are confident in their ability, focus on the long term, and pursue their missions and messages as far as they will take them, regardless of monetary gain. If you are a Million Dollar Practitioner, you will also seek out ways to pursue your mission and message with your entire community. Yes, the people in your community need you, but most of them—maybe all of them—don't even know it. Putting yourself out there is the only way to reach them. And when you do, most people will support you. Most people will say, "Yeah, that's cool. We really need this. Where have you been?"

Still, while you will generally find a supportive audience, there will be plenty of people trying to block your path: "Oh, this will never work." I have heard it too many times to count in my professional career, beginning with my own mother. When I first told her I was going into private practice she said, "You'll never make a living, David." Thirty-plus years later, here I am, writing another book, this one showing others how to build a Million Dollar Practice based upon my experience of having already done it.

So don't listen to naysayers. Let the hero's journey continue. Nobody can argue with the worth and value you have as a private practice professional and the need and ability you have to leverage your unique gifts to make a difference in the world. And when you do something for free, like giving a class at a church or a school, you are not wasting your time. You are building priceless goodwill. You are making a name for yourself as a person willing to step up and help. You are positioning yourself as the go-to person for a particular mission and message, so that whenever it comes up, people will think about you and refer to you. "Oh, you need that? Well, there was this guy that put on a class at a church recently. A lot of people were raving about it. You should call him."

Creating and sustaining a Million Dollar Practice does not mean you need to be paid for everything you do. Remember the client creation funnel from the last chapter? The things at the top are free and low-cost ways to reach people. And the larger the number of people you reach, the better and more effective your marketing funnel—and your private practice—is going to be. But you can't just sporadically string together activities without a way to gauge their effectiveness. You have to find a way to measure success.

MEASURING SUCCESS

Campbell Working Together's launch event received a lot of media attention, which is great. But media attention for its own sake doesn't do any good unless you're able to make it work for you. In our case, we were able to convert the large attendance from the media blitz into a tangible outcome that served Campbell Working Together's mission. That is, we significantly increased our membership base—and our army of volunteers working toward a solution.

At the event, we had a simple sign-up sheet: "Do you want to be part of what we are doing? If so, join Campbell Working Together. It's free." Does that sound familiar—like an opt-in on a Web site? Nearly 90% of the attendees said "Yes."

Remember, when putting on a marketing event there are three things you want to do: Make it free, come up with a compelling topic that will attract the people you want to reach, and then provide them the next step, also free, to bring them even further into your pipeline.

The tagline created for Campbell Working Together, created by Darlene, was *Join Us Today for a Better Tomorrow*. We first invited people to a free event that was compelling enough—with the help of the media in spreading the word—to get them there. Next, by asking them to join us, we put the next opportunity in front of them. As demonstrated by the high percentage of sign-ups, most of them said, "Yes, I like what you guys are up to and I want to be part of it." And that's the measure of success of creative marketing: getting your target audience to take the next step you have laid out for them.

So, what is my son going to end up doing with the rest of his life? I don't know. How will my hometown's alcohol issue be settled? I have no idea. But I am committed to posing and staying in the questions and looking at them with fresh eyes. That is how we create cool things. That is how we come up with better answers than were there before. As a parent and a member of a community, I find the issues frustrating, and I worry. But as a coach, I know that as long we stay in the question, keep exploring it, and measure the results, it will take us places. It will take us to answers that we couldn't predict. And this is what creative marketing is about—asking the question and then seeing what comes up.

But the answer is not enough. To get to the level of the Million Dollar Practice, you have to leverage it.

CASE STUDY: HEDY AND YUMI SCHLEIFER— MARKETING WORLD PEACE

Hedy Schleifer is one of my favorite people in the world. She is my most valued relationship coaching mentor, and she is a good friend. I respect and admire her work, and her as a person, tremendously. But she is, admittedly, not a great marketer. She is a prime example of someone who is charismatic, lovable, and authentic, but who has historically had a difficult time leveraging those qualities in her business.

Hedy is a child of the Holocaust and grew up in a refugee camp in Switzerland. Her parents were in a German concentration camp during World War II. Her husband, Yumi, to whom she has been married for 47 years, also comes from a family who were in a concentration camp. Hedy and Yumi have done some tremendous things with their lives. They have been involved in national politics and helped leaders communicate with each other more effectively. They have conducted workshops with couples all over the world. They speak six languages — English, French, German, Hebrew, Spanish, and Yiddish. They are involved in an effort to help ease the Israeli-Palestinian conflict. They spent a lot of time in South Africa during the Apartheid era, trying to bring people together to resolve that problem. And they have received much praise for their work and efforts, including being Jewish Holocaust survivors helping couples in Germany.

Hedy and Yumi travel extensively. They conduct workshops all over the world. They have a huge mission and message. Hedy and Yumi are leveraging their expertise, personality, charisma, and marriage to do no less than create world peace. And they are serious. They are out there doing it. They even have a date in mind: November, 11, 2012.

The vision came to Hedy some years ago. I first heard her talk about it 3 years ago. The idea revolves around a tipping point. In their thinking, all we need, worldwide, is 90 million couples to "cross the bridge" to create a tipping point that will create world peace. They are advocating and planning for an event in Jerusalem, historically the center of world conflict, to launch the event. Hedy was even invited to discuss this philosophy at TEDxTelAviv.

If you watch Hedy's TED video (available, of course, on YouTube) you will understand why people love her. She is authentic and heart-felt, and she is a good speaker. She is not playing a role. What you see is really who she is. She is the same on stage as she is when you sit down privately and talk with her over coffee.

But of course Hedy is human. She has her ups and downs like all of us. I have seen her tired and depleted after conducting full-day workshops, hanging out in her hotel room. I have seen her scared. I have seen her discouraged and frustrated. But even in a less than optimal state, Hedy's presence is still almost larger than life. Hedy has a great big heart. And she lives in it almost all the time. She is absolutely genuine, all the time. There are very few people in the world who can pull that off. And the people who can tend to be worshipped. They tend to be heroes to people because they are clearly at the upper end of the bell curve. They have tapped into the spiritual, wise energy of the universe, and they use it well.

Despite all of this, Hedy and Yumi still struggle financially, because they are not great marketers or businesspeople. They do, however, receive lots of help, support, and promotion because people love them, which is where I came into the equation.

THE MORE PEOPLE YOU HELP, THE MORE MONEY YOU MAKE

As a private practice professional, there is a guiding principle that will set you on the road to a Million Dollar Practice. It will help you make a difference in the lives of others and garner the financial freedom that comes along with it. The principle is this: The more people you help, the more money you make. But there is one disclaimer when it comes to helping others in order to make money: You have to leverage it.

Being of service to the public is a great way to get visibility, get credibility, and build the know, like, and trust factor. And if you genuinely believe in your mission, as Hedy and Yumi do, and you're not asking for money and have no apparent way of putting money in your pocket, then you deserve a lot of kudos. People receive high praise for this kind of thing, and rightly so. And the media is far more willing to write stories that feature you. Having said all that, there are many ways to leverage and monetize your offerings, and there is nothing wrong with doing so. You just have to be subtle about it.

The first product I helped Hedy and Yumi create was The Miracle of Connection, a three-CD set. If you go to Hedy's Web site, hedyyumi.org, you will see Miracle of Connection and other audio programs that I helped her create. Basically, I interviewed her, edited the audio, and mastered it. And I did it for no pay. I did it because I love her and want to support her and help her get her message out and reach more people. I also would like her to be compensated for the tremendous service she performs on a global scale. My vision for Hedy is to have her write a book called *The Miracle of Connection*, which is the brand I created for her.

Hedy and Yumi are extremely talented. They are living their dream and playing large. But they, like most private practice professionals, have their limitations that hold them back from achieving the financial rewards commensurate with the value they are providing. That's a marketing problem, not a vision problem. Hedy already has the Million Dollar Practice model in place. In fact, her impact goes far beyond the Million Dollar Practice. She just has to get creative in her marketing in order to leverage it.

Hedy, Yumi, you, me—we're all on this planet for a reason. Hedy and Yumi's goal is world peace. Campbell Working Together has its sights set on making communities work more effectively for the benefit of all. You may have another calling. The point is that as private practice professionals we all have gifts to offer the world.

Will Hedy and Yumi create world peace? Will Campbell Working Together solve the community relationship crisis? Will your venture reach its goal? Will any of these organizations ever generate a dime? I don't know. When you are called to be of service, you don't worry about the money, you just respond, stay true to your mission, do your best to be creative in spreading your message, and let the rest take care of itself.

We are all on this planet for a reason and can be wildly successful financially when we leverage that for our business. Again, the Million Dollar Practice is not about money. It's about making a difference in the world. But the more people you help, the more money you make. This formula cannot fail . . . you just have to leverage it.

MARKETING IS NOT SELLING

Here's an obvious but necessary reminder: There's a difference between marketing and sales activities. People sometimes want to just skip right over the marketing and go straight to counting their money. Practitioners naturally get antsy and look forward to the endgame, thinking, *Okay, what do I want out of this?* This self-directed question often leads to a genuine answer of, *I want more money and more of an effect on people.* As a result, they tend to ignore obvious ways to bring more value to their niche—which would ironically bring the money and effect on people they so desire—and instead push things too hard or jump in too early in trying to close the deal.

The temptation to skip steps comes in part from a lack of understanding of the steps or the process in the first place. Because practitioners often equate marketing with sales, they look too far into the future, are impatient, overlook the necessary outreach they have to do, and focus only on the parts that give them juice or energy. This is understandable, but it can also be costly. I have seen a lot of practitioners, myself included, waste a lot of time and effort and money on ineffective marketing. Remember my $8,000 direct-mail campaign? It's a classic case of barking up the wrong tree.

Here is another example: Some experts and professionals think that hosting a podcast, radio show, or Internet radio show is good marketing for them. One problem: How does interviewing other experts and guests help your credibility and help you get clients and sell your products? Other than feeding the ego, it doesn't.

Now if someone wants to build a radio show and get sponsors and leverage it in other ways, that is just fine. But if a private practice professional is trying to get clients and demonstrate expertise and become the go-to person in his or her niche, having an Internet radio show or podcast won't get it done. And this is just one example.

There are lots of ways to waste time, money, and effort in marketing. You could take a look at my Together Forever Club and the Inspirational Relationships Video project, even the Conscious Relationship Communities project, and say, "Well, that's a big black hole. That's a big waste. That's not going to get you any business. It's not going to make you any money."

You may be right. But you know what? I would do it anyway, because it is so strongly aligned with my mission and message. I consider those activities a public service, helping to solidify much-needed relationships. And ultimately, if a marketing activity does give you juice and is aligned with your mission and message, it really doesn't matter if you make any money from it. I'm not saying you don't need to make a living. You do. But if your mission and message are calling you to do something, you owe it to yourself and to the world to pursue it. Maybe a person doing an Internet radio show has fun doing it and doesn't need to make any money from it. Okay. But make it a conscious choice. Don't mistake a creative marketing venture for a fun activity or a hobby. There is a difference.

Remember: Marketing is communicating what you do. But marketing by itself doesn't create clients for you. Marketing generates prospects. Turning those prospects into clients requires a funnel, a way to bring prospects in and build your relationships with them so they end up hiring you or buying from you, which is where the next chapter, enrollment, comes into play.

But first you have to have your services, products, and programs and your funnel designed as a way to get people in the door and help them take the next steps. And you need to know what the next steps are going to be. You must have a service delivery system in which everything fits together and has a specific purpose.

The people who attend your free presentations are candidates for your workshops and classes. The people who come to your workshops and classes are candidates for your ongoing support groups or for becoming your individual clients. Those people are candidates for your advanced programs. And on and on. Everything you do in your service delivery system—and your marketing is included in your service delivery system—must fit together and make sense to those you are targeting and looking to take through the steps, always providing value, en route to your ultimate offerings.

Here's an example of how to package several marketing ideas together—in this case via a couple of conferences—into a creative marketing package.

CASE STUDY: CREATIVE MARKETING AT CONFERENCES

As with any industry, there are myriad conferences and professional association meetings. If you are new to the speaking-at-conferences concept, allow me to explain how it works. Typically, there will be keynote speakers and a mix of other invited presenters. Generally, a Request for Proposal (RFP) is put out, so potential speakers know that the associations are accepting speaking proposals. There is a set deadline and submission process. For conferences that occur every year, the dates, locations, and all other pertinent facts are published

and well publicized so that people who want to submit speaking proposals have sufficient time to give it their best shot.

Admittedly, I'm not great at planning ahead for these things, but it's
a good idea to have a list of conferences and their speaking-proposal
deadlines and procedures that you feel are worth targeting. Most
associations have mailing lists and will notify you of important and
newsworthy events.

Unless you are a keynote speaker, getting paid for your appearances
is rare. Most speakers do it for the exposure. If you have a business-
to-business (B2B) focus and something to offer the attendees at the
conference (a training program, home-study course, book, etc.), then
paying the money to have an exhibit table makes sense—it especially
makes sense to exhibit if you are also speaking. After years of exhibiting at conferences, I have decided, as a way of prioritizing my time,
that I will exhibit only at conferences where I am presenting. First,
when marketing to attendees, you have much more credibility as a
presenter as opposed to just going to exhibit. Second, going to a conference can be a major hassle, particularly if you are exhibiting.

As an exhibitor, you have a lot of materials to prepare and ship,
and then after the conference you have to ship it back. It takes a long
time to organize and make sure you have everything you need, to
strategize the exhibit and design it. It's a fine way to market, though
the return on investment (ROI) can be questionable. In fact, I'm
pretty clear that, at this stage in my career, I could get by without
exhibiting or going to any conferences at all. But going to conferences
is a good way to network and keep yourself and your organization in
the public eye.

As it happened, I recently found two back-to-back conferences
that interested me—one in Houston and the other in Albuquerque.
I submitted speaking proposals for both. For one of them, I actually
submitted *three* speaking proposals. I figured, *Well, I'll just throw a bunch
of stuff up against the wall and see what sticks. Hopefully they'll go for one.*
They accepted all three. The other organization, to whom I submitted
one proposal, also accepted. I also realized that everybody at the conferences, including the exhibitors, would be a good fit for Talky2, the
communication app and program I mentioned in Chapter 4.

If you decide to attend conferences to promote your business, please do yourself a favor: Add value, stay relevant, and stay current. When I attend conferences, my exhibit display depends upon the audience. If it's therapists, I display my *Therapist to Coach* book. If it's an audience who works with singles, I'll have my *Conscious Dating* book. For the Houston and Albuquerque events, I was appealing to both audiences. And because both of the conferences were heavily couple/marriage oriented, I also promoted and sold The Communication Map. Of course, I mainly attend conferences to promote Relationship Coaching Institute, so I pass out information about RCI. I have a free CD that people can have in exchange for their business cards, their contact information, or joining my mailing list. Additionally, I always have other valuable items to exchange for attendees' contact information, which is my main takeaway.

Speaking and exhibiting at conferences are good for marketing, but you should not expect to generate immediate sales. Sales at conferences—while they may be enough to pay your dinner—are not the endgame. What you really want to bring home from a conference is a bunch of leads to follow up. That is where you will get your new members or people who join your network and, eventually, buy your courses, books, other services, products, or programs, or refer you to others. Following up with your leads effectively is incredibly important, as each one could cost you $50.00 or more after expenses.

MULTIPLE OFFERINGS

The trick with conferences is to look for ways to enhance your presence and avoid being a one-trick pony. As a conference exhibitor, you want to give people a number of reasons to approach your booth and engage you in a conversation that differentiates you from all of the other exhibitors. Many exhibitors have candy bowls and giveaway promotional items, such as pens, key chains, and the like. I prefer promotional items directly related to my business of relationship coaching that provide value and stimulate relationship-oriented conversations. At my recent conferences in Albuquerque and Houston I created four.

The first was Talky2. I passed out flyers for it and talked up the program. The attendees had never heard of it before, so they were naturally curious. Additionally, as it was not my program, I established goodwill without coming across as self-serving. I endorsed it. I thought it was cool and that all couples and all relationships would benefit from using it, but there was no money going directly into my pocket because of it.

The second promotional item was the Together Forever Club. The two conferences were heavily couple/marriage oriented, and I had a free online membership club for couples who took a strong stand for committed relationships; it came with a membership certificate. The club was something I could point people to that added value.

The third item was an inspirational relationships card. After our conversation that spawned the Together Forever Club, Darlene and I had the idea for a card that we could hand out to couples who were affectionate and close and who appeared to have a good relationship. The card said, "You inspire us! We think you have an inspirational relationship." And then we invited them to join the Together Forever Club.

On the other side of the inspirational relationships card was item number four, our Inspirational Relationships Video Project, which can be found at ConsciousRelationshipVideo.com. The back of the card read, "Would you be willing to inspire others? Our world needs more relationships like yours. We invite you to share your relationship story to provide hope and inspiration to struggling singles and couples." At the conferences, we passed out the cards to different couples who inspired us, and we brought our video camera and some releases and filmed inspirational videos right there. These videos are now being used to inspire others.

These four items serve as an example of the kinds of services, products, and programs that you can create and offer at conferences. They are creative marketing ideas. While they didn't generate immediate revenue, these activities put us in front of almost everyone at both conferences; they helped us stand out and be visible as leaders, add value, and stay relevant and current—essential to building a Million Dollar Practice.

MARKETING BASICS

While the focus of this chapter is creative marketing, and indeed this book was written on the assumption that you are beyond entry level, I would be remiss if I didn't at least offer you a reminder of some marketing basics.

First, for the sake of simplicity, let us winnow down marketing into two categories: external and internal.

External marketing is geared toward people you don't know yet. The purpose of external marketing is to create prospects. With external marketing, you put yourself out there to strangers in your niche, and attract those who resonate with who you are and what you do. Activities that fall under this heading include advertising, speaking engagements, submitting articles for publication, publishing a book, radio and television appearances, special events such as trade shows, conferences and festivals, networking events, Internet marketing venues such as search engines, pay-per-click advertising, and banner exchanges — top-of-funnel activities.

Internal marketing is geared toward people you know and have identified through your client creation funnel, with the goal of either having them hire you or referring you to someone who will. These activities build and strengthen your relationships with your prospects.

Sales experts say that 80% of sales require five or more contacts. Internal marketing is how you engage your prospects over time and bring them closer to hiring you. Activities that fall under this heading include offering complimentary sessions, newsletters and e-zines, e-programs, e-mail broadcasts, mailings, telephone calls, sponsoring a niche community (in-person or online), free or low-cost seminars or events for your subscribers, and a membership system with member benefits. And, of course, there is the obvious — yet rarely applied — internal marketing technique of simply asking people you know for referrals.

And all of this assumes that you have invested the necessary time and effort to discover and develop your mission and message, crystalized your brand, clearly defined your niche, and performed the requisite market research to develop your initial products, services, and programs.

Primary Marketing Strategies

There are many ways to get out there—publishing videos on YouTube, publishing articles, giving presentations, and the list goes on. But as a general rule, it is best to ease into the creative marketing approach. You want it to be organic. This chapter (and this book) has been tailored to those looking to get to the next level. But as you set out on your journey toward the Million Dollar Practice, you want to be sure you have formed a proper foundation, using what I like to call Primary Marketing Strategies. I won't go into them at length here, as they are in essence prerequisite strategies for this book and aptly covered in *From Therapist to Coach*, but I will insert the basics here as a cursory reminder.

Primary Marketing Strategy #1: Speak Your Way to More Clients   Speaking to groups of potential clients allows you to reach large numbers of people you don't know. These folks are qualified leads because they're interested in your topic. Furthermore, they're interested in you, or at least they will be. When you're in front of a group, you're perceived to be the expert, and audiences are inclined to trust you—even before you start talking.

Primary Marketing Strategy #2: Write Your Way to More Clients   Writing is a potent and cost-effective way to share your expertise and information with your niche. Writing enables you to attract prospects (external marketing), build relationships, provide value to your network (internal marketing), and create products, services, and programs for passive income and multiple revenue streams.

Writing can take the form of articles, Web content, tip sheets, special reports, e-courses, booklets, manuals, workbooks, home-study programs, and full-fledged books.

Primary Marketing Strategy #3: Network Your Way to More Clients   It is well documented that the most effective way private practice professionals get clients is word-of-mouth referrals. It is basic and traditional, but the most effective and overlooked way you can get clients and build your practice. Referrals can come from friends, family, colleagues, allied pro-fessionals and organizations, and current and former clients.

Once you are ready to move beyond the three primary marketing strategies you can get a bit more creative. This chapter, through its examples and case studies, has given you the philosophy you need to devise your own methods and stand out from the crowd. But I would be remiss if I didn't give you at least a few specific creative marketing strategies that have proven effective, time and again.

Creative Marketing Strategies

Tupperware Parties Tupperware parties (to most people, a whole-some thing of the past) were in effect creative marketing activities. They were built on the premise that inviting folks into your home and offering them quality information was a positive marketing experience that both presenters and guests would enjoy.

While some may feel this practice has fallen by the wayside, it remains one of my favorite creative marketing strategies. In fact, it might be all you need to fill your practice.

You can either host the gathering yourself, or ask people you know (friends, colleagues, clients, referral sources, etc.) to host a gathering of their network for a private seminar. It can take place in a home or an office. This can be a fun, intimate gathering of like-minded friends and acquaintances who are highly qualified prospects for you.

Joint Ventures Contacting professionals and organizations and inviting them to discuss the mutual benefits of collaboration is an effective private practice–building exercise. You have your resources and platform, and they have theirs. Collectively, you can reach more people, provide more value, and create more clients than either of you could on your own.

Contests Contests are a great way to generate positive buzz while bringing leads and prospects into your client creation funnel. The idea is to start with the people in your specialty and then branch out as your practice grows.

As an example, I conduct a "Conscious Dating® Success Story of the Year" contest each year around Valentine's Day. The stories I receive are inspirational and instructive and become testimonials for my program—which helps sell my services, products, and programs by convincing prospects that Conscious Dating really works. Winners get a valuable prize, and their stories are published on my Web site and publicized in my *Conscious Dating* newsletter, blog, Twitter feed, and through press releases.

Giveaways Giveaways, like contests, are a great way to generate publicity. They also develop and deepen your relationship with your niche. Giveaways can involve services, products, and programs. They can also be time-limited to create some urgency. Otherwise, your prospects may avoid taking action, because they assume they can get the freebies anytime.

In my practice, around mid-December each year, I invite my *Conscious Dating* newsletter subscribers to order a free copy of my book to give to a friend or family member over the holiday season. As with contests, this giveaway helps promote the book and my programs for singles.

Scholarships/Pro Bono As a private practice professional you inevitably and regularly encounter people who want to enroll in your programs and take advantage of your services and products, yet claim they can't afford them. You may be inclined to offer a sliding-scale discount. Instead, I recommend you create and advertise a limited number of scholarships. This will help your community and ensure that you reserve your discounted rates for the people who indeed qualify for them, as opposed to those who don't mind spending money on a new car or the latest high-tech gadget they can't afford but want you to lower your rates.

Client Sponsors Your niche may be composed of people with limited financial means—college students, high school athletes, teenage unwed mothers, homeless veterans, and so on. To help them take advantage of your offerings, you can help them identify people in their lives (friends, family members, etc.) who might provide them with some financial help. It's a motivation issue. In my experience, if these people are truly inspired to work with you, they will either find the money to avoid asking for help or they will lean on their support system. Don't forget to target your marketing efforts to those who have a vested interest in helping your niche.

Free Starter Program   People are much more willing to sign up for a free program than a paid one. Naturally, a free starter program can be a potent marketing strategy. Once your clients have completed the beginning steps and received value, they'll be more likely to sign up to continue and get all of the benefits and results of your program.

Tele-Seminars   Conducting speaking engagements by telephone can be even more effective than in-person events for several reasons:

- Participants are more likely to fit you into their schedule if they don't have to travel.
- Low or no overhead means that your event can be offered for free.
- You can potentially reach more people, because your audience can join you from anywhere in the world.
- There's a low barrier to entry, because you don't need any infrastructure.
- Your tele-seminars allow you to create immediate products; many conference call services allow you to record the event, which becomes an instant audio product.

Attending as many different tele-seminars as you can find and paying attention to how others are structuring, managing, marketing, and following up with the events will help you with your own. Some of the things you learn will impress you; some will not. Take the good stuff and build your tele-seminar around that.

Tele-Clinics Tele-clinics are conference calls designed in a question-and-answer format, similar to a call-in radio show. Tele-clinics work well as marketing activities because everyone who participates is identifying themselves as a potential client. Your interaction with them gives them a preview of what it will be like to work with you. As a bonus, tele-clinics can give you great ideas for articles, seminars, and products for your niche.

Niche Community Niche communities were covered in Chapters 3 and 4, so please head on back there if you need a refresher.

Live Events Live events are a great way to amp up the energy of potential clients. They include socials, seminars, workshops and classes, networking, fund-raisers, and other creative ways to bring people together in a room. Live events can be tricky, though, and should be put on hold until your private practice is well on the path to becoming a Million Dollar Practice. Live events can require considerable up-front costs to produce, and if there are any key design weaknesses, they can fail—and put a serious dent in your budget, not to mention your enthusiasm. Still, live events are a powerful way to reach large groups, generate significant sales of your products and programs, and create large numbers of clients at one time. Remember, after launching my weekly Friday night social for singles, I filled my new coaching practice in 90 days.

Workshops and Classes As mentioned in Chapter 5, workshops and classes are valuable features of your service delivery system, and they are effective ways to attract large numbers of potential clients. Many graduates will join your group coaching program or hire you for individual coaching to support what they have learned in your workshops and classes.

Fund-Raisers Taking your passion and expertise to your community can be a great way to market your private practice. Schools, churches, and nonprofits are always seeking ways to raise funds, and they will most likely be open to your proposal if it fits their values and mission.

You can donate a percentage of your product and service sales to a worthy cause, or host a live event and donate the proceeds. Just remember that whatever cause you identify must resonate with your niche. Your market research will help you choose the right fund-raising partner and approach.

Public Service Campaigns   You are in the business of helping people. And it's not hard to identify a public service angle for your specialty and niche. For example, after reading headline after headline about the high unemployment rate, I put together a seminar on "Secrets of Self-Employment" and focused on tips for starting a small business. Designing a public service campaign related to your practice makes it easy to get joint venture partners and media coverage for your worthy cause. Think back to Campbell Working Together from earlier in this chapter.

Corporate Sponsorships   Corporations seeking to fulfill their community support missions are typically open to creative ways to promote their brands and enhance their images with their potential customers. While getting your foot in the door by yourself might be a challenge, having nonprofit partners can give you the clout and connections you need to make things happen.

Nonprofit Partnerships   Nonprofit organizations, including churches, schools, public service agencies, and other nongovernmental organizations (NGOs), are always seeking ways to raise funds. They are also open to partnerships, because they are continually seeking ways to stretch their resources, to more effectively provide their services, and to serve their constituencies—especially if it doesn't cost them anything. As a partner, in exchange for your services, you get access to their networks.

When pitching your ideas to nonprofits, make sure they understand the value you bring to their congregation, membership, or audience. For example, churches and schools will typically not let you "sell" or "market" to their group, but if you provide a genuine service, you can position yourself to be a highly valued information resource.

"Ask" Campaigns "Ask" campaigns serve as both market research and marketing activities. The idea is to simply ask members of your niche what they find to be the most important question or problem. In my case, the question would be, "What is your most important question about finding your soul mate?" The responses you get will generate a gold mine of ideas for your articles, seminars, products, services, and programs. Your question becomes a marketing strategy when posted on your Web site. Then set up an autoresponder and invite participants to opt in to join your seminar, to participate in a conference call, or to get a special report or other offering whereby you will give them the answer.

GET OUT THERE

There are many ways to get out there—publishing videos on YouTube, publishing articles, giving presentations, and the list goes on. But the force behind creative marketing comes from strongly communicating your mission and message. When you are reaching your target audience with that mission and message, you are authentically showcasing your passion and talents.

One way I showcase myself is telling my story. I'm honest about myself, such as acknowledging to my clients that I have been divorced twice. Showcasing yourself doesn't mean, "Look at me and how great I am. Here, I'm an expert and have all the solutions to your problems." Showcasing yourself is allowing people to see you, rather than hiding behind your office door, Web site, book, or something else.

Creative marketing is about being transparent and showing up. It's allowing people to see you so they can connect and build a relationship with you. Creative marketing is engaging in activities that strongly communicate your mission and message so that you can differentiate yourself. Creative marketing is how you get people's attention. Creative marketing is doing things differently and then asking *what works* and *what's next*—and doing so from the Platinum Rule perspective.

Creative marketing isn't easy. If it were, this chapter would have step-by-step instructions. Although there are principles and strategies, such as the ones we've covered, there is no formula. It's a challenge, because you don't always have the answers and you must stay in the question. This means you must also stay in the resulting tension, the anxiety that is, "Oh, my God, what am I going to do? I have no idea." You have to hang in there. You have to trust that nature abhors a vacuum and that you have the inner wisdom and creativity needed to fill it. You must trust that when you ask the question and allow yourself to sleep on it and let it stew for a while, answers will begin to appear. Some of them won't be so great, but they will inevitably lead you to others that *will* be great.

Throughout this chapter I have shared with you some things that I have created that are innovative. I have shared with you things that did not exist before I came up with them. I have shared with you creative marketing strategies that addressed, targeted, and reached the people I wanted to reach, and I have shared with you activities that were aligned with my mission and message. It's what helps me be a leader in my profession, specialty, and niche. And it's what will help you become a leader in yours. Creative marketing will help you become the go-to person in your field and ensure that people think of you first.

While it might seem as though I discovered this principle by accident, the truth is that my journey led me here. It led me to the place of first being helpless and then clearing the decks and starting with a blank slate and a new mind-set: *I know nothing. How can I reach these people? How can I help these people? What do they want? What do they need? What will they sign up for? What will work for them?* Ask yourself these questions regularly and consistently. This is the foundation of creative marketing for building the Million Dollar Practice.

Million Dollar Questions for Chapter 6

1. What have you done to reach your niche that has been the most successful so far? What's next?

2. What need exists in your community (or the world) that would be interesting, fulfilling, and exciting for you to address as a public service, with no thought of compensation?

3. Who is your base, your core group of people who know you professionally? How can you best be of service to them and get their support for your program?

4. What part of your business would be most effective for getting media attention? What's the most compelling story angle for highlighting your area of expertise?

5. What questions will help you create a blank slate and see your work and your niche with fresh eyes? What questions do you need to continually ask yourself to invoke the Platinum Rule and stay creative in your approach to your niche?

CHAPTER SEVEN

Making the Sale, Getting the Client

Although it is what we want most and, essentially, why we are here as private practice professionals, making the sale and getting the client is not something that can be forced. We must prepare for it and properly time it. In fact, talking about money and trying to sell your services too soon is one of the biggest mistakes you can make as a practitioner.

Go to any number of practitioner Web sites and you will usually see their services listed (complete with price tags) and a place to "register for a free consultation" or a variety of other one-to-one offerings. But let me ask you: Would you visit someone's Web site for the first time, read a few lines of text, and click a button to spend a significant chunk of your money or talk to someone you don't know, even if doing so were free? If the answer is yes, or if you have already done this, then we must be talking about a heckuva compelling offer—and I want the copywriter's number! But if you are like most people and the answer is no—you wouldn't spend your hard-earned dollars without first having established trust—then why would you expect someone else to do so? Put another way: Why would you do something that doesn't work?

Unfortunately, most private practice professionals haven't given this a lot of thought. And if they have given it any thought, it has been wishful thinking. Furthermore, if we were to ask folks who have posted such offers on their Web sites whether anybody ever, out of the blue, had come to their Web site, clicked through, and signed up for their $1,000 program, most of the time the answer would be no. So again, why would you have something like that on your Web site? The question you need to ask yourself is, "If people come to my Web site and they are clicking around, are they going to want to learn more, hang out for a while, and engage me? Or are they going to see what is there—and what is not there—and run away?"

Think of it this way: If you go to a car lot, and you are checking out a car, and the car salesman tries to sell to you without asking what you are looking for or what your budget is—or doing anything to establish a relationship and build your trust—and instead just says, "That car is $50,000. Please give me your credit card number and buy it," what are you going to do? Chances are, in some way or another, no matter how much you may have been intrigued by the car, you would start to feel bad, maybe even scared, and walk away, never to return. "Oh, I'm just looking. Thanks, anyway."

It's the same thing with a Web site when visitors see a high-dollar item. They don't yet know you, like you, and trust you, and they don't understand, nor are they convinced of, the value of what you provide. Even though they are looking for answers, all they see is something pricey on your Web site and figure it's too expensive for them, so they leave and look elsewhere.

Now, there is nothing wrong with providing a low-cost entrée into your world of services, as long as it is part of a larger plan. But if we had to decide upon a maximum amount for what somebody visiting your Web site without any enrollment efforts might buy, we could arbitrarily cap it at around $200, depending upon the product. None of us should have a "buy" button on a Web site for a publicly available item for more than that.

For instance, on my Web site, I have a home-study course for $149. And often it will be people's first foray into my service delivery system. If they are willing to spend money at all, and they are genuinely interested in the subject that brought them to my Web site in the first place, they most likely can live with the $149 price point—even without any significant enrollment effort. But for the most part, if somebody is to hire you or pay you a significant amount for your services, products, and programs, there are some preliminary steps that need to be involved that tie into a larger system. And that's what this chapter is about: the process, on a group level—because, after all, we are talking about the Million Dollar Practice—referred to as enrollment.

GROUP ENROLLMENT

In bringing in new customers and clients, the larger system to which I referred encompasses the whole client creation machine, from the top of the funnel all the way down to the bottom. But the bulk of the enrollment piece, though tied to all of the other components, focuses on the bottom of the funnel. To use a cliché, this is where the rubber meets the road. This is the place where all of your previous efforts will come to fruition.

Now, make no mistake, it takes discipline and a well-defined, comprehensive strategy to master enrollment. But I can assure you that if you spend the requisite effort on applying the principles from the previous chapters—building your system and waiting for the right moment to pitch your potential clients—you will be rewarded when applying the principles in this one.

In Chapter 1, I provided a case study on Tony Robbins. Here's a guy who doesn't have any trouble filling his programs. He has a name, he has a track record, and he has people who love him and basically sell for him, paid and unpaid. As a result, whenever he comes to town and puts on an event, it's sold out. Now, while it's entirely possible, I don't expect that many of us will ever reach that level. Still, Tony Robbins certainly gives us something to aspire to: where the members of our niche lower their resistance and we have no trouble filling a room. But it is worth noting that Tony Robbins's success came after years in the trenches and developing a highly efficient marketing and enrollment operation.

So even if we are to reach that level, we need to first pay our dues. And one of the biggest obstacles, going all the way back to when we first started our organization, is the temptation to take a shortcut and go right for the sale. The other barrier is being lulled by the bluebirds (to be addressed shortly), where we are fooled into thinking we are on track: *I made a sale! What I put together is working, so now I can just go on with my day and my business as usual, and I will someday be wildly successful.*

Despite the fact that getting new customers is what we want most, taking shortcuts will not work. Building your business takes time. It's a relationship-building process, and to reach the level of the Million Dollar Practice, you must design your marketing and enrollment to work together, as a series of steps that will be consistently refined and improved over time, taking you and your customers to the next level.

So before you swoop in for the close, as a matter of course, you must ensure that you and the prospect are ready. You must know that you have properly built your client-services funnel and service delivery system and that the client is in a position to accept what you have to offer. Fail to do this, try to sell before you have built any sort of relationship, and you risk losing the sale and scaring away any would-be customers or referrals. But expend the necessary time and effort to prepare yourself and the customer, and your efforts will pay off—big time.

You just have to know where to focus your energy. Because, while it is always wonderful when prospects jump a step and go straight from your free, introductory talk to your high-dollar program, we don't design our marketing and enrollment strategies for them. We design them for everyone else.

THREE CORE CONSTITUENCIES

When creating your overall marketing and enrollment system, there is a key concept that I find particularly helpful, which I call *bluebirds* and *boulders*. *Bluebirds* are those few but wonderful clients who are so motivated and so attracted to you and what you offer that they excitedly fly through your window and hire you without much of an enrollment process: "Oh, boy, this is great—the answer to my prayers!" And, while it's wonderful when that happens, it's pretty rare, especially in the beginning.

Boulders, conversely, are those many, and still wonderful, prospects who are interested and attracted, but who need to be coaxed and encouraged to make the leap from prospect to client.

There is also a third category, into which most others fall, that encompasses everything in between. This category comprises people who are willing to take a small step into your world, provided you present the offer properly, to test what it is like to work with you and determine your ability to deliver on your promises.

Now, bluebirds tend to fool us because they represent that which we want most: people who love us and sign up for everything we put out there. As a result, when we encounter bluebirds, we are convinced they represent a large percentage of the population. *See? This is proof. They love me and can't resist.* No, bluebirds are the exception. Bluebirds are the minority of the population, not the majority. And we shouldn't allow bluebirds to lull us into complacency and have us thinking, *Hey, my marketing's working!*

A NUMBERS GAME

Like all marketing and enrollment activities, you must take a look at the numbers. For instance if your marketing has reached 1,000 people and you only got one bluebird from that group, your numbers aren't very good. So, rather than being complacent and saying, "Ah, I made a sale, how exciting, my marketing's working," you should be asking, "What is my conversion rate and what can I do to boost it?"

And if you really want to up the ante and join the ranks of savvy marketers, you can do split testing. As an example, you can have different versions of an advertisement or e-mail message—or even different versions of a subject line in an e-mail message, Web page, or squeeze page—and evaluate them to see which one is most effective. That is a best practice, and we all should do it. Sadly, and I am the first to admit it, most of us don't, even though we may know we should.

Incidentally, we all have our weaknesses. We just need to recognize them and avoid letting them get the best of us. As private practice professionals, we have the ability to build our organizations and place people around us—staff, partners, and associates—who balance out those areas where we need help. In my case, that area happens to be numbers. I'm math impaired. I can balance my checkbook, but aside from that, numbers are like a foreign language to me. That is why I brought in a business partner who is great with numbers, among other things.

Getting back to the bluebirds, it is true that as you build your platform and have successful programs and people talking about you, you will get more of them. Bluebirds will go to your Web site already presold, because somebody they trust has told them that your service, product, or program has made all the difference in the world to them. And they will start flying in your window all over the place. It can take a while to get there, but when you do, you will know you have arrived, that you are on the doorstep of the Million Dollar Practice. And at that point, your marketing will seem almost effortless. Effortless marketing, which is directly tied to enrollment, is what we all really want as private practice professionals—we want everything we put out to be gobbled up ravenously. And that absolutely can happen, but it generally happens over time by putting out quality services, products, and programs and by doing a good job for our existing clients.

Think of your practice as you would any referral-based business. After you have been at it long enough and have built up enough of a clientele and a following and a host of referral sources, you don't have to market anymore. Every client is a bluebird after that. They just continue to call and fly through the window. But it can take 10 to 20 years to get to that point—and, at best, that will be a six-figure practice.

In Chapter 8 of my previous book, *Therapist to Coach*, I discussed the enrollment conversation and the strategy session, key components of how you actually get a client. Here, in this chapter, we are going beyond that into the Million Dollar Practice. The idea here is to take those concepts and apply them to large numbers of people on a group level. Here we explore how you fill a workshop. Here we look at how you get large numbers of people to sign up for something and then how you get them to take the next step. Here we cover group enrollment. And it starts with the campaign.

THE CAMPAIGN

As I mentioned, we need to design our marketing and enrollment for the boulders: the ones who are the hardest to coax, the hardest to move; the ones who need the most pushing and pulling and who have the most resistance, fear, and whatever else holding them back. Once we have gotten to know them well, after we have done our market research and designed our services, products, and programs, as well as our marketing and enrollment for them, the bluebirds will follow.

And as I have written in various ways and I hope made clear by now, marketing is not something you do here and there and hope for the best. It is an organized system that involves a series of coordinated efforts, a systematic campaign, of which the funnel is the model. As in the funnel, in the campaign you offer your free stuff, which leads to your low-cost stuff, which leads to your high-cost stuff. And the ones who do it properly yield huge dividends.

For starters, in any campaign, you want to schedule your marketing and enrollment period. You want to have it on the calendar. You want to have some sort of system. For instance, let's say you decide to do it on an annual or quarterly basis. You then design the campaign accordingly, which may include a free tele-seminar, which may lead to a free live event, which may lead to an upsell of a coaching program. And that coaching program may lead to an upsell of something else. So you have your service delivery system and then you have your campaign, which is how you market and enroll for your service delivery system. After each campaign, you want enough information and feedback to refine the next campaign to be more effective. You cannot ever stop. You can't ever put something in place and just repeat it the same way over and over and over.

If you are serious about making a difference in the world, about reaching as many people as you can, about having a Million Dollar

Practice, you have to constantly be refining and evolving, refining and evolving. And how do you know how to refine and evolve? It's based on the results you get. It depends on the input and feedback from the people you want to serve. Regardless of the effectiveness of any enrollment effort, there is always room for improvement—even if you enrolled three times more people than you planned, anticipated, or dreamed. Were you successful beyond your wildest dreams? Wonderful. Congratulations. You still need to refine and evolve. To reach and sustain the Million Dollar Practice level, you cannot stand in one place—"Oh, boy, this was successful. Now I can just do the same thing next time!"—never, ever. You must always be improving to play in the same league as those who do it well.

ENROLLMENT EVENTS

T. Harv Eker's organization puts on regular, free weekend workshops, *Secrets of the Millionaire Mind*. If you want to learn about financial security and wealth and managing money and your relationship with money and what to do about it, this is the place to go. Now the content itself, which is great, is in a book and could be delivered at a live event in about 3 or 4 hours. But *Secrets of the Millionaire Mind* takes up an entire weekend.

The workshop is a huge production, with hundreds of people in the room, many flying in from all over. Part of what attracts them is the perceived high value, and yet, because it's free, the financial barrier to entry is nonexistent. But even though it doesn't cost anything to get in, the organizers make clear that the ticket price is $500, except for the "VIPs" who received complimentary admission. So, not only does the content have a perceived high value, but you are given the perception that you are being specially treated, an effective strategy for filling the room.

Personal growth organizations with big promotional events often spend a lot of money up front to produce, market, and fill them. And do you know what they do once the event is under way? Yes, they share valuable content and build their relationship with you, but they also constantly present their offers. They pitch and pitch and pitch and pitch. This is similar to attending a free weekend getaway sponsored by a timeshare company—it's not really free, which allows them to pitch to you as the price of admission.

Now, as a consumer I have learned to recognize these pitch fests disguised as freebie workshops or trainings, and, as a potential attendee it's a judgment call you have to make as to whether you want to spend your valuable time learning a few gems of wisdom while putting up with a bunch of pitches. But from an entrepreneurial point of view, if done correctly, I can tell you one thing for certain: It works!

At the Millionaire Mind event that I attended, almost everybody there signed up for *something*. And almost everything they signed up for cost big bucks. The offers were strategically presented at regular intervals. They were part of a larger system, a campaign that was crafted to enroll large numbers of people in a live setting.

And as we discussed earlier, a campaign is designed from square one—from the very first thing that you do to all the way to the very end—to receive maximum numbers of clients. It's designed for all the pieces to fit together. And it can take many forms.

One very common model is an online marketing campaign in which you have a series of short videos, with high-value content, that speak to a niche's biggest problems and to what a group of people wants to learn how to do or accomplish. People opt in for access to the first video, and then, a few days or a week later, they are given access to the series' next video. And then there is a video after that and a video after that. Then there might be a conference call, tele-seminar, webinar, or even a live event (as mentioned earlier) to complement the video. And then there will be an upsell or a pitch, which everybody knows is coming.

But by the time the pitch arrives, the participants have received such value from the content, and the relationship has been built up so much, that nobody seems to care. Mind you, the people attending the event are qualified, meaning their presence is evidence that they are genuinely interested in the subject matter. You know they have a need that aligns with what is being offered because they signed up and showed up in the first place. You are not talking to random people. You are talking to highly qualified candidates for your program. And your marketing will get you to that point, because it, too, all ties together as part of a system. And then comes your enrollment.

GROUP ENROLLMENT

One of the key pieces of enrollment, though it is technically a function of marketing, is to have already laid the foundation. Everything you have done from the very beginning has been coordinated. It has been a campaign. It has led you to this point. And you now have a large group of people that are primed. So, what do you do? How do you bring them across the finish line and into your world of service offerings?

By way of inspiration and examples, this book has made a great effort to enable you to think on your feet and create your own path, specific to your business and your niche and the unique dynamic that lies between. In that same spirit, I will provide you with several common elements, which I have identified through years of experience, used by master group enrollers that you might adapt for your business.

First, successful enrollers usually go big—perceived high value and high price point. They are not thinking: *What can these people afford?* or *How low should I price this to get them to say yes?* No, they are pricing each item as high as possible, short of causing people to turn around and walk away.

A common price point you will see is somewhere around $2,000— and it doesn't matter what they are selling. The price is high enough to get people's attention, but not so high that it causes them to flee. You must also realize that the pitch at the enrollment event is the first time participants have ever seen or heard the price, which brings us to the second element: delaying the reveal of the price until a relationship has been formed and the value has been established.

BUILDING THE FOUNDATION

I began this chapter with an example of people putting high-dollar services, products, and programs on their Web sites along with a price and a buy button. In that example, visitors to your Web site, without having yet come to know you, like you, and trust you—at all—know that your program is $2,000. Chances are they are going to walk away because they are not qualified, not primed, and the relationship hasn't yet been established. You have not yet built the foundation.

Conversely, at an enrollment event, prospects are qualified and primed, and the relationship is already there. They have received value from you, they know you, like you, and trust you, and *then* they find out the upsell, the next step in order to get the big benefit, the value that they really want. They realize that all the free stuff that you have provided, while valuable, is not going to transform their lives. It's not going to deliver the results that they want. Then they see that it is going to cost them $2,000 to get the results they want. And just as you must do when properly preparing for the enrollment stage, they have to weigh cost versus benefit. *"Well, the cost is $2,000, but the benefit is that I accomplish what I really, really want to accomplish. Is it worth $2,000? Well, absolutely yes. Can I afford $2,000? Well, it's a stretch. It's going to be hard. Maybe not."*

Building the foundation is an important step in the enrollment process and sets you up for success. In this case, the members of your audience are primed and qualified, and you have given them a positive experience. They are now ready to seriously consider the upsell and take that next step and work with you. So you go over your program, and your program is everything and the kitchen sink. The program covers everything they could possibly want to know. It addresses every challenge they can possibly think of. It gives them all the possible answers and keys and solutions. They look at your program and say, "Oh, my gosh, this is the answer to my prayers."

Remember: It takes a bit of market research to design this kind of program, because, after all, before you can hit it out of the park with your pitch you need to know a few things: What are their biggest challenges? What are their questions? What do they need to know? What are the obstacles they need to overcome? Here your market research is worth its weight in gold, because during the process you have heard their questions, and now you just have to feed the answers right back to them. With all sincerity, you can tell them, "This program is going to help you do this, this, this, and this. We are going to give you this tool and this tool and this tool and this tool. This program is *exactly* what you have been looking for."

MORE MARKET RESEARCH

One of the cool things about market research is the payoff when you make sales. But it doesn't stop there. It's also wise to follow up with people who have bought from you, which provides more market research. In fact, I can't stress enough the value in doing your market research with people who sign up. "How did you find me? What attracted you to my newsletter or program? What were you looking for? What problem were you looking to solve? What information were you looking for? And what convinced you to sign up?" It makes enrollment process that much easier and more effective for everyone.

And also, equally important, is to do your market research with people that *don't* sign up. "Well, I notice you signed up for my introductory program but you didn't take the next step to continue with the series. What got in the way for you? Why wasn't it a fit? What were you looking for that you didn't get? And what could we add that would meet your needs and cause you to want to sign up in the future?"

The very nature of the enrollment process provides feedback. Sometimes the feedback will be "Yes, I want to sign up." Other times it will be "No, I don't want to sign up. It's not a fit for me." Other times the feedback will be dead air, nothing. No decision. No response. No matter the response, there is something instructive in all of that, and it is worth its weight in gold to connect with each one of your target groups. You don't have to interview everybody. Just take a sampling—three to five in each group. The information you glean from this research will help you with your next campaign.

By way of example, let's say that some people in your niche want to market their services on the Internet, but they are not tech savvy and don't know how to put up Web sites. So you decide you are going to provide them a ready-to-go Web site. Other people think,

Well, I'd like to market on the Internet, but I'm not good at copywriting. So you decide you are going to give them templates for creating marketing copy. You anticipate every possible problem and provide the corresponding solutions. Now, when you are pitching your program and explaining exactly what enrollees are going to get, you increase the likelihood that you will get the response you are looking for: *Look at this, oh my gosh, everything I need and want is here, and more — things that I didn't even know I needed and wanted!*

Letting your constituencies teach and guide you is key in pursuing the Million Dollar Practice. All you have to do is ask, listen, and respond. It's part of the Platinum Rule. It's part of market research. It applies in product development; it applies in marketing; and it applies in enrollment. In short, it's the way to guarantee your success. If you ask and listen and respond to their needs, you can't lose. And remember: It doesn't stop after the sale. It continues long after they have purchased your products, services, and programs.

Case Study: A Master Enroller

I still remember the first time I participated in an effective group enrollment campaign. I was on a tele-seminar, a conference call — one I had joined with absolutely no intention of buying anything — and the host, one of the masters of Internet marketing for experts who have a mission and a message and want to help people, made quite an impression on me. It was a free tele-seminar that I had signed up for, and it had valuable content, things that I wanted to learn — and it certainly delivered as promised. But there was one aspect that was of particular interest to me as a private practice professional.

In pitching the event, the organizers announced the time, the date, and, after I signed up for it, how to join it. But they didn't give an ending time. Nowhere did they say how long it was. I didn't ask at the time, and I didn't think to look for it later. As it turned out, the tele-seminar went on for over 4 hours. It felt like it would never end — it just kept going and going and going.

There were a couple of thousand people on the line, and the host took *everybody's* questions. He said his commitment was to be there until all of our questions were answered. So the questions kept coming and he kept right on answering them. But what did he do in between answers? Well, like T. Harv Eker and the Millionaire Mind, he pitched: "Here's a program, here's when it starts, and here's what you are going to get out of it." Additionally, he kept throwing out new incentives, enticements, and bonuses. And there was one particular bonus that caught my attention.

Remember, I had no intention of signing up for the program at this point—none. That is, until he said, "You know what? For the first 100 people who sign up, I'm going to throw in an iPod filled with recordings—the complete recorded version of my previous program and a bunch of other trainings that I've done that will help you do this and this and this and this." Now I'm perking up. Wow, that's cool. I want that. So I looked at the offer and thought: *Okay, well, not only can I participate in his upcoming live program, but I'm going to get an iPod with all of the recordings and a bunch of other really cool stuff that I want to learn about, conveniently loaded right in there.*

Now, I love gadgets, and the bonus of an iPod certainly sparked my attention. Then I ventured into territory that, as you now know, I'm not typically comfortable with: math. I thought: *Let's see . . . I know an iPod is $300–$500 . . . and the program is $2,000 . . . so right there, it's already down to $1,500 . . . hmmm . . . this is looking more attractive. . . .*

Still, despite the temptation, at that price I still didn't think I could afford it. *Well, I'm not going to sign up for that, but I'm going to hang on this call because he is continuing to deliver more and more content. He is answering all these questions, a lot of them I have myself. So it's at least worth it for me to continue to hang on this call, but I won't buy anything. . . .*

And then guess what he did? He said, ". . . and as a fast-action bonus, if you sign up right now, in the next 30 minutes, I'm going to drop the price $500. So that meant we had a $2,000 program—which in my mind became a $1,500 program with the value of the iPod— that, by taking another $500 off the price, he was offering for $1,000. And besides, the program itself was going to deliver a lot of what I really wanted to know and learn and be able to do. I thought: *Is it worth $1,000 for me? Absolutely. Can I afford $1,000 at this point? Not really, but you know what? It's an investment!*"

And that, by the way, is the kind of mind-set you want to build into your prospects. *I'm investing in myself, I'm investing in my future, I'm investing in the result I want to get. I'm investing in having the body I want, I'm investing in my financial future, I'm investing in my fulfillment* (or whatever it is to you).

So, when the host announced that for the next 30 minutes, for only those people who were still on the call, he was going to drop the price, again, we felt like a special group, because at that point we had hung on the call for 3 hours, far longer than I had ever been on the phone on any tele-seminar, any conference call, or any event, ever. What had been a group of about 3,000 people at the beginning of the call was down to about 1,000. And since we had hung in there and were special, he was going to give us a special deal—but only for the next 30 minutes, because, after all, it was a fast-action bonus. I had to decide right then and there if I wanted it.

And I'll never forget the moment, after swearing ahead of time that I wasn't going to buy anything: I got out my wallet, got out my credit card, went online, and signed up. And it was all due to the effectiveness with which the host waged and conducted his enrollment campaign. We all have the ability to do that in our own businesses.

SOCIAL PROOF

Public Acknowledgment

Master group enrollers don't just take the money and run. Successful group enrollers publicly acknowledge people who sign up for their programs. In live workshops like T. Harv Eker's Millionaire Mind, or others I have attended that include upsells, when people go to the back of the room to sign up they are applauded or given some other form of acknowledgment. This makes people feel special. On the marathon tele-seminar that I just discussed, when somebody would sign up, the host would acknowledge them right there on the phone, in real time. "Sally Jones, from Nashville, Tennessee, just signed up. Welcome, Sally. You've made a great choice . . . Oh, and

Joe Jones and Bill Jones, too. Congratulations on your investment. Welcome to the program." And, of course, it felt great when I signed up and he acknowledged me — I was now one of the club.

The principle they are using here is social proof, implying that if somebody else endorses you or says something good about you or, in this case, signs up for your program, then you must be okay and therefore it is safe and all right for others to do it, too. You're creating a bandwagon effect. Anything you can do to boost social proof helps your enrollment. When you have an enrollment event, like the ones mentioned in this chapter, social proof can work wonders — again, provided that you have already done the necessary legwork (i.e., market research, creating your services, products, and programs to address the wants and needs of your niche, and putting in place a service delivery system and client creation funnel). The conference call that I was on was an enrollment event. Sure, it was a high-value tele-seminar to teach specific content that I wanted to learn, but the goal of the host was to enroll new customers. What's more, almost everybody joining that program *knew* that was the goal. But they showed up and endured the pitches anyway, because they wanted the valuable content. And some — like me — even though they hadn't planned to do so, ended up spending significant amounts of money.

So whether it is The Millionaire Mind or some other free or low-cost weekend workshop, they are all essentially enrollment events. And if you don't know that going in, you are in for a surprise. Think about it: The hosts spend a lot of time and expend a lot of money and resources up front to deliver valuable content. And, most of the time, they deliver on their promises and you get that valuable content. But it should really come as no surprise that they are looking to get something out of it, too. Though they may have good intentions, they are not spending time, money, and resources to put on events out of the kindness of their hearts, expecting nothing in return.

Their half of the bargain is the opportunity to try and enroll you in their programs. The pitch fest is part of the deal. It's an exchange. And it's a fair exchange. The experience that I get from these events is great. Although you can get the same *content* from a book or CD set, those products pale in comparison to the energy of the crowd at a live event. The Millionaire Mind was big. It was in a fancy hotel. It was cool. There were hundreds of people there. And the social proof—if *they* signed up, it must be okay for *me* to sign up—is the beauty of what you, as a private practice professional, can do with group enrollment events like that. It will certainly help you on your path to the Million Dollar Practice.

Testimonials

Also along the lines of social proof is the enrollment strategy of using testimonials. And in one case, during a live event hosted by a successful enroller, there was an added twist. At the event, satisfied customers and clients, real people willing to stand up and explain how the program benefited them, were called up on stage—these were not videos, not photos incorporating a few kind words, but live, in-person people.

This highly effective enrollment strategy took place during a free weekend workshop on a high-value topic I wanted to learn about. Darlene and I had already spent money with the host on a middle-of-funnel program, which was to take place online, and free tickets to this live workshop were included as a "bonus." We bought plane tickets, booked our hotel room, and went to this free weekend workshop knowing that the host was going to be upselling and pitching her next thing (we didn't know what it was). We also knew that it probably would be much more expensive than the one we had just signed up to access, but we were willing to endure the pitch because, like all of the participants, we wanted to learn the valuable content of that workshop. But even knowing the offer was coming, I was in for a surprise: It turned out that she was pitching a *$100,000* coaching program!

My jaw dropped. In all of my years of attending events, I had never seen or experienced anything like that, ever. *$100,000?! That's the cost of a house. $100,000?! That's the cost of a Ferrari. $100,000?! Are you kidding me?! $100,000?!*

I had a hard time grasping the price tag. And because I had never seen a coaching program priced that high, I didn't figure that very many people in the audience would be able to afford it. But I was mistaken, or at least I underestimated the host's ability to enroll.

The host had a unique spin on the standard testimonial strategy that I had seen others do. She had live testimonials, but called them *inspirational stories*. At frequent intervals throughout the program she would say, "You know what? Let's take a break. I'd like to share with you an inspirational story." And then she would call out the person's name and that person would come onstage to tell his or her story.

What's different about this approach is that the focus is on the inspirational story of the person doing the speaking. It works because the host is not saying, in an egotistical way, "I'm great. You should sign up for my program, and this person is going to prove it and tell you why. I helped him or her. I can help you, too." It's not "me, me, me, me, me." Instead, it is having a satisfied customer or client share a personal story, which works for several reasons.

First, let's talk about the power of stories. We all love them. We learn from them. We are entertained by them. And we find them in almost every medium—movies, books, and just about everything you can think of—and they relate to people everywhere, in every demographic. Stories even capture the attention of 2-year-olds, who have the attention span of a gnat.

And what does every good story have? Well, let's break it down: First, a story has a protagonist, somebody you relate to. Next, it has a struggle or a challenge or a problem. And then it has the journey, which is what the protagonist does with the problem and how he or she tries to overcome it. And then a story has a resolution, how the protagonist solved the problem and lived happily ever after.

So, when our master enroller called client after client to the stage to share their inspirational stories, with the purpose of showcasing them and providing inspiration to the rest of us, she was tapping into the power of stories to change our lives. And it remained authentic throughout. It was the host's sincere desire to inspire us as participants. She wanted us to believe in ourselves. And so she showcased people, in their own words, unscripted, who started from nothing and accomplished great things. And, of course, in every inspirational story we see ourselves. *Here is a protagonist I can relate to. Here is a struggle or a big problem or challenge I have (or had). Here is the journey the storyteller went through, and you know what? I have experienced a lot of those same challenges that he or she was able to overcome. And if he or she can do it, I can do it, too.*

And how were the storytellers able to overcome those challenges? How were they able to come to their resolution? How did they achieve their transformation? How did they get the results that *I, too, can get* to solve the problem and achieve the level of success that they did? It's through working with this $100,000 coach, of course. And that is basically how the host sold her $100,000-a-year program.

The approach was brilliant. It was poignant. People were crying. It was genuine. These were real people just telling their stories. And it created such a powerful experience that person after person after person got up, walked to the back of the room, and signed a contract for this $100,000-a-year coaching program. It was incredible. And even though I didn't do it, I was truly amazed at how many people did.

Though not everyone bought the $100,000 program, which is common with these types of events, as I mentioned earlier, almost everybody ended up buying something, whether it was a book, a T-shirt, or some other memento. It's sort of like going to a concert, where people want to walk away with something because they want to remember the experience by taking a piece of it with them. And because event organizers understand this, often there will be a pitch for the recordings, which makes perfect sense because it is value added.

During these events, information is coming at you so rapidly, and there is so much of it that it's hard to absorb it all. There are slides being shown on the screen, and there is a charismatic speaker talking fast and telling you stories and giving you examples and strategies and tips and steps. And they give you a workbook and something to take notes on, and they even give you pens to take notes with. And you write furiously, trying to gobble up everything and take in everything. Then, when you go to the back of the room, you find a CD set of the entire thing. Naturally you might want to capture it, take it home with you and relive everything because it was so valuable.

And even though the coach that I referred to earlier had a few alternatives that were less expensive, she wasn't overly absorbed with making smaller product sales. She wanted people to step up for her

$100,000-a-year coaching program. So that's what she focused on. And she sold lots of them.

Now, occasionally she would say something like, "Oh, and I have this 'How to Be an Authentic Speaker' home-study program you might be interested in." She had packaged information products, basically taken from previous workshops, that were available for purchase at the back of the room. But again, she didn't really pitch them. She just mentioned that they were available when the subject came up. And, as an entrepreneur, marketer, and enroller, I found that interesting, as I have some experience with this.

FOCUS ON WHAT YOU REALLY WANT TO SELL

When you enroll, you have a choice of what to focus on and what you want other people to focus on. And one of the things I have learned over the years is that you never, ever, promote something if it is going to sabotage what you really want the customer to buy.

Here's an example: After several years at Relationship Coaching Institute, I saw the need for a practice-building program for my students. So I designed it, launched it, and marketed it. In time, I started marketing it outside RCI, because I recognized that *all* private practice professionals could benefit from the program. I ended up writing and self-publishing a book on the subject and put it on my Web site: *How to Build Your Ideal Practice in 90 Days*.

A couple of years later, I tackled the enrollment part of the equation by self-publishing another book, called *The How to Get Clients Toolkit*. It was 100% about enrollment: how to actually get a prospective client to say yes. Together, the two items made a nice package deal. *How to Build Your Ideal Practice in 90 Days* was the comprehensive, step-by-step overview of how to design, build, and launch your practice and how to market it, and *The How to Get Clients Toolkit* explained how to actually get clients from that effort. I marketed the two books on my Web site individually, and I also marketed them together as a bundle, kind of like Amazon does.

Now, I didn't really want to be in the business of selling books, but I figured that everybody who bought a book would be a qualified prospect for my program. After all, they were qualifying themselves with their purchase, essentially saying, "I want to build a practice and I'm willing to spend money to do it." Naturally, I figured the books would be a great way to get them into my pipeline, the perfect top- or middle-of-funnel products—low barrier to entry and perceived high value—while qualifying the prospects and bringing them into the fold. My thought was that I would end up converting some of those folks to my practice-building program, having them step up from buying the books to spending more money and participating in a live program when they realized that the book by itself wasn't the solution, because, after all, to be successful one needs more mentoring and support than you can get from a book or home-study program.

Some years later, I looked into the numbers and was shocked at the results. I wanted to know how many of the people who bought my books actually signed up for my program. And what I found was— despite all my efforts—getting people to buy my books didn't make them more likely to sign up for my program at all. In fact, people who bought my books were much *less* likely to sign up for my program. Offering those books on my Web site was actually getting in the way. It was sabotaging my desired result. So I pulled those books from my Web site, stopped printing them, and eventually stopped selling them altogether.

Again, the lesson here is that we have the power to focus our own and our prospects' attention, so we want their focus to be on where it would best serve them and also best serve us, creating a win-win. My mistake was that I thought if I focused my prospects' attention on buying a $50 book that provides value but doesn't solve all of their problems, they would take the next step. They didn't. Instead they figured, *Well, if that didn't work, then nothing else is going to work.* That's not how I imagined it, but that's what ended up happening.

It's fine to have a top- and middle-of-funnel service, product, or program that is low cost/low barrier to entry, but you have to be careful. You must track whether those offerings are creating more sales and upsells and helping people step up to your program to get the results they want or whether they are hindering your efforts. Potentially, they could get in the way, so you want to watch out for that. If your lower level services, products, and programs don't solve people's problems, and people expect them to solve those problems, they could be less likely to take the next step to your higher level programs. Your service delivery system must be well defined prior to engaging in the enrollment process. Your services, products, and programs must be lined up in a row so members of your niche will want to progress smoothly through the steps and receive the proportionate value they are looking for at the time they need it.

GROUP EVENTS, INDIVIDUAL RELATIONSHIPS

While it may seem obvious that to enroll groups of people you need to have group events, you must keep in mind that all enrollment happens at the individual level. As a result, you need to be prepared to have individual conversations with people.

The most successful enrollers have enrollment campaigns with plenty of free stuff leading up to the big, live enrollment event. And even many of the workshops or events themselves are free, or at least low cost, such as $49 for the entire weekend. But of all the enrollment events that I have attended over the years, there is one thing the best enrollers have in common: They all provide personal contact—all of them.

With the best enrollers, at a minimum I received a phone call from their staff, and in one case, I actually received a phone call from the host personally. Now for the most part, I receive a voicemail message, because it's rare for me to be available to answer the phone when it rings. But I did get a phone call directly from a host thanking me for signing up for his program, wanting to know if I had any questions, telling me that they were looking forward to seeing me there.

And in each of these cases they already had their money. But still they called to follow up. "Hey, David, this is so-and-so from so-and-so's office. I just wanted to remind you that the tele-seminar you signed up for is coming up. We look forward to having you on the call." It is a nice personal touch.

And in the case where I signed up for a program during the call, there was another thank-you phone call. "David, we see that you signed up for our program while you were on the call; you were one of the first 100 people and we are going to send out your iPod right away. We look forward to having you in the program. Remember: It starts on this date—watch your e-mail inbox. Let us know if you have any questions." And then I was given the leader's name, phone number, and e-mail. It was classy for sure.

And then, because I signed up for a tele-class program—a series of weeks over the telephone and Internet—I received a robocall prior to each one. While clearly a recorded call, it was still the leader of the program, the person I had listened to for 4 hours on the first call and to whom I had paid a significant amount of money. His voice was on my voicemail every week saying, "Hi, this is so-and-so. I'm looking forward to having you join us for our next module, on this date, at this time. Here's the phone number. Make sure to be there."

And then he mentioned other things that he wanted us to make sure to do, like download recordings and access bonuses and things like that. It was very personal. Sure, he was leveraging his time, because he had to record his message only once before it went out to his many participants. But it was a nice, personal touch, something all good group enrollers provide.

AN INDIVIDUAL AMID THE CROWD

If there's one thing I have learned over the years in conducting and participating in group events, it's that people don't want to be treated like a crowd. They want to be treated as individuals. There are a number of ways you, as a host, can do this. And you can do so in ways that do not require you to spend 50 hours a week dialing the telephone all by yourself. You can have staff. You can have a recording. And you can get creative in making a personal connection.

One of the things the host of the tele-class program did was send e-mails saying, "Click here for a recorded message from me." He realized that anything he wrote would just look like *blah-blah-blah* on my computer screen. He wanted me, personally, to experience his voice. He wanted me to experience that direct connection with *him*, not his writing. So he would send me e-mails saying, "I have an important message for you about this, that, and the other. Please click here." And then I would click and listen to his recorded message. So he was leveraging his time, but he was also providing a personal touch. He spoke directly to me, or at least that was the experience I had. As enrollers, we can all do this. Video or audio, the technology is not hard.

GROUP-SPEAK VERSUS YOU-SPEAK

Another thing to keep in mind while conducting enrollment events is the difference between what I call *group-speak* and *you-speak*. Unfortunately, many newbies rely too heavily on group-speak. That is, they don't speak to a group as if it were a group of individuals, they speak to a group as if it were a crowd: "Hello, *everybody*. How are *you all* doing today? Now I don't know about you, but I don't consider myself an *everybody*. I don't consider myself a *you-all*."

The alternative to group-speak is you-speak: "Welcome to our seminar. I'm so glad *you* are here. Thank *you* for being here. How are *you* doing today? Here is what *you* will learn." As an added tip, when addressing an audience about your program, do your best to be selective about your language. While you could say, "Here is what *we* will cover," it is even more powerful to say, "Here is what *you* will learn."

Successful group enrollers have lots of different strategies for making you feel special, some of which we have already covered, like providing a personal touch, "VIP" status, and incentives, like the fast-action bonus and discounts, and making people work for or earn them. For instance, the person who provided the fast-action bonus to me waited 3 hours into the call before offering it. And the bonus was only for the first 100 people and good for only the next 30 minutes. But all of these methods used by master group enrollers are geared toward the same goal.

YES OR NO

The primary goal of any enrollment effort is to help the prospect make a decision—yes or no. If people have qualified themselves (i.e., their very presence tells you they are interested in what you provide), then it's up to you to help them decide whether to move forward. And this is the same for an individual enrollment situation as it is for group enrollment, because if your prospects walk away without making a decision, they will be left in limbo because their lives won't change. And they want their lives to change. That's why they are at your event in the first place. In that sense, it is the worst thing in the world for them not to make a decision—yes or no. "Yes, this is a fit for me—I want to do it" or "No, it is not a fit for me—I'll pass."

And "no" is fine, by the way. We can all live with no. None of us helping professionals want people to pay us money or choose to enroll in something if it is not a good fit for them. For this reason, when it comes to enrollment, we can't be shy. We have to push people to make a decision. And there are several strategies for accomplishing this.

YOU'RE IN THE RIGHT PLACE IF . . .

One of the decision-making strategies for speaking, workshops, and seminars is what I call the *you're in the right place* strategy. I learned this strategy from one of the high-level, successful group enrollers to whom I referred earlier. And here's how it works: You make a list of three to five top benefits or biggest results that somebody would get if they enrolled in your program.

Let's take weight loss. If you wanted to help people be healthy and fit and lose weight, you could issue a series of statements: "If you want to lose 20 pounds and have seemingly unlimited stamina, you're in the right place. If you want to lose weight fast and almost effort-lessly, you're in the right place. If you've been frustrated trying to lose weight in the past and are seeking a lasting weight loss solution that really works, you're in the right place." If it's a good fit, every time you make a statement, prospects are nodding their heads, *Yeah, I want that. Oh, I'm in the right place.*

Getting buy-in from your audience is a principle of effective speaking. So every time you are conducting a seminar or a workshop or an event of any kind, whether it is free or paid, you want people to know what the benefits are. You want them to know what they are going to get out of your program, and, of course, your market research is going to tell you what they really want from you. And then your task is simply to tell them they are going to get it: "You are in the right place if . . . you are in the right place if . . . you are in the right place if . . ." Then they are in the palm of your hand. *Oh, boy, I can't wait for what happens next.*

YOU'RE *NOT* IN THE RIGHT PLACE IF . . .

The corollary strategy that I have seen work well (and it may seem counterintuitive, but is effective) is to let people know who does *not* belong at your event. "You're not in the right place if you're looking for a get-rich-quick scheme. You're not in the right place if you want to lose weight with no effort at all, or by sitting on your couch. You're not in the right place if you want to rip people off, take their money, and deliver no value."

Here you are challenging people. You are letting them know that you want to work with only a select group of people. You are not there to enroll just anybody. You are looking for certain individuals who qualify. The effect you want to create is people feeling good about themselves if they qualify. *I'm smart enough to know that this is not a get-rich-quick scheme. I qualify because I know that I'm not going to be able to lose weight by sitting on my couch. I belong here.*

Of course, many professionals are scared to death of this strategy because they don't want to turn anybody away or turn anybody off. But again, the beauty of the strategy comes in its ability to push people to make a decision. *Is this for me?* Yes or no. *Am I in the right place?* Yes or no. *Am I going to sign up or not?* Yes or no. You must shake your prospects from complacency and help them definitively decide whether to enroll in your program and change their life in ways that they want and need.

Again, the worst nightmare for private practice professionals trying to enroll clients—and for potential participants—is, "Well, I'll think about it" or, "I'm not going to make a decision right now." Remember, all of your enrollment activity is designed to get people out of indecision and into action. And you can't be quiet about it. Challenging them with what your program is *not* helps them feel good about themselves to the point where they will step up and take the necessary action, giving them the transformation that they need and that you are confident you will provide.

ENROLLMENT EXERCISES

I've also seen enrollment strategies at events framed as exercises. "Okay, I have an exercise for you. I want you to write down the top five results or benefits that you believe you could get from this program. And then I want you to write down the top five reasons *not* to do this program." Here you are walking people through an exercise that helps them make a decision. *Well, gee, these are the top five things I could get, and these are the top five things I can think of that are reasons not to do this program . . . though most of them seem pretty ridiculous . . . but hey, there is this one thing . . . maybe I need to look into it.*

You are getting people in touch with the information they need or the questions they need to have answered or the reservations they need to have addressed so that they can move forward. In any good enrollment conversation you will have anticipated objections ahead of time, and when they do come up you of course want to have a strategy for handling them. But it is even more effective to address them before they come up.

In the preceding example, you are helping prospects get in touch with whatever might be holding them back. But then comes the next step in the exercise: "Where do you imagine yourself in a year, after having done this program?" It's this line of questioning that often puts people over the top. *Oh, my gosh, if I do this program, and I get these results, and a year later my life is like this? Wow! Where do I sign?*

TIMING IS EVERYTHING

Now, I must caution you that these types of exercises would not be effective at the beginning of a seminar or marketing campaign. And they wouldn't be effective at home, over the telephone. They also wouldn't be effective as mere intellectual exercises. But they are *incredibly* effective when they are performed in the moment, at the point when participants need to decide yes or no. Here the participants have already had an intense experience with you, and of themselves, learning some cool stuff, getting inspiration from other people like them, getting in touch with their pain and their desire. That's where the power of these exercises can be found.

And just as a story has the protagonist, the challenge, the journey, and the resolution, a campaign has its own components that make it a whole system. It's analogous to a story in that it is a journey you are taking together with the people whom you attract into your pipeline. And the whole enrollment process is a story in itself, where the people have their internal struggle (should I or shouldn't I?), and you are helping them resolve that struggle. You are walking them through a process. You are giving them an experience in which you are challenging them to say yes or no. You are challenging them to take action. You are challenging them to move. The moment is here. The moment is now.

As someone who wants to make a difference in people's lives, you can't let up. You must bring out another inspirational story, throw out another bonus, and keep right on going. By the end of the event, people will surely be exhausted, and just about every person whom you could have possibly reached, who remained available to make a decision, will have made that decision. That's the magic of group enrollment.

True, there are always people who are not going to be able to make a decision. They are too scared. They are too apathetic. They are at your event out of curiosity, or they were dragged there by someone and are not really a good fit. You don't have to worry about them. But know that everybody who sticks it out for the duration of an intense experience is there for a reason. They are highly qualified candidates, and you want to work with them, connect with them, support them, challenge them, and get them to make that decision — yes or no. Of course, it doesn't end after that. Next you have your follow-up.

FOLLOW-UP

Remember, just as in marketing and enrolling with individuals, at any one point in time in a group setting you will have your three core constituencies to deal with: the bluebirds, the boulders, and those in between.

If you remember, bluebirds are the ones who are easy to sell. They love you, they are easily convinced, and they sign up for whatever you put out with very little effort. Boulders are interested and attracted enough to be there and to stick through the event for the value that they can get from it, but they haven't bought anything. And they are not going to buy anything. But they want to stay connected. They want to continue to receive value from you. They might end up stepping up and buying something a year or two later, maybe when their life situation is more ready for it. And maybe they will end up telling other people about you.

Incidentally, I have received lots and lots of referrals from people, who, when asked how they found out about me, said something like, "Oh, I found out about you from so-and-so." Yet I had no idea who so-and-so was! So-and-so was not in my database. So-and-so was never a customer or a client. What that tells me is that somebody, somehow, experienced me and thought enough of me to speak well of me to at least one other person, and probably lots more. So, if boulders don't buy from you, not only might they nonetheless tell other people about you, they might still buy from you or sign up for your program in the future. Your job is to follow up with them, keeping them informed of your latest offerings and making sure to answer any ongoing questions they may have.

The third group of people you need to concern yourself with are the ones who are there, who are interested, who are attracted, who are ready for the next step—but who don't want to take a big step. They don't want to take a big risk; they don't want to spend much money. They are ready for something small and safe.

If we realize that in any group we have these three constituencies of people whom we want to reach with our mission and our message—bluebirds, boulders, and the ones who are ready for something small and safe—we should also realize that we need to have something to offer all of them: your $100,000 a year program for the bluebirds, your $149 home-study program for the ones who need something small and safe, and your next free way to play and feel special for the boulders.

If you go to milliondollarpractice.net, you will see that I have a free membership in my practice-building network whereby I provide value to my free members. I conduct regular tele-seminars, I have free content, special reports, and recorded audio programs. If you take a look at it all together, it is a valuable selection of material and content. There is a lot there, and it would take you a long time to get through all of it.

I structure this particular Web site, for this particular business and this particular group, as a free membership for a reason. I don't even have a newsletter list opt-in. I don't want to publish a newsletter for them. I don't want them to just read something from me as a way to stay in touch. I would rather have them show up on a tele-seminar with me. I want to give the boulders the option of becoming free members. They can get something valuable, and continue to get it, until they are ready to move. And that's okay.

Looking at my database, I can see people who have been free members of my system for a decade or more. And they haven't bought anything. Chances are, if they are still in my system, they are still receiving my e-mail announcements and reminders about the free programs and other goodies. If people don't like what you have to offer and you send them stuff and they are annoyed and they get off your list, then they are unqualifying themselves, saying, "Sorry, not interested." Again, that is okay. But if they stay on your list, and they stay and they stay and they stay, and they continue to not buy, that is okay, too. They are likely spreading the word about you. They are valuable. You don't need everybody to buy from you. But you can also do your market research with them and find out why they haven't bought or signed up and what it is they would buy or sign up for. Then you can create it.

Your boulders are your most valuable asset. They are the ones who are going to help you learn the most about your niche and about how best to serve them and market to them and enroll them. Most of us practitioners think of boulders as stubborn or resistant, and we get frustrated. But our boulders are our best teachers. Design your services, products, and programs for your boulders, as well as those in between them and the bluebirds, and build things into your marketing and your service delivery system to provide value to them and keep them connected with you, like my free membership program.

After you have conducted your enrollment event, and everybody is spent, there will be a feeling of satisfaction. Your participants will have received lots of value. They will have been pushed and challenged and applauded and encouraged and inspired. For the bluebirds, the next step will be to start working with you. For a number of the people in the middle, they may buy your back-of-the-room home-study course or other product. The boulders, however, will merely stay on your list. They may even participate in the next round. And if you do an annual big enrollment event, they will be there next year, best-case scenario, which is a good thing.

FOCUSING ON YOUR CURRENT CLIENTS

There is a principle of business, with which I totally agree, stating that it is far easier and more effective to sell to your existing customers than it is to get new customers. Unfortunately, this is something practitioners routinely forget about, as they are always seeking new clients. But what we need to do, in addition to marketing to new blood, is to continue to offer things to meet the needs of the people whom we have already served or are currently serving. They are already our fans. They have already benefited from working with us. And their needs don't end with your latest program. If you really want to make a difference in the world and to be there for them in your area of expertise, you need to anticipate or determine what their next need is, as well as the next need after that . . . and the next need after that. You must continue to roll out new services, products, and programs to meet the current and ongoing needs of the people whom you have already attracted and have already served.

219

Focusing on current clients as a way to build your following, rather than make sales, is a far easier and more effective path to a Million Dollar Practice. Your following, essentially bluebirds, show up and sign up for whatever you put out there. Most everything you do and design is for them. And it's a symbiotic relationship. With them, you are not really trying to make sales. Sure, you want to reach more new people and get them to sign up and pay you money. And you will. But if you are not taking care of the people who are already following you, the ones who have already signed up and whom you are already serving, then you will have a revolving door. If your current customers are not deliriously happy with you, continuing to buy from you, and continuing to work with you, your business will suffer. Not taking care of your existing client base results in churn, in which you always need new people to sustain your business. And that's a very hard way to go.

Again, you will know you're doing a good job when your clients don't want to go. As private practitioners, we don't want to encourage dependence, but we also believe it is hard for our clients to be successful without ongoing support of some kind. So we need to design a system that continues to support ever-increasing levels of functionality and accomplishment for the people we want to serve. That is not dependence, it is leveraging the support of others.

Besides, new customers will be much more attracted to you and willing to sign up for your programs when they see that your existing customers are such rabid fans, who won't go away, who think you are great, and who talk you up. On the one hand, potential clients might be suspicious, thinking your customers are drinking the Kool-Aid or that they are being brainwashed. *What's going on here? Is this some sort of cult?* On the other hand, if they are genuinely interested in the result that you promise, the result they see other people getting from you, they will be more willing to check you out.

So, anytime you are engaging in the enrollment process, you want to have happy customers, and continue to sell to those happy customers, because those happy customers will attract other customers. And those happy customers will do your enrollment for you. Every new customer has unlimited potential and is that much closer to becoming a bluebird. It all depends upon what you do with them once they are in the door. Remember, at some level, as long as you are delivering at or beyond the level of your promises with each transaction, your marketing will become effortless. When you have enough people who are happy with what you do and talk you up, and when you have a large enough organization and have reached a large enough number of people, you will become the go-to person in your niche, and people will start coming to you. You won't have to go to them. They will start signing up on their own, with very little effort, which is what we private practice professionals often dream about: that time when our marketing becomes effortless and we don't have to worry about it anymore.

SYNERGY

My first experience with group enrollment was conducting weekly singles events. Over time, I built a following and had a regular stable of participants. Those were the people who signed up for my classes and workshops. And they got a lot of value from those classes and workshops and from meeting other singles and being part of a singles community. As a result, they continued to show up every Friday night. When we would announce our next class or workshop from the front of the room at those events, I generally was not the one announcing them. I was in the back of the room. At this point, I was letting other people run the show. I was there. I was still the leader. It was my organization. But I was empowering other people to take functional roles. I didn't want to be in the front of the room all the time. I didn't want attendee relationships to be just with me.

After a while, as I was in the back of the room and somebody else was in the front of the room announcing the next workshop or class, I would notice time and again one person leaning over to the next person, giving that person a little nudge, and saying things like, "Oh, you've got to take this class. It's really cool." It was a wonderful validation and endorsement to have somebody who took our class or participated in one of our workshops willing to sell and promote us to somebody else. I witnessed this right before my eyes. And it was heartwarming. At the same time, it struck me how powerful it was, as a private practice professional, to provide a way for existing customers to intermingle with people who have not yet signed up.

This is an effective technique employed by most personal growth organizations. They host regular events in which they invite their participants and members to bring guests. When you get true believers together in a room with people who are finding out about you for the first time, and then they see how people love you and how much benefit they have gotten from working with you, the endorsement is priceless. There is a lot of powerful synergy in creating an enrollment event in which you have existing customers in the same room with potential customers and somehow you get them talking.

In my case, I didn't plan to get them talking. It just happened. Existing customers were sitting next to potential customers, and they just felt a need to share. *Hey, this is a cool class. You should check it out.* When you take care of your existing customers, not only are they your best customers for anything else you put out, but they are also your best salespeople. Sometimes this translates into promoting affiliate programs or multilevel marketing, whereby your existing customers sell your services, products, and programs and get a percentage.

But in the case I just mentioned, it wasn't done for money. The people who endorsed our programs were not motivated by commissions. They were just honest fans looking to spread the word in the hope that someone else could benefit like they did. And, given the opportunity to talk to somebody else who may be interested in what you do but who is undecided about whether it's a good idea, they are happy to share their experience.

At Relationship Coaching Institute, we go so far as to invite prospective members to contact any of our current members—anybody. In fact, we tell them "Do your due diligence. Check us out. Go on our Web site, choose a couple of our members at random, contact them, and ask them about Relationship Coaching Institute. Ask them if they would recommend it." Almost always, as a result of their research, prospective members are convinced to sign up. In a way, it is almost unfair. Our members are happy with our trainings and our programs and our support. Most of them are true believers; otherwise, they wouldn't stay members. They are existing customers and wouldn't be in our community unless they were satisfied. Still, it speaks to their level of satisfaction. And if you are a consumer considering paying money or making a commitment and signing up for something, it is inarguably a good idea to talk to somebody who has already done it. "What was it like for you? What did you get out of it? How did it work for you?"

From the other side of the equation, as a private practice professional in pursuit of new clients, it's a powerful and effective enrollment technique to have existing clients or customers talk with prospective clients or customers. You can facilitate that. You can coordinate that. You can extend the invitation. You can make it happen. You just have to decide how you want to structure it.

In my case, I will never forget the first time I witnessed the synergistic phenomenon in the back of the room during my singles events. And as soon as I started noticing it, I also realized that every one of our classes filled up. They didn't fill up because we were pitching them and convincing anybody to sign up. They filled up because our past participants were helping us promote them. They were talking up our classes to the prospective participants.

So, if you are providing a community for the people in your niche, not only is that service beneficial to them, but it provides an ongoing way that your fans and followers can talk you up and promote you to the people you want to reach so that they can benefit from your services. What a wonderful win-win—when the best way to market and enroll also happens to provide great value for the people you want to serve. As long as you do the necessary prep work, outlined in the previous chapters, and then apply the lessons here on a group level, you, too, can become a master enroller and join the ranks of those who have used these skills to build a Million Dollar Practice.

Million Dollar Questions for Chapter 7

1. What is it about "selling" that is uncomfortable to you? What approach to "enrollment" would feel good to you?

2. Why have your prospects not enrolled in the past (if you don't know—ask!)? What can you do differently next time?

3. What are the top five benefits or results your niche wants most? (Use this in your marketing and enrollment. For example, "If you want _____, you're in the right place.")

4. What are the 10 most common questions or reservations your prospects have about your program? (Create a FAQ and prepare effective answers.)

5. How can you connect your satisfied customers and clients with your prospective customers and clients to support your enrollment efforts?

CHAPTER EIGHT

Building Your Million Dollar Practice

Philip Reynolds Jr. came to Campbell from East San Jose, a notorious gangland in northern California. After seeing firsthand the destructive turn a community can take, he made it his mission to stop it.

Phil is a good guy with a passion. He believes in the power of neighborhood associations not only to create great environments for the residents of those neighborhoods, but to create them for the good of the community as a whole, one neighborhood at a time. And he speaks from experience.

A telephone lineman by trade, Phil has donated much of his spare time over the years to community activism. He has a history of organizing residents into neighborhood associations, cleaning up areas, getting the gangs out, creating neighborhood watches and neighborhood events, and creating cohesive, vital, family-friendly communities out of areas where nobody wanted to walk alone at night.

When he moved to Campbell, Phil ran for city council, advocating for strong neighborhoods. Though he lost his bid for public office, largely because he didn't have the necessary budget or business-oriented backers, he didn't let that quell his passion. Today he continues to volunteer his time helping people put together neighborhood associations, making a difference in the community as a private citizen.

Phil's passion—though until recently he had never thought of it this way, and in this regard he is no different from many of us—is a seed that, if properly nurtured, could potentially grow into a Million Dollar Practice.

FILLING A NEED

I got to know Phil over a period of several months and came to appreciate him. He has been helping us out with Campbell Working Together and has been involved with several other community initiatives. In fact, it seems that whenever I turn around now—because I, too, am involved in the community—he is there: city council meetings, community events, you name it.

The more I learned about Phil and his passions, the more I saw his potential for effecting change. I even did some research trying to find books, articles, or other information on how to create and develop neighborhood associations. And while there was lots of information about addressing gang problems, really severe stuff, there was almost nothing on run-of-the-mill neighborhoods and communities. This is a real shame, as many areas could benefit from creating neighborhood associations to deal with regular, functional—or slightly dysfunctional—community issues. And Campbell is a perfect example.

Everybody loves Campbell. It is considered to be a family-friendly place; it has a nice downtown; and the residents tend to be happy. People come from neighboring communities to take part in a variety of festivals and see what else we have going on. We are generally a functional bunch, but like most communities made up of a collection of human beings, we have our share of problems. They don't rise to the level of gangs, but we do have challenges. And Phil lives and breathes this stuff. His passion, combined with his sincerity, knowledge, and willingness to help, position him well to own this niche.

LEVERAGING YOUR PASSION

Over the course of several conversations, I planted the idea with Phil that perhaps he was missing his calling by being a telephone lineman and could in fact build a business around his passion: building better neighborhoods and communities. And he could do it on a global scale.

While Phil made it clear that he wasn't yet ready to let go of his job at the telephone company—and all of the benefits and security that come along with it—he did say that he would be retiring in a few years and wanted to look beyond retirement. He was excited about my idea and requested a meeting to discuss it further.

Darlene and I met with Phil over coffee and talked for a couple of hours, and our discussion unfolded like any other marketing and business-building consultation. We talked about all of the different ways that he could monetize his passion, market his business, and build a Million Dollar Practice. We talked about how he could write a book, put together a "toolkit" with forms and instructions for starting a neighborhood association, do workshops and seminars, get consulting and speaking gigs, conduct trainings, even start a nonprofit and pursue corporate sponsorships. We explored the many ways that he could leverage his passion, experience, and track record of cleaning up bad parts of town through neighborhood associations and make a larger difference in the world.

My general take was that if Phil became the go-to person who owned the niche for how to create and build great neighborhood associations and turn them into great neighborhoods, he would attract more clients than he would know what to do with. As our meeting evolved, it became apparent that Phil had a strong and clear mission and message and was excited about the potential to one day build a Million Dollar Practice.

As our discussion was coming to a close, I asked Phil, "If you had to come up with a domain name or a title of a book around your passion, what would it be?" After brainstorming all sorts of ideas, as we were standing up and about to finish, Phil said, "How about the Neighborhood Guru?"

We all loved it.

Now What?

Here is a man who is sincerely being of service, who has a mission and a message that strong neighborhood associations help create strong neighborhoods and that strong neighborhoods help create strong communities, and who really wants to promote that. And it's all there right in front of him—I even had one of my Web guys put up a Web site for him, www.neighborhood-guru.com, as a way to support and inspire him into action. He is now on the cusp of going from Phil Reynolds Jr., good guy with a passion, to building a national or international brand—The Neighborhood Guru—around a mission and a message that can make a big difference in communities throughout the world.

Phil Reynolds's story is a wonderful example of somebody who discovered his passion, mission, and message and who is at the beginning stages of doing something about it. And remember, Phil works for the phone company. He is one of those guys you see climbing up telephone poles, trying to find the disconnection in the grid. He is not somebody who thought he would ever be an expert in anything, be invited to speak anywhere, or have anything of real value to offer anybody. And if he did, he certainly didn't think he could find anyone willing to pay him for it. But now he's getting it: *Hey, I have something of value that not very many people have, and there is a need and a market for it. Now what?*

While our degrees, licenses, and expertise may vary, we have a passion and a mission and a message inside all of us, even when we least suspect it. And we have the power, with a little help from good mentors and the tools in this book, to act on our passion. This model can work for anybody and everybody. We all have the inherent ability to build a Million Dollar Practice. We just have to be aware of some fundamental principles—which, as we close out this book, we will now reiterate from previous chapters, with some new concepts thrown in for good measure—starting with reaching the necessary level of entrepreneurial development to use them.

ENTREPRENEURIAL DEVELOPMENT

Over a recent holiday weekend, my wife and I took our family up to the mountains to enjoy the snow. Sitting and relaxing one day, we began talking about our kids and how they are still partly "little kid" and yet partly very mature. As parents, it is clear and obvious to us when our kids are being self-centered and when they are being considerate of others. And you applaud the steps that your kids make when they evolve to the point where, instead of saying, "I don't want to go to that party because it's boring," they say, "I'll go to that party because it's family. And Mom and Dad want to go, so I'll do it for them." It takes a higher level of development for a kid to embrace that kind of thinking.

As an entrepreneur, it takes a higher level of development to focus on the needs of your clients and their reality than to focus on the reality of you as the expert. After all, you have so much schooling and education and training, and you have that title, and you have that license or certification or whatever, right? Ego often causes us to believe we know what we are doing and what we are talking about.

LONGBOARDING

Let me take the analogy a little further. Recently, I was having a conversation at dinner with one of my sons. His birthday was coming up, and he told me he wanted a longboard. At first, my wife and I thought he was talking about surfing, a common thing to do in our part of the world. But no, he was talking about something else.

As my son dutifully explained, a longboard is a long skateboard.

"Oh, I've seen them on the street," I said. "What would you do with a longboard that you couldn't do with a regular skateboard?"

I can't say I remember his exact response, but I can tell you that whatever it was, I essentially processed it as, "My friends and I are going to go down steep hills and around treacherous curves at 90 miles an hour."

"No way!" my wife and I said. And my wife, a former nurse, promptly began relating firsthand accounts of teenagers showing up in hospital emergency rooms with dangling limbs and horrific cases of road rash — and worse. She soberly added, "You could die."

My son, to our astonishment, responded, "Well, my friends go down Highway 9 on their longboards."

Highway 9 is a mountainous, curvy road, and it's one of the major routes to get you over the hill from Silicon Valley to Santa Cruz. As the name implies, it's a highway, for crying out loud! *Wait, these kids are actually going to skateboard on a highway?!*

In my son's mind, and it is glaringly obvious, *Nothing bad's going to happen to me. I know what I'm doing. I'll be fine. It'll be fun.*

My wife and I, however, are of course looking at this as an accident waiting to happen. *If this kid gets on a longboard on Highway 9, he's going to tumble over a cliff, he's going to get hit by a car, he's going to take a fall, and wind up in the hospital—and he could die!*

While not quite as dramatic, I liken this scenario to what I often see while mentoring private practice professionals. "Oh, I know what I'm doing. I know what's good for my clients. Nothing bad's going to happen." And in my head I see them on a longboard, winding down Highway 9, a disaster waiting to happen.

REMEMBER THE PLATINUM RULE

Practitioners headed for disaster haven't quite grasped the Golden Rule versus the Platinum Rule. It's ego versus truly being of service. It's being blinded by what you know and what is going on in your own head versus learning what your niche wants and having an open mind to providing it.

Conscious Dating was developed because I truly had an open mind. I had a blank slate. I knew nothing, and I wanted to learn. As I write this 15 years later, I am launching a Conscious Dating app, which I discuss in more detail in the epilogue. When I first set foot on this path, I had no idea that I would one day publish a book, or start a certification program for professionals, or launch an app that can potentially reach billions of people across the planet.

As a private practice professional, you must resist the urge to live in your own head and, as I like to say, believe your own bull****. When kids do it, it just seems so ridiculous. "You're going to skateboard down Highway 9? Are you crazy?" And yet, as private practice professionals, we do it all the time. "Oh, this is the best way to go. This is what will work. Why? Because I think so." No, instead you should consider the best interests of your target audience.

MAKING THE CASE

The best and strongest case I can make for the Platinum Rule is that it works. For people who need to wake up and shift how they are thinking and what they are doing, I need only ask them a simple question: "How is it working for you?" If it's not working for you, then you need to change what you are doing, how you are thinking, and how you are approaching things.

If you are being responsive to what people want and need, it will work. If you are putting out what sounds good to you, what you want to do, if you are practicing the Golden Rule and it's not working, if they don't want to buy it, that's why your business is coming up short. If you find yourself feeling stuck and frustrated and experiencing a ceiling with your earnings because you are doing the same thing over and over and over, because that is what you are trained to do and that's all you want to do, and then you find that your practice is dwindling, well guess what? You are not being responsive to your target audience—maybe you haven't even chosen a target audience. You are still focused on what it is you want to do rather than who you want to serve and how best to serve them. And that's a problem.

One of the goals of this book has been to bring clarity to what works and what doesn't work, how to serve people and what doesn't really serve them, and how we get in our own way. That clarity is valuable and important, because without it we are going to believe that we are doing great work and that people should hire us. But they are not going to hire us, and they are certainly not going to pay us what we think we are worth. As a result, we are going to be angry and frustrated at them. But it's not their fault. It's our fault. We alone as private practice professionals have the capacity to craft for our niche the best services, products, and programs to address their needs and wants and to price them accordingly.

THE LAW OF ATTRACTION

There comes a pivotal point, a fork in the road, in the life of every private practice professional where you must determine whether to stick to your price point or open yourself up to negotiation. On one path is where you cater to people's anxieties and stories about how much they think they can afford or whether they trust that you can deliver. That path is fear-based. The other path is the path of abundance, where you believe all of the resources, including money, that you need to be successful will appear. It's the path of success. The path of fulfillment. The path of realizing your vision.

If what you want is 100%, only one path that will take your there: the path of self-confidence. The path of getting into action. The path of learning what it is you need to know and getting the support you need and staying focused and making progress toward your goals. The other path is where you settle for less than you want or deserve: *Well, I really want 100%, but I don't think it's possible or that it is really going to happen for me, so I'll just take whatever I can get.*

In the relationship world, I have learned that those of us who have low self-esteem or don't think we deserve love tend to get involved in relationships that don't meet our needs. That's all we know. As a relationship coach, especially working with singles, I support people going after what they really want, not what they think they can get. It's no different with building your private practice. Identify what you want, go after it, and don't ever settle for less. Don't be content in your relationship or your business with 80%. Go for 100%. Don't tell yourself, *This is the best I can find, and I have to take this or nothing.* And certainly don't tell yourself, *This is the most I can charge, and I must accept this offer or my business will fail.*

When we open the door of settling, then that is what the law of attraction brings us: less than what we really want, and more and more settling. When you open the door to negotiating your rates with a client, what does that bring? It brings more clients who want you to negotiate your rates. When you draw the line in the sand and say "This is how much I charge. If you want to work with me, this is what it takes," then you attract clients who step up to that, who want that, and who respect that. And those are the clients you want. You don't want to work with the clients who question your value, who don't trust that you can deliver on your promises, and who want to negotiate your rate down to as low as possible and still work with you. Working with those folks isn't good for you or them.

Again, it's the law of attraction in action. And the law of attraction can work for you or against you. When you set the bar high and stick to it, you become successful and ultimately better positioned to help your clients become successful. You can build that Million Dollar Practice and help them with their problems and goals. But you hit a slippery slope the minute you start negotiating, thinking, *Oh, well, what can they afford? How low do I need to go to make them say yes?* Those are the wrong questions. The right questions are, *What can I do to motivate and inspire them—the ones who really want it, the ones with whom I really want to work, the ones who can best benefit from this program—to say yes to a high price point? How can I motivate and inspire them to say yes to my $2,000 offering?* It's not, *Well, I really want $2,000, but I don't think people will pay more than $495.*

While true helping professionals are not in business for the money, there is a need for us to make money. And there is a phenomenon at work in which people benefit from what they invest in. And the more money they pay, the more benefit they tend to get, as long as we do a good job, hold them accountable, and support them to get there. Money is an exchange of value; it is something we need to pay our bills and achieve our goals, but it is not the primary objective or motivator.

Still, there is a pivotal decision point that everybody encounters, in some form, multiple times in their lives. When you reach the crossroads, what's it going to be? Right or left? Toward abundance, success, and what you really want? Or toward scarcity, mediocrity, and *Well, no, I don't think that's really going to happen, so this is the best I can do.* Only you can decide.

INTEGRITY

Along the way, you must identify and stick to your core values and apply them to determining whom you want to help. I have seen, for example, practitioners choose niches because they think those niches will be more profitable; because they think the people in a given niche can afford a particular service, product, or program; or because they think it will be easier to market to them. These are the professionals who sign up for "Marketing to Millionaires" workshops. And I have seen them altogether dismiss the niche that they really want to serve because they don't think their desired target audience can afford them, or they don't see a path to creating a business with that niche. I see people talk themselves out of what they really want to do all the time. And it is always out of fear. Our clients do this as well. That's why our clients need us. But we are human, so we are like our clients. We do this to ourselves. We need to ask ourselves, *What would I recommend to clients who are experiencing fear and are at risk of sabotaging their goals and making choices not in alignment with what they really want?* And when we determine the answers, we have to consider doing that for ourselves.

All of this is part of integrity. It's realizing how similar you are to your clients, rather than being superior to them. And it's being willing to do the work yourself, not expecting your clients to do anything that you haven't done or are not willing to do. If you haven't paid $2,000 for a program, I wouldn't expect anybody to pay you $2,000. If you haven't hired a coach for $500 a month, I wouldn't expect hoards of people to pay you $500 a month for your coaching services. It's called walking your talk.

WALKING YOUR TALK

In my office, I have three computer monitors on my desk, and on one of them is a sticky note with a principle relating to walking your talk and being in integrity as a practitioner. I keep that note in front of me whenever I'm working. It is my wording and paraphrasing of something I heard somebody else say, and I don't even know who that somebody else was, but it goes like this:

> *Investing in yourself will help your prospective clients see the value of investing in you.*

Being willing to invest in yourself and your own learning and your own growth and your own need for support, and addressing your own vulnerabilities and weaknesses, gives people confidence in you. If you are not willing to invest in yourself, if you are going to be in the business of helping people yet are not going to work on the challenges that you are expecting to get paid to help others face, then it should comes as no surprise if they run away from you. Again, the law of attraction can work against you. Yes, you might get clients if you don't invest in yourself, but you are not going to be successful. Your performance and credentials are likely not going to build positive buzz or word of mouth. People are not going to get excited about you. Chances are, they are going to be slightly uncomfortable with you, and they won't be sure why. And the reason is that you do not have integrity. You are not walking your talk. You are not on the path that you expect them to take. If you are truly keeping at heart the best interests of your clients and not just trying to make a sale, your self-investment will shine brightly.

THE PRACTITIONER VERSUS THE SALESMAN

There is a difference between a practitioner and a salesman. A practitioner is somebody who really wants to be of service and help people and who sees the value in what he or she does for him/herself as well. Practitioners have experienced what they are doing with others. They have worked on healing. They have worked on personal growth. They have walked their talk. They have been on a path similar to or the same as the people whom they help. They have training. They have experience. They have expertise. Therefore, people are willing to pay them, and they deserve to be paid well because they are genuinely able to help people achieve the results that they really want.

The salesman, however, is somebody who simply wants to make the sale. Salesmen are after the money. They don't care what it is they are selling. It could be a car. It could be a house. It could be a $2,000 program. They don't really care. All they know is they want people to buy it so they can get paid. They will mold themselves and do or say whatever they think they need to say. In the business of helping people, though, where you have to have that know, like, and trust factor, salesmen are not trusted. You don't get the genuine vibe. People are intuitive. People know whether something feels good, right, and in alignment—and whether it doesn't—even if they don't know why.

I'm not saying salesmen can't build a Million Dollar Practice, but the odds are against them. You are much more likely to become wildly successful if you can appreciate that we are all in the people business. And you are best positioned to leverage that fact if you are a true practitioner.

THE HERO'S JOURNEY — MAKING IT NECESSARY

Now I don't mean to suggest that any of this will be easy. It can be scary, and there is a lot at stake. But that's why I refer to it as a hero's journey. Along the way, we will certainly experience fear and doubt. But the question is, "What do we do with that?" Remember, the short way is the long way, and the long way is the short way. Going the long way might seem daunting, but it is the shortest, most sure path to success. You must be willing to embrace that long path. And you know what? As the adage points out, it is never as long as we fear it is going to be.

When I launched my relationship coaching practice, I had no idea whether it would succeed or fail. I tried to increase the odds of success by doing some market research, conducting a pilot project, and getting people on board even before I launched. And it was motivated by fear: *What if I have a party and nobody comes? What if I offer a relationship coaching service and nobody wants it?* After all, it was a profession that few knew about at the time.

So, when I launched my new venture, I had no idea whether it would be successful, but I did know I was committed. I knew it was what I wanted to do, and I didn't want to do anything else. And when that is where you are coming from, you have no choice. In my case, there was no other job I wanted or was willing to do, so I had to make it work. And as it happened, I filled my practice within the first 3 months. It surprised me, and I was ecstatic about that, but when I first launched I was scared to death. I didn't want to go back to doing therapy. I didn't want to go back to working for nonprofit agencies for minimal wages. I didn't want to take a job in restaurants or in a high-tech industry. Working to build relationships was the only thing I wanted to do. So it was necessary. And necessity is the mother of invention.

Despite what happened with me, I see and have worked with a lot of people — many of them are even in my organization at

Relationship Coaching Institute—who don't make it *necessary*. They want it, but their fear causes them to take timid steps forward. They don't really commit. They don't take that risk, and they don't take that leap of faith. Now, I don't believe that you should jeopardize your ability to provide for your family and to pay your bills. On the contrary, I respect that, and it was part of what made it necessary for me to succeed. But you must ask yourself, *Am I making this choice out of fear? Or am I making it out of wisdom? Is this the wise course, or is this the fear-based course? And if it's fear-based, am I appropriately channeling that fear?*

Getting Support

Often we have trouble gauging things for ourselves. We fool ourselves. We think we know, but we don't. It's pretty opaque. We need a coach or a mentor, somebody who has accomplished what we want to accomplish, who understands our plight, who has walked the path and can clearly see things that we can't see. Coaches and mentors can be our guides, and they can tell us whether we are coming from fear or from wisdom and how best to proceed.

We function best when we don't try to do it all by ourselves, because we tend to talk ourselves into and out of things. We create stories that come from fear. And because this is a hero's journey, and because we all have fear and doubts and self-doubts, we must get support so that we are not staying in our comfort zones, holding back, playing it safe, pricing things affordably because we are afraid that nobody will pay a higher price for it—all because we are afraid it might not work. These are all self-fulfilling prophecies.

And when you have the necessary support and you are focused on the needs of your clients, you will gain the necessary energy and strength and get into action to overcome your fear and doubt and play a bigger game. This will allow you to help more people and make the kind of money you deserve in the process.

The root of it all lies in being customer-service-oriented, in doing it for your clients. Speaking from experience, I know that if I focus on me, then all of my stuff comes out. *Can I really do this? Do I deserve this? Is this really going to work? What if I fail?* But if I focus on being of service to them, it is freeing. It gives me the energy and inspiration to show up for them, help them, and meet their needs. This mind-set and approach has always propelled me into action and helped me make the hard choices that will pay off in the end.

THE RIGHT FIT

In my experience, when you are the right person—meaning that you have expertise, you have experience, you are coming from a place of service, you are passionate about your niche and how you want to help them, you are connecting with the right people, and you are committed—then you will be successful. If you are struggling, you must answer these questions: Are you the right person? Are you ready? Are you prepared? Do you have the expertise or experience? Do you have the track record? Do you have the commitment? Do you have the passion? Are you connecting with the right target audience?

If your answer to any of these questions poses a problem, it is solvable. You can *become* the right person. You can modify your target audience. True, if you take a series of marketing and enrollment tactics, and you are not the right person or you are not connecting with the right target audience, it's not going to work. However, given those same marketing tactics, if you are the right person, connecting with the right target audience, it will work.

When you are the right fit, success happens a lot faster than you can imagine. This is the filling-your-practice-in-90-days phenomenon. When I developed my singles events, I was the right person, connecting with the right target audience, and it happened more quickly than I could have ever imagined. But I didn't know it was going to be that quick. I didn't know it was going to be successful. All I knew was that I was committed, because there was absolutely nothing else I wanted to do. But it turned out that I was the right fit.

Now, you should certainly set a long-term timeline. You should expect it to take a long time. Don't bank on fast results. Expect incremental results. But there is nothing wrong with adopting a philosophy of optimistic pessimism, or *"hope for the best, but prepare for the worst."*

I'm prepared for my ideas not to work at all. But I am always hopeful that they will be great. And I am always committed to whatever it is I do. I am going to do it no matter what. But be prepared to be surprised. If you are the right person, connecting with the right target audience, success can happen really fast, in a big way. And it's wonderful when it does.

THE UPHILL CLIMB

Choosing the downhill trail, the one that seems easy in the short term, is often chosen when we are feeling lazy and full of fear that we won't be able to make it all the way up the uphill trail. But when we focus on our clients, it is much more palatable to take the uphill trail, even though we know it is fraught with obstacles and challenges. Now, I suppose there are charismatic people who are great salesmen and who are successful at getting other people to carry them to the top of the mountain. I would say they are the exception, not the rule. But for the rest of us, when stepping onto the uphill trail, we at least know that we are doing it for the right reasons: *This could be very successful very quickly, or it could be a long road and it could fail. But it doesn't matter, because I'm doing it for them.* And when you have discovered your passion and know you are doing right by your niche, you will often be surprised how quickly things fall into place.

The task before you may seem daunting. The uphill climb might seem scary, full of hard work, and risky. But consider this:

How do you get to the top of the mountain? By going uphill.

Sure, the downhill trail might seem nonthreatening, easy, and devoid of risk, but it likely will not take you where you want to go. Conversely, choosing a wiser course will put you on the path toward fulfillment. And if you are committed to that path, you will find a way to make it work. Sure, you will have fears, but you won't let them run the show. Instead, you will get the support and the resources you need to fulfill your mission and build your Million Dollar Practice.

SUMMARY

At the beginning of this chapter I told you about Phil Reynolds. In many ways, he is no different from you or any other practitioner. If you have a mission and a message and a passion, the world needs you. And you now have the means to reach your goals—from branding, to creating services, products, and programs, to generating multiple revenue streams, to incorporating the one-to-many model, to creative marketing, to enrollment. And as one final recap, here are the highlights, summarized for you, to allow you to effectively leverage the principles in this book and to go forth and create your Million Dollar Practice.

CHAPTER 1: IS A MILLION DOLLAR PRACTICE RIGHT FOR YOU?

Your capacity to endure the road to the Million Dollar Practice is based on *the Litmus Test*: "If you were offered a job, making a comfortable living, doing exactly what you wanted to do, with whom you wanted to do it, would you take it?" If your answer is "No," then it is likely that you are up for *the Hero's Journey* and willing to take the necessary *Leap of Faith* to play the *Inner Game and the Outer Game*, using the *Seven Habits of Million Dollar Practitioners*:

1. *Passionate*
2. *Positive*
3. *Entrepreneurial*
4. *Playing Large*
5. *Creative*
6. *Service-Oriented*
7. *Walking the Talk*

Do not take on the role of the *Lone Ranger*; instead, get the necessary help and support to step out from behind your security blanket, even if means *Public Speaking* and getting over your *Fear of Success and Fear of Failure*. But you must first know whether you are a *Technician* or an *Entrepreneur*. It's the *Entrepreneurial Mind-Set* that will guide you on your way to a Million Dollar Practice, as shown in the *Case Study: The ScreamFree Institute*.

But remember, this is not always easy. Sometimes *the Long Way Is the Short Way and the Short Way Is the Long Way. It's an Evolution*, and you must go through the *Seven Stages of Practice Building*:

Stage 1. Student
Stage 2. Intern
Stage 3. Apprentice
Stage 4. Practitioner
Stage 5. Master Practitioner
Stage 6. Teacher
Stage 7. Leader

And before you can pursue it, you must first answer the most fundamental question about it: *What Is a Million Dollar Practice?* It is helpful to answer this question by *Comparing the Six Figure Practice and the Million Dollar Practice*.

SIX FIGURE PRACTICE	MILLION DOLLAR PRACTICE
The Six Figure Practice typically exchanges time for dollars (one-to-one)	The Million Dollar Practice has multiple revenue streams (one-to-many)
The Six Figure Practice typically provides a standard service commonly found elsewhere	The Million Dollar Practice provides unique and creative services unavailable anywhere else
The Six Figure Practice typically emphasizes quality services and benefits	The Million Dollar Practice emphasizes life-changing results
The Six Figure Practice is typically composed of one practitioner and a few staff	The Million Dollar Practice is a collaboration of motivated partners providing complementary talents and contributions
The Six Figure Practice seeks to make a comfortable living	The Million Dollar Practice seeks to make a social impact

Along the way, you may wonder, *Is a Million Dollar Practice Possible?* To help light your path, you need only cite those who have gone before you, people like Deepak Chopra, Anthony Robbins, and yours truly, David Steele.

So, *Is the Million Dollar Practice Right for You?* Only you can make that decision, but if you are interested in *Leveraging Your Expertise to Build a Successful Business That Makes a Difference*, my guess is that you have come to the right place.

Chapter 2: Your Mission and Message

In building your Million Dollar Practice, you must be clear on *Your Purpose, Your Vision, Your Mission, Your Message,* and *Your Passion.* And to put your *Mission in Practice,* you must fully understand the principle of *Resonance* and what sets you apart from the crowd. *You Are Unique. Embrace It. Use It.*

Passion and Service will guide you on your path to a Million Dollar Practice as long as you are not *Coming from Ego* and viewing things only through your own *Lenses and Filters.* And you must know that *Trust Is Key to Success* and *a Productive, Long-Term Relationship.* You must keep focused on the needs of your clients and watch out for *The Razor's Edge,* because *You Don't Know What You Don't Know,* but you can always come back to *Your Passion Speech.*

Chapter 3: Owning Your Niche

You need to know the answer to *What Is a Niche?* It helps to understand niche in the context of several other classifications: *Profession, Specialty, Niche, Services,* and *Brand.*

- A profession answers, "Who am I?"—Example: relationship coach
- A specialty answers, "What do I do?"—Example: coaching singles

- A niche answers, "Who do I help?" — Example: personal growth–oriented singles in Silicon Valley
- A service answers, "How do I help them?" — Example: workshops, classes, coaching, and the like
- A brand answers, "What do I call my business or service?" — Example: Conscious Dating or Unstoppable Women of Silicon Valley

A Million Dollar Practice Is a Business Fueled by a Niche. There are *Seven Benefits of Choosing a Niche*:

Benefit #1: You Get to Push the Boulder Downhill.
Benefit #2: You Get to Follow Your Passion.
Benefit #3: You Get to Be Creative.
Benefit #4: You Get to Be of Service.
Benefit #5: You Get to Create a Legacy.
Benefit #6: You Get to Be Unique.
Benefit #7: You Get to Make More Money.

A Niche Is a Business … and You Can Have More than One. There are *11 Strategies for Choosing a Niche*:

Strategy #1: The Mirror Strategy
Strategy #2: The Calling Strategy
Strategy #3: The Testimonial Strategy
Strategy #4: The Attraction Strategy
Strategy #5: The Life-Story Strategy
Strategy #6: The Serendipity Strategy
Strategy #7: The Pipeline Strategy
Strategy #8: The Gateway Strategy
Strategy #9: The Replication Strategy
Strategy #10: The Unmet-Need Strategy
Strategy #11: The Quick-Start Strategy

All of these are centered around *The Platinum Rule of Marketing* and the *Seven Steps to Owning Your Niche—Making the Platinum Rule Work for You*:

Step 1: Do Your Market Research. There are five steps for conducting market research:

Step 1: Research your niche for their demographic information, other professionals/organizations that serve them, other approaches to helping them, Web sites, online social networking groups, books, and workshops. Call or meet with similar and complementary professionals and organizations to learn more about how they help the people in your niche. Do your homework and become an expert on available information about your target clients.

Step 2: Put together some ideas for programs, branding, and services. Come up with a variety of program names to find out which they prefer. A great exercise is to brainstorm answers to this question: "If I were to write a book or deliver a workshop for my niche, what would I call it?"

Step 3: Identify three to five people who fit your niche. Ideally, these are people you know. If not, then ask your network for referrals. Contact them for informational interviews.

Step 4: Conduct your informational interviews and ask for feedback about your ideas from Step 2. Ask what they read, where they hang out, which groups and organizations they join, and which publications they read. Ask them about their experiences, needs, goals, and challenges. Ask them about what they have done, where they have gone, and with whom they have worked to get support for the need or goal you will address in your practice. Listen closely to the language they use to describe their needs and goals. Ask for their top three problems and top three goals. Ask them to describe their ideal support services or programs to address their needs or goals.

Step 5: Compile your data and ideas, and use them to design the services, branding, and programs for your niche. Follow up with your market research participants and get their feedback on your ideas, plus ask them for referrals. Remember, "people support what they help create," and when you follow up with those who helped you along the way, you will be pleasantly surprised by their excitement and support. In fact, a common and delightful by-product is that some of them might sign up for your program!

Step 2: Conduct a Pilot Project.

Step 3: Create a Brand Identity.

Step 4: Design a Service Delivery System.

Step 5: Host a Niche Community, of which there are 11 benefits:

Benefit #1: External marketing

Benefit #2: Internal marketing

Benefit #3: Stimulate word of mouth

Benefit #4: Build strategic alliances

Benefit #5: Increase visibility

Benefit #6: Generate low-cost marketing

Benefit #7: Increased credibility

Benefit #8: Increased effectiveness of your service delivery system

Benefit #9: Increased traffic

Benefit #10: Attract partners/collaborators

Benefit #11: Transform your practice into a business

Step 6: Provide Group Services.

Step 7: Leverage Your Niche to Build Your Platform.

Chapter 4: How to Create Services, Products, and Programs That Promote Change

Use the organic approach on your road to success. Here's a snapshot of what it looks like: Choose your specialty and your niche; conduct market research to identify its wants; come up with an idea for a service, product, or program to address those wants and needs; launch a pilot project to test your offering; and continually add value by identifying and addressing any ongoing needs in response to working with your clients.

The idea is to *Sell Programs, Not Sessions*, and there are *Two Questions for Organic Program and Product Development*: *What Works?* and *What's Next?*

You want to always *Create Leverage*. There are various ways to do that:

Creating a Service — Online Membership Program
Creating a Service — Groups and Coaching Teams
Creating a Product — Specific Solutions
Creating a Product — Mobile Apps
Creating a Product — From Workshops to Home-Study Courses
Creating a Program — Ecosystems
Creating a Program — Niche Communities

CHAPTER 5: CREATIVE BUSINESS MODELS AND SERVICE DELIVERY SYSTEMS

Creating a System is vital to building a Million Dollar Practice, but you must learn to properly put your *Systems in Action*. It helps tamp down the *Allure of the Mystery Novel*. Be aware of *Having a System — Benefits to the Client* and *Having a System — Benefits to the Practitioner*. *Systemizing Your Business* is vital, and you must recognize *The Importance of Creating a System*.

Getting to Yes is imperative, as is *Building Your Service Delivery System/ Creative Business Model*. And you must always bear in mind the needs and language of your clients for the following reasons:

1. *Your Target Market Doesn't Define What You Do in Your Terms.*
2. *You Don't Buy Your Own Services.*

The key is to view *Your Service Delivery System as a Client Creation Funnel*, as demonstrated in the following graphic:

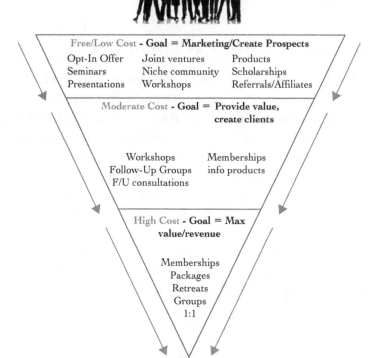

There are three things to note about *Top of Funnel: Your Marketing Activities*:

1. *They're Free.*
2. *They're Valuable.*
3. *They're Designed to Build a Relationship.*

Top-of-Funnel Activities: Prospect Generation include *Speaking, Writing, Networking, Free Information Products, Workshops and Seminars,* and *Niche Communities.*

When considering *Middle-of-Funnel Activities: Client Enrollment,* the principle ways to do this are *Workshops, Seminars, and Classes; Paid Information Products;* and *Paid Memberships.*

The *Bottom-of-Funnel Activities: Your Client Services* include *Individual Services, Groups, Retreats,* and *Packages.*

CHAPTER 6: CREATIVE MARKETING

There is *Good News, Bad News* when it comes to creative marketing and you must make *Incremental Progress,* starting with a *Blank Slate.*

Creative Marketing and the Coaching Point of View is successful because you are *Putting Your Target Audience in the Driver's Seat.* And solutions will come to you because *Nature Abhors a Vacuum.* As a way of viewing this principle in action you can look to this *Case Study: Staying in the Question and Creative Marketing—The Inspirational Relationships Video Project* and this *Case Study: Staying in the Question and Creative Marketing—Campbell Working Together.*

Leveraging Your Experience and Expertise—Creatively can help you succeed and contribute as we did with our four-pillar philosophy for Campbell Working Together, which looks like this:

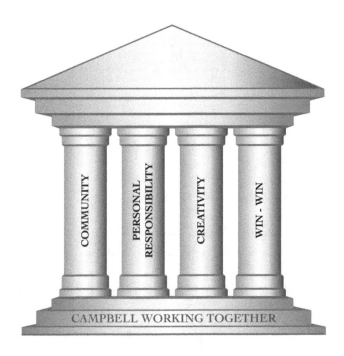

Chapter 6: Creative Marketing

Creative Marketing and Your Relationships play a huge role getting out your message and pursuing your passion to form a win-win situation and best reach and serve the people in your niche.

You must utilize fundamental principles for *Going Live* with your services, products, and programs, and *Reaching the Media* and making sure that you practice *Creative Marketing Alignment*.

The Hero's Journey Continues as you pursue your message and you must find appropriate ways of *Measuring Success* along the way.

You can absolutely make a living and affect lives in pursuing your passion, as shown in *Case Study: Hedy and Yumi Schleifer—Marketing World Peace*. And *the More People You Help, the More Money You Make*, but you have to leverage it.

Marketing Is Not Selling, but it is a necessary and effective tool for getting where you want to go. There are many ways to do it; consider the *Case Study: Creative Marketing at Conferences* where you can have *Multiple Offerings*.

While you must get creative in your marketing, you cannot forget both external marketing and internal marketing, and utilize three *Primary Marketing Strategies*:

1. *Speak Your Way to More Clients.*
2. *Write Your Way to More Clients.*
3. *Network Your Way to More Clients.*

As for *Creative Marketing Strategies*, there are a host of things you can do, such as the following:

Tupperware Party
Joint Ventures
Contests
Giveaways
Scholarships/Pro Bono
Client Sponsors
Free Starter Programs
Tele-Seminars
Tele-Clinics

Niche Communities
Live Events
Workshops and Classes
Fundraisers
Public Service Campaigns
Corporate Sponsorships
Nonprofit Partnerships
"Ask" Campaigns

Marketing is a huge topic that deserves an entire book by itself—or several. But you can get creative and start with the ideas in this chapter to build your Million Dollar Practice. You just have to *Get Out There*.

CHAPTER 7: MAKING THE SALE, GETTING THE CLIENT

Group Enrollment is a key to building your Million Dollar Practice, and along the way you will need to be aware of your *Three Core Constituencies*.

Getting clients is *a Numbers Game* that hinges upon *the Campaign* and a series of *Enrollment Events* leading to *Group Enrollment*.

Building the Foundation requires *More Market Research*, which will lead you to a becoming a shining example, as in our *Case Study: A Master Enroller*.

Social Proof can take the form of *Public Acknowledgment* and *Testimonials*, but never lose sight of your goal. You want to *Focus on What You Really Want to Sell*.

Group Events still require *Individual Relationships*, because each person is *an Individual Amid the Crowd*. You must understand *Group-Speak Versus You-Speak* and challenge each person to answer *Yes or No*. This can be accomplished by framing events with *"You're in the Right Place If …"* or *"You're Not in the Right Place If …"* and a series of *Enrollment Exercises*.

Timing Is Everything in group enrollment, and you must not forget to *Follow-Up*, whether you are addressing the bluebirds, the boulders, or those in between.

But you always want to be *Focusing on Your Current Clients* and fostering *Synergy* at your events, where you have existing customers in the same room with potential customers and somehow get them talking.

CHAPTER 8: BUILDING YOUR MILLION DOLLAR PRACTICE

Filling a Need and *Leveraging Your Passion* are essential ingredients for building your Million Dollar Practice, but without the necessary tools you will be left asking, *Now What?*

The proper level of *Entrepreneurial Development* will keep you from *Longboarding* toward disaster and help you to *Remember the Platinum Rule*, the effectiveness of which can be used in *Making the Case*.

Leveraging *the Law of Attraction*, maintaining your *Integrity*, and *Walking Your Talk* are pillars of building your Million Dollar Practice and will determine whether people see you as *the Practitioner Versus the Salesman*.

Remember, you are embarking on *the Hero's Journey—Making It Necessary*, and this can increase your odds of success. *Getting Support* and being *the Right Fit* will also bolster your chances of making *the Uphill Climb*.

DO'S AND DON'TS

Additionally, if you keep in mind the following Do's and Don'ts, you will remain on track to creating your Million Dollar Practice:

Do's

- Do be willing to take risks.
- Do be willing to stretch.
- Do get help with things that you don't know how to do or that you resist.
- Do your market research.
- Do follow the Platinum Rule.
- Do capture testimonials and endorsements.

- Do leverage your efforts, making sure they fit together in your system.
- Do be willing to price your services, products, and programs so that the people that you are serving have to stretch to enroll.
- Do be willing to require people to invest in themselves, and invest significantly, by working with you.

Don'ts

- Don't assume your constituencies and target audiences are like you.
- Don't be trapped or seduced by the Golden Rule.
- Don't try to leap too far before you are ready—the "stars in the eyes" phenomenon.
- Don't make things up off the top of your head because they sound good to you or you are convinced that they work. Make sure that everything you do and put out there is tested and proven.
- Don't outsource blindly. You have to be involved.
- Don't sell yourself short.

Will You Pull It Off?

Phil Reynolds, like all of us, is human and has some serious obstacles. He has his own sense of inadequacies and insecurities. He wonders, Who am I? He has his distractions. He busies himself with a lot of things. He volunteers for everything. He is a procrastinator. He puts off things he really doesn't want to do, such as learning how to update the WordPress Web site I put together for him.

In Phil's mind, he'll definitely be motivated and have the time when he retires, which isn't that far off. But that is what he is say-ing now. When he retires, maybe he will continue to be so busy with his volunteer endeavors and continue to avoid things he doesn't want to handle. He is gifted. He is talented. He is respected as a leader. But he is human. He has a passion, but he has yet to leverage it fully.

What is the difference between the guy who is passionate, yet giving it all away, and the guy who is playing a bigger game with his passion? It's creating a business around it. And that is what is so exciting to me. It's the fact that we can take our expertise, our passion, our mission, and our message, and build a business around them that makes a big difference, helps a lot of people, and generates a lot of money. That's what this book is about: showing you how to do that.

Will Phil Reynolds ever realize his potential? Who knows? Will you?

Million Dollar Questions for Chapter 8

1. Are you the right person to help the people in your niche?

2. Do you have the experience and expertise to help the people in your niche?

3. Are you committed and willing to stretch, to go "all in," and to take risks?

4. Will you get the support you need to make it to the top of the hill?

5. Are you ready for the success that you want, and do you believe it is possible?

My best wishes in leveraging your expertise to build a successful business that makes a difference.

David Steele

Epilogue

It has been my observation that there are three kinds of helping professionals attracted to working with me to build their practice: the go-getters, the dabblers, and the secure, scared, and stuck — I call them the *Triple S's*.

And I bring it up because it might be helpful for you to identify which category you belong to — or are at risk of belonging to — as you pursue your Million Dollar Practice.

Go-Getters

The go-getters are the ones who are excited and positive. The go-getters move forward, are self-disciplined, and will take enough risks to make things happen. Go-getters are not going to let anything hold them back. They are motivated. They are going for it.

In my experience, the go-getters account for maybe 5–10% of professionals seeking to build a private practice. This is, unfortunately, a small number of the participants who have gone through my practice-building programs.

Dabblers

The dabblers start out looking like go-getters: They are motivated; they are excited; they are engaged. And then they lose steam.

The dabblers get distracted. Life gets in the way; they encounter an obstacle, and it stops them in their tracks. They don't work on overcoming it. So they are easily obstructed, like a train with an obstacle on the tracks. The obstacle is there, the train stops, and it's not going anywhere.

The dabblers make up the majority of the participants of my practice-building programs.

The Secure, Scared, and Stuck

The secure, scared, and stuck are the ones who want to change their practices, want to make more money, want something different and something better; they sign up for my program, but they don't do anything with it. They have a way of paying their bills, so they are secure. They are scared to risk that. They do want to transition to better practices or expand their existing practices, and they want the kind of results that my programs can deliver for them, but they are absolutely not willing to risk their existing source of income. And since they are not willing to take a risk, they don't go anywhere.

THE BELL CURVE

Through 15 years of conducting practice-building programs with hundreds, probably thousands, of participants (remember, I'm math impaired), and even before that, when I was mentoring interns on launching and building their practices, I've noticed that there is a bell curve. The go-getters are on the forward end of the curve, representing 5–10%; the dabblers make up the majority, or the middle of the bell curve; the secure, scared, and stuck constitute the other end of the curve, making up the remaining 5–10%.

I liken it to buying a book. You bought this book because you wanted the information in it. You wanted the benefits that this book could give you. The secure, scared, and stuck put the book on the shelf and didn't even open it. The dabblers opened it, read a little bit, and then put it down and never looked at it again—or they might even have read the whole thing, but didn't do anything with it.

And then there are the go-getters—like you, perhaps, if you've read this far—who bought the book, read it all the way through, worked on the "Million Dollar Questions" at the end of each chapter, acted upon the information to build a Million Dollar Practice, and perhaps even availed themselves of additional services, products, and programs in the Selected Resources section to take their business to the next level.

This goes for your clients, too. You will inevitably have clients who are go-getters: really motivated and excited to get into action. They are the easy ones, the ones who are fun for us to work with. Then there are the clients who are dabblers, the ones who talk about it and may even take some action, but who lose steam pretty quickly. They get frustrated and stop easily. And then there are the ones who are secure, scared, and stuck; the ones who need you, but for the most part won't even show up to work with you. And the ones who do are your nightmare clients, the ones who are hardest to work with. They tend to be the most challenging boulders, both in terms of enrollment and in terms of getting them into action, getting them to benefit from working with you.

THE DIRTY LITTLE SECRET OF TRANSFORMATIONAL PROGRAMS

I bring this to your attention, especially as it relates to you as a practice builder, because over the years I have learned that we helping professionals, by nature, want to understand people and want to understand ourselves. We need to understand the process of growth and change, and we need to understand what works and what gets in the way. So now we have this paradigm, and we should be able to look in the mirror and say, *Okay, well, what is going on for me? Where am I in my practice-building process? And what type am I fitting into or looking more like?* When you are looking in the mirror, you can also make a conscious choice. You can choose to be a go-getter. And that is my desire. That is what I want for you and why I challenge you with this. I want you to be a go-getter, because that is what is needed for you to benefit from this material and achieve your goals. And you must realize that most people won't. It's the dirty little secret of transformational programs. Most people who are motivated enough to sign up and pay their money don't follow through far enough to get the benefit they want and paid to achieve. Being a go-getter is the only way to realize your full potential and build a Million Dollar Practice. It also keeps you going for the future, as you can never stop evolving.

The Evolution and the Organic Process Continue

Everybody has a smartphone in their hands nowadays, far more so than computers. People sit in front of their computers for a few minutes or a few hours a day, but they are never more than arm's length from their cell phones, and they always seem to have their noses in them. So smartphone apps are huge, and they are becoming more and more prevalent and used.

As a result, I had been thinking for a long time about developing a Conscious Dating app or finding ways that private practice professionals could use apps to market themselves or make a difference with people in a given specialty or niche. Finally, I directed my head tech guy to become familiar with apps and to determine whether we should develop them ourselves or outsource this task.

We found that there were plenty of people who will develop apps for you, so I first decided to look at using apps within my own stable of services, products, and programs. I wanted to explore what would lend itself to an app, how to design the app, how the app might work, and what features it might have. A company I respect, one that always seems to be on the leading edge of making technology easy and affordable, hosted a webinar on developing apps. Again, I know and trust this company. It is the one from whom I private-labeled Easy Seminar. On the webinar, the company had a fast-action bonus and all the enrollment strategies that you can imagine—they actually sold it a lot harder than it needed to be sold—and when they gave the link to buy, I went ahead and jumped. Now I'm in the app development business. I went ahead and developed my first app, Conscious Dating, then helped a few of my colleagues build their apps, and then I built a company to develop apps for private practice professionals, at EasyProApps.com.

THE PROCESS

As is customary with the process that I have developed over the years, and as I suggested with Phil Reynolds, any time I start a business I think about a brand for it. So far I have come up with and registered two domain names. Sometimes I'll register eight, nine, or ten domain names, and I might end up throwing eight out, not renewing them the next year. But registering a domain name is seven bucks, so it's not a major expense, and it is part of my creative process.

To date, the domain names that I have registered are easyproapps.com and privatepracticeapps.com, and I have been using the former. The niche clients I am targeting for the development of apps are private practice professionals. Certainly, with this platform, I can develop apps for any business. The platform has templates for restaurants, for example, so that all you have to do is walk down the street, walk into a restaurant and say, "Hey, have you ever thought about promoting your restaurant with an app?" A lot of them would perk up, and if you showed them how an app could really help them, it would be an easy sell. Darlene and I talked about getting a salesperson on board, and we might do it, but my expertise and my passion is for helping private practice professionals get out there and make a difference and reach more people. In today's world, apps are definitely the way to do that.

So the evolution and the organic process continue. This is real-time breaking news. Do you want to conduct professional tele-seminars and webinars and conference calls? I have a wonderfully easy, effective platform for that at EasySeminar.com. If you want to put together an app to promote your business and serve the people in your niche, I now have an easy, affordable solution for that, too. So the entrepreneur in me is very excited.

MAINTAINING THE INTEGRITY OF THE BRAND

But I must issue a word of caution as you are rolling out new services, products, and programs. You must be careful to maintain the integrity of your brand. Here's an example: As I was getting ready to launch and promote my app development offering, I was putting together a webinar at mobilemediamarketingrevolution.com that was meant to orient professionals to the huge potential for incorporating mobile technology into their overall marketing plans by getting their e-books on e-reader platforms, creating and launching apps, and making their Web sites mobile compatible. Despite the huge trend in this area, I have noticed that there is currently nobody in my space talking about it and showing others how to do it.

So for me, one of the challenging things is that while I very much want to put on an event to inform people, provide value, and help them get started, I also see a tremendous opportunity to put together a mentoring program. Once people truly see the value of mobile technology in marketing, they are going to want help and will be willing to pay for it. They need to be walked through it step by step. And as much as I would like to do it, I can't, because I don't want to dilute my brand. I don't want to distract from my main mission and message, even though it is an area of interest and passion for me.

It would be like wanting to join the Peace Corps if you are the CEO of a start-up company. If you join the Peace Corps and are not available to nurture your start-up, to be present, to be the face of it, and to support it, it's going to suffer. And I don't want RCI to suffer.

So even though it would be fun, even though it would probably be very profitable, even though the apple is ripe and ready for the plucking and I am the closest one to it, I have to pass it by. And you need to bear this in mind as you go forward in pursuit of your Million Dollar Practice. You can't be distracted by all of the shiny objects. There are times when you must pass by an opportunity or not make as much money as you could in order to stay on track with your mission and your message. But that doesn't mean that you can't get creative and find a way to play.

In my case, ever the entrepreneur, I am not going to just sit back and let somebody else take the reins. I am going to put it out to the universe, let my joint venture partners know about it, and see what kind of opportunity we can create. I could provide a lot of the specific expertise and content, and they could help put together the program and market it in their network and platform. We could conduct it together, yet it would be under their umbrella so as not to dilute RCI's brand, thus allowing a win-win.

When you are in the flow of creating services, products, and programs, you are going to come across opportunities to be a leader, to be first in something. But you have to be careful of what takes you away from your mission and your message. When you are starting out and you are hungry, you might be tempted to say yes to everything and anything. But eventually you have to stick with what you have. You can't spread yourself too thin; you can't go in too many directions. You can't be all things to all people. These are some of the choices, struggles, and challenges that you will encounter. Entrepreneurs who are pursuing the Million Dollar Practice will all go through this eventually. It comes with the territory. You just have to know and choose what is right for you at any given time.

THE FUTURE IS NOW

At the time I am writing this book, apps are the wave of the future. Five years from now, that could change. Maybe something else will be the new cutting-edge concept. Yet my foray into app development is an example of how things continue to develop organically. As I said, I have wanted to develop an app for a while, and I finally stumbled upon the resource that could help me do that. I was prepared to go through a lot of effort and spend a lot of money, and this resource made it a lot easier and a lot more affordable. And that's the way the organic approach to building a business can happen.

If you know what direction you are going, if you have a vision, if you have a mission, if you know what it is you want to create and build and grow—and you stick to it—then you must always be on the lookout for resources, next steps, and ideas that can help you get to the steps beyond that to reach the Million Dollar Practice.

PAYING ATTENTION

I bring this to your attention because it is an example of keeping up with the times, evolving, and finding and always being open to creative ways to reach people, serve them, and market your services, products, and programs on the way to building a Million Dollar Practice. I'm getting lots of compliments for being on the leading edge for creating this app, but to me, it's nothing special. You must pay attention to what's going on in the world as it relates to your niche and respond to it. So to me, this is not leading edge. Leading edge would be having launched an app two years ago. This is simply an example of getting on the bandwagon when it's completely obvious where things are going.

Many business owners have blinders on and just focus on what is; then they are surprised when things change. But things change all the time, so how do you keep up with that? How are you even aware of the changes? You pay attention. That's the simplest advice I have. That's what I do. I pay attention. This is a passion for me, so I read newspaper and magazine articles, I watch movies, and I buy new books when they come out if they seem intriguing. I set Google Alerts so that my trademarks and keywords are brought to my attention when they appear on the Internet.

If you stay in the flow of serving your target audience, they will tell you things. "Hey, have you heard about this cool new app?" Again, it is not hard to do. You just have to pay attention—and then, of course, act on the information. You must always be in development mode. Sure, there are practitioners who don't want to do this. They want to practice. They want to serve a client and then the next client and then the next client and then the next client. They want to slowly grow their business and make their money and make the difference in the world that they feel called to make in their own way. They don't want to be in business development mode all of the time. This is where the entrepreneurial spirit comes in, because an entrepreneur is never satisfied with the status quo. An entrepreneur is always looking to develop and grow and stretch and do things better.

BREAKING THE DAM

When I was a therapist, working in the area of relationships, I was completely frustrated and wished there was a better way to go. I desperately sought a more effective and fulfilling way of helping people with their relationships. I wanted things to be different. And finally, after 10 or 15 years of being frustrated and feeling stuck, I made a move and the dam broke loose. Now I am all about new and better and more effective ways to reach people and help them with their relationships, where before I couldn't see any way—that is, until I stumbled across coaching. *Wow, there's a possibility of a different way to help people with their relationships!* Prior to that, as a therapist feeling frustrated and stuck and burned out in my practice, I didn't know about coaching. I didn't know there was any other way. I had to keep my eyes open and be prepared to act when I saw it.

Some practitioners will be attracted to this model and some won't. But as far as I'm concerned, the Million Dollar Practice depends upon having an entrepreneurial spirit and continually being in development, because that's how you grow. Yes, it is possible to grow doing the same thing over and over and over. We can serve our target audience in the same way again and again and just expand and do more of the same. But eventually, what we do is going to become obsolete, because things change all the time. The field is ever growing and evolving. And if we become stuck in our ways, we are going to become dinosaurs in our chosen fields while customers looking for new and better solutions go elsewhere.

As far as I'm concerned, survival in any business is about continuing to evolve, because we as a species continue to evolve. If you are the kind of person who likes what you do and wants to do the same thing over and over and over again, you could be in for a rough road with your business. If you are a cabinetmaker or other craftsman, that approach might work, but in most businesses, it doesn't. In most businesses, you must evolve.

PAVING THE ROAD TO YOUR FUTURE

The other day I saw a clip on TV about this guy who developed a completely self-contained system for repaving roads. It breaks up the old asphalt and concrete, processes it, and then lays new asphalt, using the old asphalt and the old concrete to lay the bedding and the asphalt for the new road.

As a result, all of the other paving businesses — based on trucking in new dirt, concrete, and asphalt, breaking up the old stuff, trucking it out, and dumping it — are behind the times. The guy on the show built a completely self-contained system that recycles the road and renews it at the same time. The machine is huge and expensive, but it is fast and far cheaper per mile than the old-fashioned way of breaking up the road, carting off the old debris, and carting in new materials.

If you are in the paving business and you are not going to look at paving roads any differently, you are going to be left behind. You are going to become obsolete. No city, no transportation agency is going to want to pay you to break up the old road, cart it off, and bring in new materials if there is an alternative to that. And it is no different in your field.

Human beings are growth oriented. We develop new things all the time. We grow. We evolve. The universe expands. And if you are a private practice professional, you just have to keep up. This is why we go to conferences, have continuing education requirements, and read professional journals and other materials.

But my problem with this is that it is preaching to the choir. It's professionals talking to each other. The trick is to evolve in response to our target audiences. We need to be asking those development questions: *How can I better reach them? How can I better serve them?* Sure, there is a time and a place for professionals to talk to each other, to share experiences, to share expertise, and to share new ideas. But those new ideas need to come from somewhere — they need to come from serving clients and asking, *"How can I better market to them? How can I better reach them? How can I better serve them?"* Answer those questions and you will be well on your way to success.

As a private practice professional you have priceless expertise that can solve significant human problems, enhance quality of life, and make the world a better place for all of us. You deserve professional and financial success. Your audience needs you and is waiting for you to show up. What are you waiting for? Your Million Dollar Practice awaits.

Afterword

Typically, when I write books, I lay them out as how-to manuals, chock-full of practical tools and tips and loaded with immediately applicable steps and ideas. This book, too, is loaded with value, though it has taken a different turn than I had planned. This book, like the primary means of developing a Million Dollar Practice, has truly used the organic approach. It came from the inside. It came from being creative. It didn't come from some cookie-cutter business strategy formula.

Additionally, this book has been designed to use stories, examples, principles, questions, and information to make it an easy, fun, and engaging read. This book was created with the intention of showing you the path and giving you the inspiration and direction needed to get into action. And I hope you feel I have succeeded in doing that.

Still, I have had to make a little adjustment all the way along this book, reminding myself that the purpose of this book is to provide a broad road map. It's sort of like taking a road trip and breaking out the atlas: You have pages that give you the big picture, so you can get the lay of the land and a sense of where you are going and how best to get there; if you want the surface streets and the micro view, you have to turn to other pages and dive a little deeper.

And while it was not realistic for this book to give the micro view of every step and strategy, nevertheless it was an adjustment for me as a writer, and perhaps for you as one of my readers. But I am hopeful that you have enjoyed and received value from this book for what it is and because it supports your desire to leverage your expertise and bring it to another level. It is not meant to give you the unrealistic expectation that *"all I have to do is buy this book and follow the steps and that will be the end of it."* The road to the Million Dollar Practice doesn't work that way. There's more to the story. You can expect a long journey, with many bumps along the way. But I can assure you it's well worth the ride.

David Steele

Selected Resources for Building Your Million Dollar Practice

- Hosting conference calls, webinars, and teleseminars: www.easyseminar.com
- Affordable mobile apps for private practice professionals: www.easyproapps.com
- Autoresponders: www.coachautoresponder.com
- Copywriting for print and Internet: www.getresultswithwords.com
- Done-for-you Web site solution: www.besttherapistcoachweb sites.com
- Do-it-yourself Web site solution: www.easywordpresssolutions.com
- Practice management console: www.managemycoachingprac tice.com
- Accept credit cards: www.bestepaymentsolution.com
- Shopping cart with affiliate program: www.bestcoachshopping cart.com
- Newsletters done for you: www.bestcoachnewsletters.com

- Marketing help for coaches and therapists: www.bestcoachmar keting.com
- Marketing and building a successful practice: www.milliondol larpractice.net
- Comprehensive practice-building information: www.private practicemarketingonabudget.com
- Effective, ethical client enrollment: www.naturalclientenroll mentstrategies.com
- Develop signature audio/CD program: www.privatepractice magic.com
- Free audio series "How to Earn Six Figures as an Expert Who Speaks": www.relationshipcoachinginstitute.com/speakingbiz.htm
- Free quick-start program "Using Conference Calls to Grow Your Business": www.easyseminar.com
- Free comprehensive resource bank for private practice professionals: www.milliondollarpractice.net
- To schedule a personal consultation with the author: www.consultwithdavid.com

About David Steele

AUTHOR, RELATIONSHIP COACHING PIONEER, AND GLOBAL AUTHORITY ON GROWING A PROFITABLE PRIVATE PRACTICE

After two decades serving as a couples therapist in full-time private practice, David Steele grew weary of trying to save marriages and chase insurance reimbursements to survive. He discovered personal life coaching in 1996. Within 3 months of completing his initial coach training, he had transformed his therapy practice into a thriving and profitable coaching practice. He subsequently created and tested a standardized model for relationship coaching that is the foundation for the curriculum taught at the Relationship Coaching Institute (RCI), the first and largest relationship coach training organization in the world. Steele and his team at RCI have since trained thousands of relationship coaches and mentored hundreds of therapists and coaches to build successful, sustainable practices that guide their clients to enjoy more satisfying, functional lives so they can make a difference in the world. His practical advice about how to grow and sustain a profitable, rewarding coaching practice gives struggling therapists cause for hope and celebration.

A prolific writer, including *From Therapist to Coach: How to Leverage Your Clinical Expertise to Build a Thriving Coaching Practice* (Wiley, 2011), Steele is creator of proprietary and proven coaching models, mentoring programs, and practice-building products such as *Private Practice Magic* and *Private Practice Marketing on a Budget*. Steele is an industry pioneer and a sought-after speaker and trainer who is passionate about showing therapists a better way to achieve lasting success and significance. As he often says, "It doesn't matter where you've been. What matters is where you're going and how you'll get there."

Steele is happily married to his soul mate Darlene and is parent to three children, including twin boys. He lives in northern California.

For a private consultation with David Steele to get his input and support for building your Million Dollar Practice, visit www.consult withdavid.com

Notes

NOTES

Notes

NOTES

Notes

NOTES

Notes

NOTES

Notes

NOTES